MW00756774

WITHDRAWN

ZERO FOOTPRINT

ZERO FOOTPRINT

THE TRUE STORY OF A PRIVATE MILITARY CONTRACTOR'S COVERT ASSIGNMENTS
IN SYRIA, LIBYA, AND THE WORLD'S MOST DANGEROUS PLACES

SIMON CHASE
AND RALPH PEZZULLO

MULHOLLAND BOOKS
LITTLE, BROWN AND COMPANY
NEW YORK   BOSTON   LONDON

Author's Note: Names have been changed to protect privacy.

This is the story of one man's experience as a private military contractor, but it's really much more than that. I hope readers understand that there are thousands of men and women like me from various countries fighting to advance and protect the interests of the United States and Great Britain in war zones all over the world. They all have stories similar to mine. They've all lost friends and teammates, and shed their tears and blood. In their honor, I'm donating my profits from this book to the veterans mental health charity Combat Stress, located at combatstress.org.uk.

Mulholland Books/Little, Brown and Company
Hachette Book Group
1290 Avenue of the Americas, New York, NY 10104
mulhollandbooks.com

First Edition: January 2016

Mulholland Books is an imprint of Little, Brown and Company, a division of Hachette Book Group, Inc. The Mulholland Books name and logo are trademarks of Hachette Book Group, Inc.

The publisher is not responsible for websites (or their content) that are not owned by the publisher.

The Hachette Speakers Bureau provides a wide range of authors for speaking events. To find out more, go to hachettespeakersbureau.com or call (866) 376-6591.

ISBN 978-0-316-34224-7
Library of Congress Control Number: 2015948814

10 9 8 7 6 5 4 3 2 1

RRD-H

Printed in the United States of America

"If all men were just, there would be no need for valor."
— Agesilaus

Dedicated to my fallen PMC brothers
and their families

CONTENTS

CONTENTS

LIST OF ABBREVIATIONS

AQI—al-Qaeda in Iraq
AQIM—al-Qaeda in the Islamic Maghreb
BDU—battle dress uniform
CASEVAC—casualty evacuation
CHU—containerized housing unit
COB—collocated operating base
COBR—Cabinet Office briefing rooms
CONOC—contractors' operation center
COP—close observation platoon
CP—close protection
DBA—Defense Billing Act
DFAC—dining facility
DIA—Defense Intelligence Agency
DL—drill leader
DOD—Department of Defense
DOS—Department of State
DS—Diplomatic Security
DShK—Degtyaryov-Shpagin, large-caliber machine gun
EFP—explosive force penetrator

ENDEX—exercise termination

EO—executive order

EU—European Union

EVAC—evacuation

FFD—first field dressing

FIBUA—fighting in built-up areas

FN—foreign national

FOB—forward operating base

FSA—Free Syrian Army

GPS—global positioning system

GRS—Global Response Staff

GUF—graduated use of force

HH—His Highness

HRH—His Royal Highness

HVT—high-value target

IED—improvised explosive device

IFAK—individualized first-aid kit

IMO—information management officer

ISI—Islamic State of Iraq

ISIS—Islamic State of Iraq and Syria

KMS—Keenie Meenie Services

LN—local national

MANPADS—man-portable air-defense system

MBITR—multiband inter/intra team radio

MI6—Military Intelligence, Section 6

MRE—meal, ready to eat

MT—mobile security team

MWR—morale, welfare, and recreation

NA—Northern Alliance

NGOs—nongovernmental organizations

NRO—National Reconnaissance Office

NVGs—night-vision goggles

OBE—Order of the British Empire

OBL—Osama bin Laden

OIC—officer in charge

OP—observation post

OPSEC—operational security

ORBAT—order of battle

PCH—Pacific Coast Highway

PCO—Project and Contracting Office

PKM—Pulemyot Kalashnikova, modernized machine gun

PMC—private military contractor

PO—presiding officer

PSC—private security contractor

PT—physical training

PTI—physical training instructor

PTSD—post-traumatic stress disorder

QRF—quick-response force

RLT—reconstruction liaison team

RPG—*ruchnoy protivotankovyi granatomyot*, handheld antitank grenade launcher

RTA—road traffic incident

RV—rendezvous point

SAD—Special Activities Division

SAF—Syrian Armed Forces

SAS—Special Air Service

SBS—Special Boat Service

SCIF—Sensitive Compartmented Information Facility

SET—security escort team

SF—special forces

SIR—serious incident report
SOCA—Serious Organised Crime Agency
SRT—security reconnaissance team
SSG—Syrian Support Group
SVR—Sluzhba Vneshney Razvedki, foreign intelligence
  service of Russia
3IC—third in command
TL—team leader
TOC—tactical operations center
2IC—second in command
UP—urban observation post
USACE—US Army Corps of Engineers
USAID—US Agency for International Development
USF-I—US Forces–Iraq
USFI—US Forces, Interior
USG—US government

ZERO FOOTPRINT

CHAPTER ONE

QATAR

IF YOU haven't found yourself in the middle of the shit in places like Iraq, Afghanistan, Somalia, Pakistan, or Syria recently, you probably have little understanding of what we do. Or that we're sometimes called upon to perform missions too sensitive and top secret for even Delta Force or SEAL Team 6.

We're mostly guys, and some women, who live in your neighborhoods, drive fast cars, work out a lot, and spend long periods of time away from home. We tend to keep to ourselves and avoid socializing with the neighbors. Some of you probably suspect that we're spies or former convicts, drug dealers, or maybe even Internet entrepreneurs.

What we really are: PMCs—private military contractors, or operators. There are hundreds of thousands of us living in the United States working for companies like G4S, DynCorp, Unity Resources Group, Erinys, Triple Canopy, and Aegis Defense Services. They hire us to do the dirty and dangerous jobs the military and intelligence services can't or don't want to do. Some of us are former Tier 1 operators—SEALs, Delta Force, marines, or Army Rangers—with extensive combat experience. My background includes fifteen years of service in the British Royal Marines, British special forces, and the Special Boat Service (SBS).

We defuse terrorist bombs, guard dignitaries, protect convoys traveling through perilous territory, battle drug runners, provide security to oil facilities, fly manned reconnaissance planes, and maintain military aircraft and equipment.

In my case, I've fought beside Afghan and Syrian rebels, rescued kidnapped children from inside Pakistan, battled Somali pirates, shoveled the ashes of my best mates off the streets of Baghdad, tracked down al-Qaeda high-value targets (HVTs)—including Osama bin Laden—and performed other "zero-footprint" missions for the US government. One of those zero-footprint missions put me in Benghazi on September 11, 2012, the night Ambassador Christopher Stevens and three other Americans died.

It's a hard transition from military to PMC. In the former, we were hailed as heroes. As private operators, we're regarded as shadowy figures or mercenaries who are in it solely for the money, which isn't always true. Maybe the pay is better, but we're pretty much doing the same work and employed by the same governments. And we're motivated by the same standard of service to the ideals we hold true.

As PMCs we operate deep undercover without government backup or air rescue, public credit for what we do, or military honors when we die in combat. Maybe, as some commentators have suggested, we're unsung heroes in the war against terrorism. That's not my call.

My decade-plus career as a military contractor began during a black-cab ride to London in 1999 with my mate Pete. My first assignments were cakewalks with a laugh or two along the way compared with some of the brutal missions that would follow after 9/11. But that was okay with me, because I was learning the ropes and developing a sense of the moral dilemmas I would face going forward.

Pete and I had been through thick and thin together, starting as young toughs from Romford in the East End to the time we spent in juvie. At five foot nine apiece, neither of us was physically imposing at first sight, but we were both workout fanatics. While I was faster on my feet, Pete was the toughest man I'd ever met and training to become a UFC fighter.

From juvie we had both recruited into the Royal Marines. After fifteen years of British military service, we were now two East End blokes going up the smoke, as we called it, on our way from Portsmouth to London in a cab with no idea what we were going to do next. That's when my big, ugly NEC P100 cell phone rang.

It was Marvin C., our former PTI (physical training instructor), who had gone on to the SBS—the naval partner of the infamous Special Air Service (SAS)—where I had served.

"Simon, what are you doing?" he asked. "You still in your RDP?" RDP was the four-month "rundown period" the Brit mil gave us to transition into civilian life.

"We just got out, Marvin. And as for the future, I have no idea." It was the truth.

"I'm in Qatar working for Nigel R." Nigel had been my former commanding officer in the elite Royal Marines—a charismatic man in his late fifties and former commander of 42 Commando, which had played a major role in the Falklands War in '82. Marvin told me that Nigel was now running a company called SERAC Ltd., which I'd never heard of. General Nigel R. was someone who immediately commanded respect.

"Nigel and some of the boys—Dolly Gray, Topsy Turner, and

Bob Marley—are in Qatar now," Marvin continued. All of them were former colleagues in the Brit mil in their late twenties and early thirties.

"They helped the sons overthrow the old man in '95. The coup was bloodless, and the sons are now in power, one as the prime minister and the other as the foreign minister. We're working for Sheikh Abdullah bin Khalifa Al Thani. He's the PM and the boss. He wants us to act as his protection detail when he travels around the world and to train a local security team."

I'd run multiple personal-protection courses during my years in the Brit mil. Though I'd been to nearby Saudi Arabia and United Arab Emirates, I'd never set foot in Qatar. It was one of those places nobody ever talked about.

"It's a good gig," he said. "There will be ten of you all together. Pays real well."

I said, "Yeah. I'll have some of that."

After that it was pack the gear, hop on a flight east, and welcome to Qatar (pronounced KUT-ter), one of the smallest, most conservative countries in the Arab world, where Wahhabism (a strict interpretation of Islam) is the official religion and falconry and camel racing are national pastimes. It's also one of the wealthiest nations on the planet because it sits on vast fields of oil and natural gas.

We were in the sweltering capital city, Doha, where the average temperature from May through October topped a hundred degrees. We lived in a villa in the western compound, complete with pools, gyms, and tennis courts. Everything was provided for us—food, drink, cars.

An adjoining villa housed a team hired by Scimitar Security out of London, whose job was to provide security to the boss's brother, the foreign minister. The guys on the SERAC and Scimitar teams all knew one another, so we cut a hole through the adjoining wall and turned a spare bedroom into a bar where we could hang and drink together. Since Qatar is a strict Muslim country, booze is forbidden.

One afternoon soon after I arrived, we were grilling lamb kebabs and drinking beer in our makeshift bar when a Scimitar chap named Dave told us that the foreign minister was conspiring against his brother, the prime minister—the man we had been sent to protect.

Thinking the heat may have affected my hearing, I asked, "Are you sure about that, mate?"

"Yeah, next week we're supposed to overthrow your boss," Dave answered casually.

I looked at Dolly, the leader of our team, who turned to Dave and said, "That's not going to happen."

Here we were, drinking beers together, same league, different teams, and now we were being asked to go up against one another with automatic weapons on behalf of the Al Thani brothers. Obviously, we weren't going to allow that to happen. But it was a serious mind-fuck to a newcomer like myself and a rude introduction to the murky world of private military contracting.

Lesson number 1: Stick close to your teammates and develop trust. They're the only people you can depend on to have your back.

Our first task was to train a CP (close protection) unit made up of locals—a kind of Praetorian Guard—that would protect the boss when he was in Qatar. (In the Middle East, it's considered a sign of weakness to have FNs—foreign nationals—guard a leader in his own country.) We coordinated with a commander of one of the local Qatari elite military units, a guy with a thick black mustache named Musraf who spoke directly to the boss.

My mates and I designed an eight-week training program that we hoped to run in a timely manner. It was the same program that we did in the regiment and included small-unit tactics, counterinsurgency, antisurveillance, and passive surveillance.

The Qataris did the vetting process, drawing men from their elite special forces units. Though I speak Arabic, I used a local interpreter (called a terp) so that we could move through the lessons quickly.

The first morning, I stood outside the training room waiting with my cup of coffee at 0755. All I saw in front of me was sand, crickets, and tumbleweeds. None of the twenty men we were scheduled to train in the first of the three groups had appeared.

Turning to Musraf, I asked, "Where are the men?"

"They're all at the mosque," he answered calmly. "They're praying now. They'll be here."

The mosque? Trainees in the UK or United States would have already been lined up in their uniforms, eager and ready.

Around 0830 the Qataris started drifting in. One guy was wearing an old Manchester United T-shirt and a pair of flip-flops. Another had no teeth; a third looked like he was about ready to drop dead on the spot; a fourth had brought his goat to the party. Several wore old, ratty sweatpants and carried their belongings in plastic shopping bags. Not a single one had a uniform on.

Confounded, I asked, "Musraf, these guys are elite military, right?"

"Oh, yes. Yes," he answered like it should have been obvious to me.

"They've been vetted?"

"Oh, yes. Of course."

"They've been through local training and done military service?"

"Yes. Yes."

It was clear right away that we had to scrap military training for the time being and spend a week or so on husbandry—basic things like how to take care of your uniforms, how to fold them, how to sew on a button, how to store them in your locker, and how to wash yourself.

Next day, five of the twenty Qatari trainees didn't show up. When we located them, they said they didn't realize that they had to return. The guys who did appear weren't wearing uniforms.

To maintain our good humor, my buddies and I started taking bets on how many would show up on a given day and what they'd be wearing. A guy we called Elvis stood on the parade ground one morning in his uniform and bare feet. Through the terp, I asked him, "Where are your boots?"

"My brother's got them."

"Why?"

"Because he needed something to wear."

We had issued every trainee a full military kit, complete with G1 respirator (the kind that fits fully over the head and face and filters out gases and other noxious airborne particles), but we hadn't shown the trainees how to use them yet. One morning Elvis lined up at 0815 wearing his respirator for no apparent reason. Another guy had his on backward.

The physical training part of the course wasn't intense, but we had to factor in a certain level of fitness so that, if required, the Qatari CP unit could hustle people out of a car or a bus or pick up the VIP they were guarding and run him or her away from danger.

We took the trainees out for a short run, and within one hundred meters all of them were dying, and Abdul was wearing flip-flops.

"Why, Abdul?" I asked, trying not to lose it. "Why don't you wear the sneakers we issued like the rest of the guys?"

After a couple of weeks, we selected ten of the best trainees out of the first group of twenty to graduate to vehicle and arms training. Instructing these gents how to care for their uniforms and do push-ups was one thing. But teaching them how to spot an ambush and drive through it without getting killed was quite another.

It was like letting highly caffeinated five-year-olds loose on the bumper-car ride. Guys were driving over cones and crashing into walls. The shooting range was a melee of negligent discharges, magazines falling out of rifles because they weren't loaded properly. Miraculously, no one was killed.

In the middle of the course, we had to peel away because the boss, HRH Abdullah bin Khalifa Al Thani, wanted to travel. Since Qatar is a desert that's almost unlivable during many months of the year, he spent most of his time as head of state out of the country, in places like London, Paris, Saint-Tropez, and Barcelona. So our training team transformed into HRH's overseas security detail, and the instruction was handed over to Qatari officers. Not the ideal way to run a training program, but the best we could do under the circumstances.

Lesson number 2: Stay flexible and alert, because the mission can change any minute.

Now we were going to guard the boss, who was short and physically weak but eloquent and charming, fluent in English and French, and educated at the Royal Military Academy Sandhurst, which is the British equivalent of West Point. Nigel R. had been one of his instructors there. They built a friendship, and when Abdullah decided it was time to oust his father, who had developed an unseemly fondness for opulence and alcohol, he called Nigel.

The traveling security detail expanded to eleven men and two women, the latter to protect HRH's two wives—one named Leila, a nineteen-year-old with supermodel looks, and the other a grumpy, short, overweight woman in her forties named Fatima. Because the Qataris are strict Muslims, a woman isn't allowed to be in the company of a man who isn't a blood relative.

We traveled first class in two specially outfitted Qatar Airways

Boeing 737s, with all our kits, weapons, radios, surveillance cameras, and laptops. Weapons included Glock 19s carried in covert holsters and HK MP5 submachine guns and shotguns stored in the trunks of our vehicles.

We took over entire floors of five-star hotels like the Savoy in London and the George V in Paris. Because the boss was a prime minister, he met often with religious and other dignitaries. Trips to Buckingham Palace, the White House, and 10 Downing Street were common. Since the boss wasn't an important target, the only real threat was that someone might try to kidnap one of his six sons and hold them for ransom.

This, I learned, was the light side of PMC work, moving every four days and living out of a suitcase. If the boss wanted to go to Cannes to take his boat out, and the kids, meanwhile, were staying in London with one of his two wives, we divided up the team.

Wherever we were, we'd get up at 0600, work out, then meet and go over the day's schedule, check the drivers, the radios (comms), and divvy up the team if necessary—figuring out who'd be with the boss, the wives, the sons. For those guarding the boss, a suit was required; business casual for the wives; jeans and a polo for the kids.

We traveled in Qatari embassy vehicles—Mercedes S-class sedans and G-wagens (short for *Geländewagen*), all armor plated and flying diplomatic flags. When in London, we'd get two officers assigned to us from Scotland Yard's Diplomatic Protection Group and a motorcycle escort.

I roomed with a guy called Nick (or Stumpy, because of his diminutive size) who was straitlaced, generous, and always prepared. The two of us found novel ways to amuse ourselves. We'd get up early, train, return home, shower, dress, and make up the beds so they looked immaculate. We knew that whichever cleaning woman was working that morning would be arriving precisely at 0800, so I'd set the alarm for 0805. Stumpy would then slide under the bed, and I would hide in the closet. The cleaning woman would knock on time. When no one answered, she'd let herself in with the key and start to clean. At 0805 the alarm would go off, and I'd emerge from the closet stretching and yawning as though I'd slept there, and Stumpy would come out from under the bed doing the same.

The confused look on the cleaning woman's face was bloody priceless!

We had a character on the team named Phil, who was a tall, very likable penny-pinching Scotsman. There was more chance of having a pint with the pope than seeing Phil take out his wallet.

Once when we were with the boss in Hong Kong, we found out he was attending a state function. Needing a new suit, Phil found a cheap tailor in the Temple Street Market who said he could make him a silk one in four hours for forty dollars.

I said, "Phil, nobody makes a decent suit in four hours."

He replied confidently, "You'll see, mate. I found a guy."

We were lodging on the fifty-second floor of the swanky Mandarin Hotel. At 1600 the tailor showed up with Phil's suit. It looked sharp and well made until Phil tried it on and discovered that the pants were four inches too short.

The tailor said through our terp, "No problem, sir. I left plenty of fabric. I'll let them out."

Now, Phil and Justin H., who was another member of our team, hated each other. Justin was a hard East End boy with a face that looked like it had been pushed through a meat grinder and back—a result of his many bouts as a bare-knuckle fighter. Any chance one of them could prank the other, they'd jump at it.

We were scheduled to leave for the event at 1900 hours. At 1800, we held a Chinese parliament in my room to go over all assignments. I noticed that Justin had a huge grin on his face.

"What's up, Justin?" I asked.

"You'll see."

At 1830, the tailor showed up with Phil's suit. Phil went to his room to try it on.

Meanwhile, Justin, who was dying, led us into the corridor outside Phil's door.

I whispered, "Justin, what did you do?"

He whispered back, "Wait for it. Just wait..."

We heard a loud scream from Phil's room, and immediately Justin exploded in hysterics. A moment later Phil came out with his pants cut above his ankles—like women's capris. Justin confessed that he told the tailor before he left that what Phil really wanted was to have the pants shortened a few more inches and to cut away the excess fabric.

"What the fuck do I do now?" Phil asked.

"Borrow some pants," I answered, trying not to laugh in his face.

At 1900 the rest of the team stood waiting downstairs in their suits by the cars. I came down the elevator with the boss, saying into my wrist mike, "Stand by. Stand by."

As we emerged and passed Phil, I glanced at his trousers, and they appeared okay.

I helped the boss to the limo, nodded off the other guys, climbed in the limo, and boom, we were off to the conference center. When we arrived, I watched Phil get out of the lead car and saw that he was walking with this weird gangster shuffle. I was thinking to myself, *What's up with that?*

I escorted the boss to his seat in the auditorium and backed away because the event was going to be televised and the room was already secure.

Upon finding Phil in the lobby, I asked, "What happened, mate? How'd you fix your trousers?"

He glowered at me and said, "Don't even ask."

"Seriously, how'd you fix them?"

He lifted up his jacket. What he'd done was to use his holster belt to cinch his trousers near the bottom of his pelvis. That's why he was shuffling when he walked.

All night, he complained, "My back is fucking killing me."

I laughed my head off. Still, Phil didn't learn his lesson. Two days later, he came to me and said that he needed a pair of shoes and heard that they made good handmade ones in Hong Kong.

"That's true, Phil. If you talk to one of the terps, he'll tell you where to go."

"No," Phil said. "I'm going to the Temple Street Market. I can get some oxford brogues that would cost a hundred pounds back home for twenty dollars."

I warned him, "Keep in mind that you get what you pay for."

Phil, being Phil, went straight to the Temple Street Market and ordered the shoes. When the brogues came back they looked good, and I thought that maybe he had proved me wrong.

The next day we were out with the boss shopping, and it was pissing rain. As we stood waiting outside a department store, I glanced at Phil's shoes and saw that the soles were curling up so that his socks showed through.

I asked, "Phil, what's up with your shoes?"

"You're not going to believe this," he answered. "The soles are made of fucking cardboard!"

*   *   *

While we were in Hong Kong, we learned that the boss's old man was conspiring to seize power back from his sons. Apparently he had hired a group of former French Foreign Legion and German special forces blokes from their GSG-9 to sneak back into Qatar and start causing trouble.

It just so happened that my old friend Pete knew one of the Corsicans who had been recruited by the father. One night they were chatting on the phone, and the Corsican said that he was headed to Qatar to work on a project for the sheikh.

Pete said, "That's a bit strange, because my mate Simon is currently working with the sheikh. Which sheikh are you working for?"

"I'm working with the dad," responded the Corsican.

"Where's the dad?"

"He's in Switzerland feeling put out by his sons and wants back in power."

Pete called up Dolly, and Dolly spoke to Topsy, who went to see the boss. HRH decided that for the next six months anyone entering Qatar with a French, German, or South African passport would be stopped and questioned.

Then we escorted him to the sumptuous Le Richemond Hotel in Geneva for a sit-down with Dad. The boss slapped the old man on the wrist and reminded him that he had plenty of money and needed to stop mucking around. Matter settled.

Lesson number 3: The PMC world is a tight one. Chances are you're going to run into the same operators numerous times in various places. They can help you navigate the murky waters of contract jobs and international politics.

*   *   *

At that point, I'd had enough bouncing from one city to another with the Qataris. So I returned to East London and was there two weeks looking for something more long-term when I got a call from Nigel R.

Nigel said, "Simon, I've got another gig, if you're interested. It's a security manager job for a mining company in Malaysia. It's good for a year initially, with the option to extend longer if you like."

"Sounds good. I'm interested."

"You're going to need another guy to work with," Nigel added.

"I'll get Pete." My childhood mate Pete was an excellent sniper and marksman, and the type of guy you wanted with you in a fight.

"Fine. Tomorrow after lunch come to Kensington; on King's Road there's a pub called the Chelsea Potter. When you get there, give me a ring on my cell, and I'll tell you where to go."

Pete and I knew the pub well. We met and ordered a plate of chips and two pints of Guinness. After spending a few minutes catching up with Pete, I called Nigel.

"When you get to the corner, turn left onto High Street," Nigel instructed. "It's the first house on the left."

"Sounds a bit cryptic," Pete commented.

"You know Nigel."

Outside we encountered a beautiful spring day—complete with flowers, butterflies, and girls in summer dresses. We were two blokes walking through one of the poshest neighborhoods in London in our best suits, clean-shaven, and with military haircuts.

Feeling good about life, I knocked on the door of an impressive-looking town house. A big, heavily muscled man answered. He passed a metal-detecting wand over our bodies and shot us funny looks.

"What was that about?" Pete whispered as we climbed a grand staircase to the second floor.

"A bit odd for a job interview, isn't it?" I whispered back.

We entered a second-floor living room handsomely decorated with expensive leather sofas, oriental rugs, and flat-screen TVs. A middle-aged woman sat on a sofa next to slim, gray-haired Nigel R. in a Savile Row suit.

She stood, greeted us, and introduced herself as Susan—no last name.

"Thank you for coming," she said, very businesslike. "Have a seat." No offer of coffee or tea.

"General Nigel R. has spoken very highly of you," said Susan. "Clearly, you're qualified for the job. Do you have any questions?"

I leaned forward and answered, "Quite a few, actually. The general hasn't told us much except that it's a security job for a mining company."

"Do you know where the mine is located?" she asked.

"The general told us Malaysia."

"Have you been?"

"No, but I've traveled extensively throughout the Far East."

"The job is to provide security for a gold mine my company is opening and to train a security team and guard force. You're happy doing that kind of thing?" Susan inquired. "You've worked with foreign nationals before?"

"Yes, I have."

"What would you do in terms of training a guard force?"

"I see that basically as a four-week course, teaching guard technique, perimeter security, quick reaction time, and so on. Guarding the transit of the gold to its exfil point is a separate course in mobile security. Sounds like you're going to need two teams—one for the mine and one for the mobile bit."

Susan folded her hands in her lap and nodded.

"That all sounds good," she said. "But that would be the second part of the job."

"What's the first part?" I asked.

"Currently, there's a small tribe living on the land. We need to move them on so we can commence groundbreaking and deforestation. They don't want to move," said Susan.

I glanced at Nigel R. and Pete, both of whom looked surprised.

"We've offered to relocate them to better housing with schools and a clinic, and even offered them jobs in the mine," she continued. "But they want to stay. So the first part of this is to move these people on."

I sat slightly flummoxed. "You just told me every way I can think of to do that in a legal fashion. So what would you propose?"

Susan's mouth tightened, and her tone turned slightly snippy. "I don't care how you move them on," she said. "We just want them gone."

A chill passed through my body. I said, "Okay, I think I understand. Probably the best thing to do now is for Pete and me to go off and have a think about how we would best do this."

"Fine."

We all stood and shook hands. Susan said, "Everything will be handled through the general. You probably won't see me again."

Turning to Nigel, I said, "General, we'll get back to you as soon as we figure out how to proceed."

Pete and I walked back to the Chelsea Potter. We went straight to the bar, ordered two more pints of Guinness, and returned to the table we had been sitting at before.

Pete sipped his pint, looked up at me, and asked, "You know what we're going to need for this job, right?"

"Yeah," I answered. "Shovels and lime and a lot of nine-millimeter ammo."

"Fuck that," Pete offered.

"Fuck that is right. I'm not going near this with a barge pole."

"Me, neither."

If working with the Qataris was on the light scale of PMC, Susan had just introduced us to the dark side.

I dialed Nigel R.'s cell phone and, when he answered, asked, "General, what the hell was that?"

"I had no idea about the indigenous personnel issue. It was pitched to me as a security management gig for a mining site."

"You know we're not doing it."

"Of course," Nigel offered. "Don't worry about it. Just walk away. I'll give you a call in a couple of days."

Pete and I drank our pints. I found out later that some other guys took the job and executed it.

It was a real eye-opener. Those jobs exist, and people are doing them. Not me. I've developed my skills and am willing to risk my life to protect people from harm and defend the principles I believe in, not to liquidate inconvenient people for multinational companies. But as I was learning, PMC work is wide in scope and full of surprises.

Lesson number 4: You have to bring your own skills, mates you can trust, and your own moral code. Because you're going to be asked to do all kinds of crazy shit in an assortment of dangerous places—some of it laugh-out-loud funny, some of it shocking and controversial, and some best described as heartbreaking.

CHAPTER TWO

ROMFORD

I WAS born and raised in East London, in a rough, grimy suburb called Romford, a dozen miles east of central London. Built on the back of burgeoning light industry that began in the 1800s, Romford is still commonly referred to as "Slag Town"—slag being the waste from coal mines but also meaning "slut" or "scumbag." It's the kind of place where if you look at someone you don't know on the street, you're likely to be challenged, and teenage pregnancy and rhyming slang are common—such as "rub-a-dub" for "pub," "bees and honey" for "money," and "brown bread" for "dead."

Back in the seventies when I grew up, it was known for its outdoor market, dog races, and rows and rows of housing estates—or government housing projects. My dad worked in the massive Ford Motor plant, which employed most of the male adults in Romford and nearby Dagenham. Common were flocks of angry young men heading to the pubs every night to get gartered, girls with dodgy makeup looking for a shag, geezers on push bikes, rundown council flats, and thick cockney accents. Think *EastEnders,* and you won't be far off.

As gritty and common as Romford was, it prepared me for dealing with the underside of life. Nothing was as it appeared, the men were hard and violent, and you had to be clever and quick with your fists in order to survive. At the same time, though Romford was low income, people nurtured a sense of community. Neighbors left their front doors open as kids played tag and football (aka soccer) on the broken asphalt and cobblestone streets. Mornings, my mates and I would walk with little packs through town to our old redbrick school named Crownfield, past cobbler shops and bakeries selling scones and bread.

Ours was a terraced house with other houses glued to either side of it—not a semidetached, which was reserved for the better off—which cost a mere fifty pence (less than one US dollar) a month. It consisted of three bedrooms, a little backyard, and a patch of grass where you'd usually see two or three good cars tightly parked. Entering the living room was like stepping into Aladdin's cave. Crammed helter-skelter in the little space were brand-new TV sets, Betamax video machines, pinball machines, Ataris, and other goods still in boxes. In my six-by-six-foot bedroom upstairs I'd jimmied in a huge pinball machine that blocked the door.

Nothing in our house added up, because my dad, though nominally employed by Ford Motors, derived his main income from membership in the local firm, or gang. Each housing estate was run by one, and most of the dads were members. Mine was a hard man without a loving bone in his body, and a notorious ringleader.

This was the midseventies, before the drug trade blew up. My dad's firm made its cash the old-school way—robbing postal offices and savings and loan associations with hoods and shotguns, collecting protection money from mum-and-pop stores, and racketeering. He'd purchase ten slot machines and force the local pubs to take them in. All the profits from the machines would go to the firm, and the pubs would have to pay rent on them, too. If another firm tried to slide its machines in, my dad and his mates would smash them to pieces, then treat the blokes to a beating with tire irons and bats.

Back then a lot of electric goods were shipped through England on lorries. My dad and his mates would wait in a van on the side of A3 or M25 motorway for lorries coming from the docks. They'd hijack it, threaten the driver, then drive the lorry into town, strip it down, and sell the goods inside.

I've blocked out most memories of my father, who seemed to solve every problem with his fists. Evenings, he'd come home from work, shout at my mum, smack me and my brother, kick shit, then go out with his mates to plan another robbery. One of the few things I remember is hiding under the kitchen table while he went on one of his rampages. He was in and out of prison constantly, and most of my relationship with him was through iron bars during 2:00 p.m. visiting hours at the lockup.

The fact that my mum married him still confounds me, because she and my dad came from opposite ends of the social universe. Mum was raised in an affluent family from a town called Brentwood, four stops farther out from London on the tube. Her great-granddad started the printing trade in London and had once been mayor of West Ham. She grew up on country estates surrounded by cricket lawns. But the wild in my dad attracted her. So she gave up that life, moved to Romford where she still lives, and stuck by him until he died in 1994.

I've got a brother who's five years older than me. Today he's a member of London Metropolitan Police, which is ironic, because growing up all our role models were criminals. It wasn't like your friend Billy's dad was, say, a lawyer or a dentist. His old man worked in the same factory and was a member of the same firm. Rough blokes and crime were all we knew.

So we drifted into it. I started at age eight. I'd find out what kind of novelty erasers the kids in my school wanted (*Star Wars* figures were the craze), pinch them from a store, and sell 'em for eighty pence when they cost a pound each in the store. The kids would save twenty pence; I'd pocket eighty. Pure genius.

As a teenager, I took the same business model I'd used for erasers and applied it to cars. We called it ringing. A client would come to me looking to buy a black 1985 911 Porsche. He didn't want to go to a dealer and pay seventy thousand pounds. So he'd ask me, Can you fix me up?

Sure, sir. Right on it!

My mates and I would cruise through London looking for that particular make, model, and color. Back then all you had to do was drop a jockey strip down the window and pull the lock. Later, when the Germans developed central locking, my mates and I came up with our own ingenious feat of engineering. We'd cut a tennis ball in half, press it against the driver's side lock, and push it down until it created a vacuum. Then we'd smack the ball with a Ping-Pong paddle to force air into the locking system and pop the locks. The funny part was when guys like us who clearly weren't from the level of society to play tennis went into the hardware store to buy twenty tennis balls.

After hot-wiring the car, we'd drive it to a shop we had in one of the tunnels near the East London locks. The archways there housed various mechanics and members of the motor trade. You might have seen them depicted in the 1971 film *Get Carter,* where Michael Caine plays a British gangster revenging the death of his brother. Bloody brilliant.

We'd back the car in, pop the hood, chisel off the old plate with the VIN number on it, and replace the plate with a new one with a new number. We had a friend called Twinsey who worked at the Brit version of the DMV, known as the DVLA. We'd ring up Twinsey and read him the new number. Twinsey would type it into his big clunky computer and reregister the car, so everything appeared on the up-and-up.

The new owner would get a logbook or certificate in the post. For a car of that quality we'd charge twenty thousand pounds. Ten would go to the firm; ten would land in our pockets.

The point was to flip the cars as quickly as possible. No new paint jobs or changes of tires or hoods. Just pop off the old plate and reregister it. Nice and tidy.

I started this at fourteen. My crew consisted of myself, Curtis, Barry, and Gary. Curtis is now a reputable real-estate agent in London. Barry is a fireman and still a total character. He's the kind of guy who, if your house is on fire, and he shows up, throws extra gasoline on it, and files an insurance claim. Because Barry ain't saving it.

Gary remained on the dark side and became one of the biggest drug dealers in East London. Last time I saw him, about ten years ago, he was living large with a big house in the country and an estate in Marbella, Spain, on the Costa del Crime. We call it that because all the criminals went there before Spain and the UK signed an extradition treaty. Now guys like Gary go to Florida—better weather, thongs, and Latin booty.

Cocky men about town with money in our pockets and wearing our new Fila tracksuits, which were the rage at the time, we'd hang with Darren C. and his sons Michael and Tony. Darren, who was my dad's age and a firm guy as well, had invested his money in pubs and nightclubs, building a reputable business. One Friday night, my mates and I stumbled out of one of his clubs in London—completely shit-faced.

We'd arrived by tube and didn't have a car to get us back to Romford. So Gary said, "Let's just jack one."

Seemed like a reasonable suggestion given our line of work and our current state of inebriation. Around the bend we found a '76 Mini Clubman Estate station wagon, which we were into and hot-wiring in seconds. We were laughing our way back to Romford, pissed out of our minds, Run-DMC's "Hard Times" blasting through the cheap little stereo, trying to keep the car between the lines, until we saw the flashing blues lights of a cop car behind us.

Gary, at the wheel, said, "Hold on, it's gonna get hairy," and hit the gas. His intention was to outrun them. What he didn't realize was that the max speed of the Clubman was about sixty. Still he gave it a go, zipping through one housing estate after another, trying to lose them. We entered Romford with the cops still tight on our tail. Gary swerved onto a street lined with new tower blocks.

The Clubman was running low on petrol, so we ditched it, and followed Barry as he bolted like a man possessed to the top of one of the apartment towers. As soon as we got there, Curtis said, "Well done, wanker."

Looking around, we realized that we had done a stupid thing and trapped ourselves. The cops were waiting downstairs. They knew we had to come down eventually, one way or another.

After two hours, I had to take a piss and went downstairs. The cops grabbed us, handcuffed our wrists behind us, and took us to the Romford police station. It was my first time in jail. All the macho talk my mates and I had been exchanging minutes before quickly faded.

Two days later, my mum posted bail. She was annoyed, but not angry. My dad was in prison at the time at Wormwood Scrubs. In a sad voice, she said to me, "You've stepped onto that ladder now."

Two weeks later, I appeared in court and was sentenced to eight months in Borstal, more politely known as a youth custody center, which is the British equivalent of juvenile detention. I was sixteen.

All four of us were taken to a place called Rush Green, which later was transformed into a mental home and then demolished. It was about the size of three terraced houses knocked into one. Each boy had his own little room. Downstairs consisted of a living room with TV, dartboard, pool table, and a classroom where we were supposed to continue our studies.

My mate Pete, who would follow me into the British military and my PMC adventures, was in already for theft. He showed me the ropes. Borstal was more boring than awful. We took lessons in English, history, math, and literature, but I didn't pay attention and learned nothing. Afternoons, we were sent out to clean up graffiti or pick up trash — stupid jobs like that. You could also choose to help the OAPs (old-age pensioners) in their homes under the supervision of a social worker. Pete and I always chose an old-age pensioner named Mrs. Miggins, a Margaret Rutherford–like character who treated us like grandchildren. She didn't like seeing us slaving around her house. Instead she'd fix tea, set out cakes, and invite us to chat with her.

A month or so in, recruiters from the army, Royal Navy, and air force (or air farce, as we later called it) paid us a visit. They were looking for energetic, aggressive boys like us that they could mold into soldiers, or cannon fodder.

First, they did a short presentation involving lots of cool pictures and a video that talked about all the exotic travel that we could be doing. I remember the video showing this guy skiing down a mountain one minute, then lying on a chaise longue drinking a cocktail with some girl in a bikini draped over him—all very James Bond. Then anyone who was interested could have a one-on-one with a recruiter.

Being somewhat intrigued and a cocky young punk, I walked straight up to a very intimidating guy from the Royal Marines named Corporal Bob—a former semipro rugby player and the epitome of a kick-ass drill sergeant. He was the size of a small house with a badger of a mustache under his broken nose.

Corporal Bob had my file with him and got straight to business. He said, "Your family history is here, Simon, and I can see that you're following the plan."

At that time, the trade in illegal drugs was starting to pick up. Local firms were moving away from armed robbery and making more money dealing coke, Mandrax (or meth), and LSD. Before, if you stepped on the toes of someone in a rival firm, you'd get a beating. Now blokes were getting gunned down, and turf wars were growing more frequent and violent.

Corporal Bob said, "Simon, you keep doing this shit, and you'll end up doing a twenty-year stretch in Wormwood Scrubs like your dad. Either that or you'll end up dead in some back alley with some cat pissing on you. It might not happen for a couple of years, but it's going to happen."

I knew he was telling the truth.

The marines, he said, would channel my aggression in a positive direction. I'd get regular pay, housing, and a chance to travel the world. I'd see the Middle East and Africa. I'd feel proud of myself, and I'd be respected.

I was sold. But still sixteen and a minor, I needed my mum's permission first.

I expected her to be excited. But when I told her, she said sadly, "The marines might keep you off the streets and out of prison, but I'll never see you. I'll lose you to your new family."

"No, Mum," I countered. "It won't be like that. I promise."

It turned out that Mum was right.

Lesson number 5: You can never go back.

And why would I choose to? My childhood in Romford wasn't a walk in the park. Between the beatings from my dad and the shouting in between, I don't have a lot of happy memories, and most of those that remain have been burned away and replaced by the violence and conflict in the many places I've visited since.

CHAPTER THREE
ROYAL MARINES/SBS

I **HAD** signed up to join the British Royal Marines—a relatively small unit of amphibious, highly specialized commandos capable of deploying on short notice in support of Her Majesty's government's military and diplomatic objectives overseas. In the mid-1980s, it consisted of roughly seven thousand men, half of whom were support staff, command personnel, and trainers.

But I was sent by mistake to the naval recruit training center, near Torpoint on the southeast tip of England. I remember leaving home and getting on the train for what seemed like the longest journey of my life, and one that I didn't want to end. Even though I was a cocky punk, I was nervous, getting up from my seat every five minutes to get a bite of food from the cart, wondering what my mates back home were up to, watching guys my age boarding at the stops along the way looking anxious.

Upon arrival at Plymouth, we were greeted by a friendly navy petty officer, who checked our names on a clipboard and showed us to a bus that took us to Torpoint, where we got on a ferry that carried us to a land base called HMS Raleigh. Once we walked through the main gate and met our training team, petty officers started screaming in our faces: "Bags here! Fall in! Three deep! Toes on this line; heels here! Back straight; face forward! Answer when your name's called! Then pick up your bloody bag and hurry over there!"

We split into three classes. Mine included a number of thieves and ruffians like myself, including Neil Hart (Nidge, we called him) from Manchester, who had been on track to become a professional footballer until he hurt his leg; Harvey Langman from South London, a former Olympic swimmer; Ian Robertson (Robbo), who became my lifelong friend; and Gordie from Newcastle.

Our class teacher was a woman officer or Wren (for Women's Royal Naval Service—formed in World War I), who hated us. We loathed her with equal relish. The first eight weeks were super basic and involved learning ship husbandry, how to take care of your uniform and your kit, how to fold stuff, how to polish your shoes properly, how to sew on a button, how to wash yourself, and that kind of nonsense. There were bits of physical training (PT) thrown in as well.

I thought to myself: *Getting into the corps is really quite easy.*

What Robbo and I didn't realize was that we had been sent to the wrong place. It was only when our instructors told us that we were going to be weapons operators on a ship at sea for six to twelve months at a time that we ran to see PO (presiding officer) Wren in her office.

Robbo said, "Ma'am, we think there's been some kind of mistake. We signed up for the Royal Marines, not the navy."

"No, no," she replied. "I've got your paperwork here. This is what you signed up for. You're in the proper place."

So we went to see our drill sergeant—a six-four marine brick shithouse named Sergeant Stanner. Everyone was afraid of him on account of his intimidating manner and loud voice. But he turned out to be quite sympathetic.

After looking into our situation, he said, "You two lads are in the wrong place, and you have two options. You can either pull out now, reinterview with the Marines, and go through the whole process again, or finish the last four weeks of training here and put in for a transfer."

Robbo and I chose the latter and became the only two blokes in British military history to go through both sets of recruitment courses. After graduation, with my mum and stepdad in attendance to watch me receive the Best Recruit Award, I returned home to Romford to wait six months for the next Royal Marine intake class.

When September rolled around, I was on another train, this time to Exmouth in Devon. All the recruits turned up with shaved heads this time. A massive drill corporal, called a drill leader (DL), Jumper Collins, lined us up and frog-marched us through a barbed-wire fence and past a barrier. A gray-looking sixties-era building sat to our right. To the left was Bottom Field, where another class was getting thoroughly trashed. I saw wankers sprinting with huge packs on their backs; others were falling off of ropes and diving into water tanks.

Myself, my childhood mate Pete, and thirty-three other recruits made up 607 Troop. Robbo fell in two troops behind us. Day 2, week 1, we marched to see Alfie Bass, who had once been a marine sniper in the Suez but was now a wiry grandfatherlike figure in his sixties. He issued each one of us two pillowcases, two sheets, two blankets, and one counterpane, or bedspread. The next two weeks we spent learning how to iron them correctly so the creases ran straight up the middle. Then we spent whole days learning how to make our beds. It was maddening.

Mondays we had to have a "closed bed"—sheets pulled up covering the pillows, the counterpane laid out full so you couldn't see the sheets. Tuesdays were slightly different—counterpane folded down and wide, across the exact middle of the bed, with two blankets stacked one on top of the other at the end. Wednesday, the counterpane was placed halfway up the bed with the blankets stacked side by side at the bottom.

Day 3, we marched back to see Alfie Bass to collect our rig—combat boots and pants, two green shirts, two sets of white shirts, one pair of white socks, one pair of white taps. Next came a lesson on how to iron our pants with white creases down the front of each leg.

After two weeks of induction, we met our training team. A friendly looking corporal in a green beret stood before us and said, "Hi, I'm Fish. To my left is Trev Thomas, he'll be your troop sergeant. Standing to my right is Paul Horrigan, one of the other training-team guys."

Fish gave a little spiel about the importance of keeping our heads down and pressing forward. He said, "We're here to drive you to your limits, but it's never as bad as it seems."

Yeah, right. The minute we walked out of the induction room, the smiles disappeared, and the shouting started. "Everybody get in line and march. Stop and give us fifty push-ups!"

Those first two weeks broke each one of us physically and emotionally. I called my mum every night from a pay phone and told her I wanted to quit. She asked me to stick it out.

Week 2 we moved to the second floor, and a new class (608) slipped onto the first. Every class was given a T-shirt with a team slogan on the back. Ours said HAD ENOUGH? which was totally apropos. One kid in 608 failed the swimming test by drowning. So 608's motto became "It pays to be a swimmer."

One kid on 609 committed suicide by slitting his wrists. The corps had a slogan that went "A cut above the rest." The slogan for 609 Troop, displayed prominently on the back of its T-shirts, became A CUT ABOVE THE WRIST.

We worried about some of the guys in our unit. Like Archie, who was so small we used to put him in his rucksack, or bergen, as we called it, and carry him around the yard. All of us looked out for Archie, because we were afraid he would crack as the physical challenges grew progressively harder.

But Archie gutted it out. He went on to 45 Commando, sergeant, in the SBS and retired several years ago with full honors.

Our days started at 0600. After breakfast, we'd stand for inspection. All the gear in our lockers had to be color coded, clothes ironed and folded to fit an A4 board, shoes at the bottom, cap up top with the peak facing out. If Fish or Sergeant Thomas found anything wrong, the whole team would be punished. At the end of inspection, they'd ask, "Anybody got any questions? Anyone want to go home yet?"

We all had questions, but none of us dared open his mouth, fearing that he'd be throttled before he got the first words out.

All of us would be wearing the rig of the day. If we were wearing rig 1, and the training team felt like messing with our heads, Sergeant Thomas would scream, "Outside, two minutes, rig number two!"

So we'd run back inside, tear off our training clothes, dump them on the bed, pull on the pants and shirts that made up rig 2, and run outside. Sergeant Horrigan would go in the room, throw all our training clothes on the floor, and start jumping on them with his dirty boots.

Then Sergeant Thomas would shout, "Go back inside. You've got two minutes to change back into your training rig."

Now we had to change back into the soiled, wrinkled training rig. Outside, Sergeant Thomas would bawl us out for wearing dirty clothes. We also knew that anything we wore that day had to be washed, ironed, folded, and placed back in our lockers before we could turn in. So we wouldn't be getting to sleep that night before 0200.

After inspection, we'd be off to our classes. Maybe field craft or military law or regular courses like English and math, subjects I had failed in school but was acing now. In addition to the course work, we did lots of PT and team drills, with some weapons handling thrown in.

After week 15, 607 Troop had been whittled down from thirty-five to fifteen recruits. That's when the commando phase started, and we traded our blue berets for cap comforters, which looked like World War II–era beanies. This new phase involved less time in the classrooms and more hours doing field exercises—like night-time navigation, map reading, weapons handling, infantry tactics, hill drills, pack runs, and fitness tests—our bread and butter.

Instructors amped up the PT to bring everyone to the same level. They had us doing obstacle-course runs, fireman's carries, leopard crawls, and rope work. All of this built up to test week, when they trucked us out to Woodbury Common for the beginning of what was to become a colossal thrashing. First, we were submerged in pairs in a water-filled tunnel known as Peter's Pool. After we succeeded pulling ourselves and our mates through, we then ran the murder mile back to camp soaking wet with our weapons and all our gear.

From there we were directed straight to the firing range for the next test, first checking to make sure our rifle sights hadn't been smashed off in the previous drill. We had to put down five lots of five shots each from different distances—twenty meters, twenty-five, fifty, one hundred. All the time the instructors were shouting questions at you.

"What year was the corps formed?"

"Sixteen sixty-four!"

"What month?"

"October!"

"What day?"

"The eighteenth, sir!"

"Wrong! Try again. And don't call me sir, I work for a living!"

You were trying to concentrate on the target and answer correctly, which was mentally exhausting. And the tests weren't over. Because we still had to complete basic fitness, and after that the brutal thirty-miler, which we had to finish in less than six hours carrying all our gear and rifle—staggering uphill, tumbling down the inclines, and trying to run on the flat. Once I stumbled across the finish line, I passed out.

Coming to, I looked up to see Sergeant Thomas standing over me, handing me a green beret. I had graduated.

My mates and I had gone from induction troop to recruit troop and were now members of the king's troop. Suddenly, there was no more PT or thrashings or inspections.

Instead, the instructors talked to us about pensions, pay scales, and promotions and asked us to fill out paperwork for the trades we'd like to learn. We found out that the corps wasn't all about fighting. In addition to armorists and heavy weapons specialists, there were also vehicle mechanics, guys who illustrated maps, navigators, swimmer canoeists, and sports marines who were on the corps' rugby, cricket, football, rowing, field gun, and bicycling teams.

I checked off "top-tier fighting unit" and was assigned to 40 Commando. At seventeen and a half years old I was packed off to Northern Ireland to do surveillance on IRA members, guard outposts, and go on secret missions. Real adult stuff for a scruffy lad from Romford.

*   *   *

While in 40, Pete and I did a stint in Commachio Group, guarding the transit of nuclear weapons. After that I completed the Junior Command Course to become a corporal and put in to join the Special Boat Squadron (renamed the Special Boat Service a few years later), which was considered the crème de la crème of the Royal Marines and the maritime equivalent of the British Special Air Service. The SBS was like the US Navy SEALs, only smaller (approximately 250 strong) and less well funded.

Entry into that very elite unit involved another six months of training that included diving, learning how to operate swimmer delivery vehicles, small-unit tactics, beach reconnaissance, and maritime counterterrorism. Each member of the SBS had to have a specialty. I chose combat medicine. My medical training included weekends in a local civilian hospital sewing people up and treating the drunken wreckage that came into the ER on Friday and Saturday nights. I dare say the hospital staffs were glad to have us there on a few occasions. An ER full of rowdy drunks isn't singing and dancing.

Having completed training, I was assigned to X Squad, whose mission was land-based counterterrorism. That's where I learned the fundamentals of working in a small unit where teamwork was imperative and each of us understood that we were never going to be the toughest or the smartest guy in the room.

If I happened to be running a four-man unit that was given a mission, I would put a plan in place and present it to the rest of team. Since I was the medic, I'd make sure we had someone else on the team with medical skills to back me up if I got nicked. Same with other skills like radio operator, navigator, or explosives expert.

After presenting the plan to the unit, I'd ask: Does anybody have any questions? Or do any of you have a better way of doing it?

Someone in the unit might say: We tried it that way last month, Simon, and it didn't work.

I'd amend the plan—always open to suggestions.

Working as a team, we snatched war criminals off the streets of Bosnia and Serbia and deposited them in The Hague. We trained DEA agents in Colombia in how to conduct jungle warfare and did a ton of work in Northern Ireland, which was a hotbed of violence in the early 1990s.

Much of what we did to counter the IRA involved surveillance and gathering evidence for the Serious Organised Crime Agency (SOCA) so government prosecutors could make criminal cases in court. This work took me throughout Northern Ireland, to Spain, and into South America. In the process I watched the IRA transform from a terrorist group into a criminal enterprise making boatloads of money.

Clever IRA Belfast Brigade commanders hired their men out to teach cartel members in Colombia and Mexico how to do countersurveillance and defend their turf. IRA terrorists actually taught courses in IED (improvised explosive device) making and deployment, sniper skills, and close-quarter assassination from cars and motorcycles. They advised on how to move illegal consignments through customs. It was a regular curriculum in how to succeed as an international criminal.

They also trafficked drugs and arms, laundered money, and were making serious bank. I remember following one IRA Belfast Brigade commander, Paddy, who was staying on a farm in Northern Ireland. He also owned houses in London, Cork, and Belfast and a villa in Spain and had been under surveillance for months when we got the order to kick his door in.

My team did the hard knocks, which involved breaking down the door and arresting the target. We had a second SBS team protecting the SOCA auditors who had been in Belfast going through Paddy's finances. He sat handcuffed on the sofa when the blokes from SOCA marched in to inspect the place. They found three new cars in the barn, some fancy TV sets, and a few handguns. Nothing much.

One of the guys on my team tried to turn the TV on to check the score of the Chelsea–Manchester United football match, but the TV didn't work. He tested the plug. The TV still didn't come on. So he unscrewed the back of the cabinet and saw that the electronics had been removed and the space stuffed with cash.

Same thing with the cars. The engines had been lifted out and the space packed with shrink-wrapped euros and pounds. The money was hauled off on pallets, and Paddy wasn't getting it back.

A lot of the work we did at the time took us to cities like Belfast, Armagh, and Newry, where we did surveillance, snatch and grabs, or taking out bad guys. Some of it was bloody deadly; most of it I still can't talk about; and other ops didn't go as planned. Like the time Shaun, Carl Kresey, and I were working in a hide, or urban observation post (OP), on Falls Road, doing surveillance on a high-ranking IRA brigade commander.

We hid in the attic of the terraced house adjoining the brigade commander's. One of our tech guys had drilled through the ceiling and run a fiber-optic cable down and across into his bedroom. Missions like these were extremely high risk because we knew that if the IRA got its hands on someone from our unit, it would torture him and drill his kneecaps out before applying the coup de grâce.

The three of us worked with another three-man unit on a seven-day rotation. Super clandestine. We'd carry in all the food and drink we'd need at the start of the week and carry out all our waste in plastic bags at the end.

All week we'd lie on individual mattresses near the little attic window, which provided the only light. We worked in one-hour shifts, with one guy listening through earphones and watching the monitor, one guy resting, the third catching some z's. Since the walls were extremely thin, we couldn't make any noise. If nature called, we'd carefully roll off the mattress, retreat to a dark corner, and do our business in a plastic bag or bottle, which we immediately capped or tied up.

As the op drifted into early July, the temperature climbed into the upper eighties.

One afternoon I was reading a thick book in the light from the attic window, when Shaun, who was slightly older and as serious as a heart attack, whispered, "What's that smell?"

"Don't know, mate."

As the afternoon wore on, the stench got stronger until it started to bother me, too.

"What the hell *is* that?" Shaun asked.

Evening came, and the room turned dark. Shaun spoke up again.

"You hear that?" he asked.

"Not really. No," I whispered back.

Then we both heard a little squeaky noise from the dark corner to our right.

Shaun whispered, "It's a fucking rat!"

I didn't know that rats were his pet peeve. Minutes later, I was recording something in my notepad, when I saw a shape scurry across the mattress. It was a five-inch-long rat covered with something that stuck to its fur.

"Fucking A!" said Shaun. We spotted four more, bringing the total up to five.

"Guys before us must have left some garbage behind, which attracted them," I offered.

"Yeah. What are they eating?"

That's when I recognized the smell and realized it came from the same substance they were covered with. I said, "They've been eating through our bags of shit."

"Fucking hell!" Shaun exclaimed. "Those fuckers are riddled with disease. We've gotta find a way to rebag it."

"With what?" I asked. "We've got three more days, and I've only got three bags left. How many have you got?"

"Three, too," he whispered back.

"Wake Carl and find out how many he has."

Carl was down to three as well.

We suffered through. At 0300 the seventh day, we did a handover to the next team and gave our tapes and notes to the boss.

"What'd you get?" he asked.

"Sir, we've basically been covered with feces the last four days, fighting off rats, listening to this guy bang his Page Three model girlfriend," I reported.

"That all?"

"That's all we heard and saw, sir. Yes."

The next team took traps with them to deal with the rats. But in terms of surveillance they got the same results.

We learned later that the IRA brigade commander had known about the surveillance all along because one of the neighbors had seen us going over the fence at 0300 and warned him. Hardly the Tier 1 commando stuff you see in movies.

*   *   *

Another time Steve J. and I got orders to do a surveillance job at a country estate just off the A3 south of London. Steve was a tough East End lad who had done a lot of bare-knuckle fighting. He had scar tissue over his eyes and talked kind of slow but was super smart. The commander said, "We think there's an IRA cell moving about, and we think they're using local barns to conceal their equipment."

We built a hide on the estate and stayed there—two days on, two days off—for a week without seeing anything. Week 2, night 1, Steve J. woke me and whispered, "I think we've got movement."

"Where?"

"It looks like a Range Rover's approaching without lights."

I put on the night-vision goggles (NVGs) and checked it out. "Yes," I reported. "Two pax [persons] up. Two males. Twenty to forty-five years of age."

They parked the Range Rover and disappeared into a barn.

"You see any weapons?" Steve asked.

"No longs, mate. Maybe they're concealing shorts. Couldn't tell."

Twenty minutes later they came out carrying something, which they loaded into the back of the Range Rover.

"Can you see what they've got?" asked Steve.

I squinted through the NVGs and answered, "Looks like saddles."

"Saddles?"

"I'm no equestrian, but they look like saddles. Yes."

Next day, I left the hide and reported to the boss. "About two in the morning, these two boys got out of their vehicles, went into a barn, and came out with saddles. Couldn't get a good description."

"Saddles?" the boss asked.

"Definitely."

"You sure it's saddles. How many?"

"Two."

"That all?"

"One of the guys went back in and came out carrying a load of straps."

"What did they do then?"

"They drove off."

"Did you follow them?"

"No. But I informed the street team."

"Great work," the colonel said in his upper-crust accent. "Same thing tonight."

Later, when I met up with Steve, I said to him, "This job is weird. No one in the unit knows anything about it. And what are these blokes going to do, raid London on horseback?"

That night, we returned to the hide in the pitch black. The daytime team reported that they had seen people working at the main house. We decided that maybe terrorists were using the barn of this prestigious home as a hideout or a place to store arms.

I said to Steve, "Tonight we're going balls out."

"Roger, mate."

Again at two in the morning, a Range Rover pulled up to the barn, headlights off. Two dudes got out and emerged fifteen minutes later carrying saddles.

I wrote it all down in my notebook and radioed the boys in the street. "All call signs stand by; they're going to hit Blue One in about five minutes. It's all yours from there."

Next morning the colonel had a big grin on his face.

"Fantastic job last night. Fantastic job!" he exclaimed.

"Colonel," I said excitedly. "I think Steve and I figured out what's been going on. Those blokes have been hiding weapons in the barn for some kind of attack. Or they're cleaning it out to get ready to move things in."

"No. No, no, Corporal. It's nothing like that. These guys are professional saddle thieves. They raided a couple estates in the area. I figured mine was next, and I wanted to catch them red-handed."

I had heard that the colonel was from a wealthy family, but had no idea it was his country estate.

"I'm sorry, boss? That's your estate?" I asked.

"Jolly well is. I thought you fellows knew all along."

"No, sir. We've been working twenty-four hours nonstop, one shift during the day, one shift at night. We've been doing this for almost two weeks now."

"Well, good job. When they went out, the mobile team caught them. Do you know what a good saddle is worth?"

"No clue, sir."

"Tens of thousands of pounds. The local community is going to be extremely pleased."

It was a total misuse of regiment time.

Lesson number 6: Nonsense of that sort happens all the time both within the regiment and in PMC work, and upper-class eccentrics like the colonel get away with it.

Steve and I ran into him ten years later when we were both working for a private security company, and he needed guys to guard the racehorses he had running for Queen's Cup.

We drove down the A3 to the same estate, parked, and watched the former corps colonel walk out wearing his riding ensemble—jodhpurs, green riding pants, boots, jacket.

"I don't know if you guys know," he said, "but at this time of year there's a lot of thieving in the area."

"Is there?" I asked.

"Yes. Yes."

"Saddles?"

"Yes, by jove. How do you know?"

"You don't remember us, do you, sir?"

He looked confused.

"Steve and I did a job for you about ten years ago when we were in X Squad."

"By jove, yes, I do remember. You're the guys who saved my saddlery!"

What a fucking wanker.

A few months later my time in the SBS was cut short by a crash-landing on a routine training parachute jump. One frosty November morning I stood at the back of the transport plane watching the green and gold colors of the Devonshire countryside pass beneath me. Funny part of it was, I didn't have to jump that day; I just wanted to, because I loved it.

I waited a little too long to pull the cord and was traveling too fast, which caused me to land heavy on my left side and smash my left knee and thigh, resulting in a hematoma. A one-way trip to the naval med center, two months of rehab and home leave later, I was sitting across from the doc, who told me there would be no more leaping out of planes for me or long marches with one hundred pounds of kit.

"That's all very good, Doc," I said, "but I'm a marine; that's what I do."

"Not anymore," he replied.

After that it was a trip to see my commander and discuss a way for me to stay in the corps. As nicely as he could, he told me that in terms of continuing on the teams, I was finished. He offered instead to keep me on as a training officer.

Being in my early thirties and still eager to mix it up, I considered that no more than a glorified desk job. If I couldn't deploy on operations with my mates, there was no point staying in the regiment. So I decided to hand in my notice.

Pete, who had also decided to leave the corps, asked me, "What will you do now, mate? In civvy street?"

"No idea. Haven't even thought about that, frankly."

Turned out that there was no need to, because Marvin C. rang my cell during the taxi ride home.

CHAPTER FOUR

SCIMITAR

A COZY relationship had existed between the SBS (and the SAS) and private security companies for years by the time I showed up on the scene in 1999, which made sense, because we possessed skills that could easily be transferred from one to the other. Many of us spoke multiple languages, and our proficiencies included counterinsurgency, hostage rescue, snatch and grabs, and security and surveillance, skills that became increasingly in demand in an era of terrorism and asymmetrical warfare.

One of the first SAS officers to transfer the expertise he had acquired in the regiment to private business was Major David Walker. A bright gent with a sterling reputation and political connections high up in the Conservative Party, he had served as a battalion leader on difficult deployments in Northern Ireland and South America, experiences that made him an expert in fighting rural and urban terrorists.

Seeing an opportunity to provide security services to private companies and high-profile individuals, Major Walker retired from the

Brit mil in 1974 and became managing director of a company called Control Risks. Three years later, Walker bought out the small outfit within the company dedicated to covert paramilitary operations and renamed it Keenie Meenie Services (KMS). *Keeni meeni* is Swahili for the movement of a snake through the grass.

His new company quickly landed a lucrative contract to train and supervise the special forces of the new sultan of Oman. Coincidentally, a few years earlier Walker had helped the new sultan depose his father in a bloodless coup. As General Nigel R. had done with SERAC in Qatar, Major Walker used his relationship with the sultan to help get KMS off the ground.

Filling the company's ranks with highly skilled veterans from the SAS, SBS, and Royal Marines, Walker signed contracts with King Fahd of Saudi Arabia to guard the king and his advisers and with the governments of Pakistan and Sri Lanka to train their special forces. President Nimeiri of Sudan hired KMS to help conduct paramilitary operations against insurgents, and the Aga Khan hired it to track down his kidnapped racehorse Shergar.

In 1987, after getting caught up in the Iran-Contra scandal, he abruptly shut down KMS, which had been located at 22 South Orderly Street, and moved one stop up the tube to 7 Abington Road in South Kensington to reopen it as Scimitar Security Ltd. Walker also bought a place up the block, called the Wendy House, where blokes in his hire stayed between assignments.

I took my own turn at Wendy House twelve years later, when, after turning down the job for the mining company in Malaysia—the one that wanted Pete and me to "relocate" an entire community—I entered into Scimitar's employ.

These were still the easy days of private security work prior to 9/11. My job this time was to guard US-born philanthropist, book collector, and billionaire Sir Paul Getty, the eldest son of one of the richest men in the world. Sir Paul, as we called him, had lived a wild and dramatic life. He and his second wife—Dutch model and actress Talitha Pol—had been fixtures on the swinging sixties scene in London, hanging with Mick Jagger and his then-girlfriend Marianne Faithfull. Compton Miller, who chronicled the scene, described Getty as "a swinging playboy who drove fast cars, drank heavily, experimented with drugs, and squired raunchy starlets." In his 2010 autobiography *Life*, Keith Richards fondly recalled that Getty and his wife "had the best and finest opium."

In 1971 Talitha died of a heroin overdose in Rome. Two years later, his eldest son, John Getty III, was kidnapped in Rome by Calabrian mobsters, who demanded a $17 million ransom. Getty paid the money after receiving one of the boy's severed ears in the mail.

When I met him, he struck me as a friendly, down-to-earth man with serious health problems. Due to alcohol and drug abuse, his circulation was bad, his kidneys were failing, and he was wheelchair bound. While he was receiving weekly dialysis treatments in a clinic near his big estate in Oxford, his third wife, Lady Victoria, had started to receive death threats.

So Scimitar organized a twelve-man mobile security team and put me in charge. The MT, as we called it, was added to the eight-man residential security team Sir Paul already had securing his twenty-five-hundred-acre Wormsley Estate. The residence itself possessed state-of-the-art security with cameras, infrared motion sensors, and two-pronged panic buttons that connected directly to the Metropolitan Police.

Now every time Sir Paul left the estate, which happened about two or three times a week, our MT would take over. We'd pick him up at the residence in an armored, kitted-out minivan, me in the front seat next to the driver, Sir Paul in his wheelchair and a couple nurses behind us, and the rest of the lads following in a Range Rover chase car.

Sir Paul had a passion for antique books, fine art, and cricket. He was also a devout Roman Catholic and flew in a monsignor from Rome every Friday to hold private Sunday mass. First time we escorted him to the little chapel on the grounds of his estate, he turned to me and asked if I was going in with him.

Being a nonbeliever, I answered, "If I go in there, boss, I'll burst into flames."

Once, while we were driving through London, he asked us to stop at Harvey Nichols, a posh department store across the street from Harrods on Knightsbridge. As we were walking through the elaborate food market on the ground floor, packed with imported cheeses and other delicacies, he turned to me and whispered, "Simon, this is the first time I've been in a supermarket."

I said, "Sorry to piss on your parade, boss, but this isn't your typical supermarket. This is Harvey Nichols."

Sir Paul maintained one of the greatest private libraries in Britain. With the help of the antiquarian book dealer Maggs Brothers, he acquired what may be the earliest English manuscript, the seventh-century *Historia Ecclesiastica* by the bishop of Caesarea Eusebius Pamphili; four leaves of the remaining medieval illustrated biography of Saint Thomas à Becket; first copies of the King James Bible; and hundreds of modern first editions, including everything by Ian Fleming.

While I was on the MT, Maggs Brothers rang him up to tell him that one of the four copies of the Magna Carta in existence was coming up for bid at Sotheby's. Sir Paul decided to add it to his collection.

Prior to the auction, David Walker called me and said, "Simon, Mr.

Getty is thinking of buying a copy of the Magna Carta. Do you know what that is?"

"I know I didn't go to college, David," I answered. "But I'm not stupid."

David said, "The document is in London and will need to be transported back to the estate."

"We can hire a Brinks truck and load it," I offered. "But that might be too obvious and set us up for a hijacking. Let me talk to the boss."

I met with Sir Paul and the two Maggs brothers in the library and asked, "At the end of the auction, if you've won the bid and the brothers sign all the paperwork, will I have the right to take the document away?"

"Yes, we can arrange that, Simon. How are you planning to do it? Are you going to take some of the boys with you?"

"Boss," I replied, "I'm going to take a Tesco plastic shopping bag with me. After the Magna Carta is secured, I'll put it in the bag and carry it to the train station. I'll have one of the boys meet me at the station here."

The Maggs brothers looked horrified. They had just finished explaining how they wanted the document sealed and placed in a special climate-controlled cabinet. Sir Paul leaned back in his wheelchair and nodded. He liked my plan.

The following Thursday afternoon, I sat on the train to Wormsley Park with eleven million pounds' worth of English history on my lap, and no one had the slightest clue.

I remained on the Sir Paul Getty mobile security detail for a year and a half, until David Walker offered me a higher-paying job guarding Aga Khan IV, who needed extra protection during his biannual *mulaqats*. I took it even though I had no idea who Aga Khan IV was or what *mulaqat* meant.

I quickly learned that the Aga Khan IV (His Highness, or HH, as we called him) was a British business magnate, racehorse owner and breeder, as well as the forty-ninth and current imam of Nizari Ismailism, a denomination of Shia Islam that consists of an estimated 15 million adherents (under 10 percent of the world's Shia Muslim population). The Aga Khan claims to be a direct descendant of the Islamic Prophet Muhammad through Muhammad's cousin and son-in-law. As the imam of Nizari Ismailism, Aga Khan IV is considered by his followers to be the proof, or *hujjah,* of God on earth as well as infallible and immune from sin. Because of his large following in Pakistan, Uzbekistan, Kurdistan, Afghanistan, and other Middle Eastern countries, he's treated as a head of state without portfolio.

The sect he ruled was extremely wealthy and maintained huge public relations, communications, and philanthropic branches at his headquarters in Chantilly outside of Paris. I traveled there with Phil, Pete, Marvin, and others on what was to become our sixteen-man team to be briefed.

It was the biggest, most lavish estate I'd ever seen and run like a mini-country unto itself. Off to the right of the main house, HH had constructed a large office block from which he ran his Ismaili empire. We were ushered into an ops room as state of the art as something you'd see at the White House—officers manning phones and monitoring computer screens, massive monitors with live maps.

The Aga Khan's head of security, Brigadier Tony Hunter-Choat, greeted us—bristle mustache, maroon beret, stiff upper lip. He reminded me of Lieutenant Colonel Nicholson, the character portrayed by Alec Guinness in the movie *The Bridge on the River Kwai,* and turned out to be one of the dodgiest characters I'd ever met.

Though British through and through, Brigadier Hunter-Choat had begun his military career in the French Foreign Legion fighting against Algerian freedom fighters. In 1958, he was a young machine gunner dropped behind enemy lines in the bloody battle of Fedj Zezoua, earning his first of three French Croix de la Valeur Militaire. He also was awarded the French Médaille Militaire.

In April 1961 he took part in the coup against President de Gaulle. He returned to England in '62, joined the Royal Artillery, fought in Borneo and Indonesia, and worked his way up to command of the 23 SAS regiment. Upon retirement from the Brit mil in '86, he was appointed officer of the Order of the British Empire (OBE) by the queen.

That's when he went to work for David Walker in Oman. He left ten years later with the Omani Order of Achievement.

I now sat before him as he explained that *mulaqat* means "audience" in Arabic. It was essentially a large traveling tent show where the Aga Khan could speak to and be seen by his millions of followers in different parts of the Middle East and South Asia. They'd be staged in remote parts of countries like Afghanistan and Uzbekistan.

First, a crew would fly in and construct a massive stage with lights, sound, backstage tents, a long U-shaped walkway that would extend into the audience, and a plinth in the middle to display the Koran.

We could expect as many as 150,000 followers to converge on the site. Some would walk for days from remote mountain villages. Many would be armed. The crowd would include the weak, elderly, infirm, people missing limbs, and newborn babies, all coming to be blessed by the man they considered to be God. None of them would be required to buy tickets, nor would they be screened through metal detectors.

Our sixteen-man security contingent would arrive with HH by Black Hawk helicopters leased from the Afghan military. HH would be wearing a blue suit tailored at Huntsman in London, white shirt, and powder-blue tie. We would escort him into an enormous tent set up backstage, which had been outfitted with lavish silk carpets and furniture and bathrooms complete with marble walls and floors and gold fixtures.

Once in the tent, HH would remove his suit and put on an elaborate gold-filigreed cape and crown. He'd walk onstage and deliver a forty-five-minute sermon. After that, Tony Hunter-Choat explained, he'd step onto the red carpet and complete a long loop through the crowd. He'd end the *mulaqat* with another fifteen-minute blessing.

"Under no circumstances are your shoes to touch the red carpet during HH's walk," Brigadier Hunter-Choat announced.

"So we stand off the carpet to the sides?" I asked.

"No, you have to stay with him the whole time."

"You mean we're surrounded by one hundred fifty thousand people who want to touch him, some of whom are armed, and we can't walk on the carpet?"

"Not with your shoes on. No. Your shoes come off when you walk around with HH."

We had already been told that we would be wearing suits and armed with MP5Ks and pistols in pancake holsters. Each one of us would carry a mesh satchel over our shoulder with extra mags, spare batteries for our radios, and our cell phone.

I asked, "Tony, what do we do with our shoes?"

"You carry them."

"I'm not trying to be funny," I responded, "but when I'm on the boss's shoulder, I need to keep my right hand on my weapon."

"It's not rocket science, mate," Tony retorted. "Hold your shoes in your left."

"But I need my left to hold people back. And if something happens, I might have to draw fast. I can't do that if I'm holding a pair of shoes."

He frowned and barked, "Work it out."

Phil asked, "What happens if we have to do a runoff with HH in our socks? Some of the terrain is loose shale, which cuts like bloody razor blades."

"Work it out," Tony repeated, his frustration building.

"But, Tony," I added, "if someone fires a shot, we can expect panic. Now we've got to get the boss through one hundred fifty thousand hysterical people in our socks to the vehicles parked, say, a hundred meters away, behind the stage."

"That's correct."

"Don't you see it's fucking madness? Can we get some sort of special dispensation to wear our shoes?"

"Absolutely not."

In the end we had to do the whole walk with our shoes in a carrier bag. The experience itself was transporting. We were men looking after someone the crowd perceived to be the direct descendant of Allah, and as such we were considered holy warriors (or mujahideen).

After HH gave his sermon in a field near Bishkek, Kyrgyzstan, and we started to escort him into the crowd, I realized that nearly every person in the crowd—women, children, handicapped, and hardened warriors armed with AK-47s—was weeping. As we walked on the red carpet, people leaned in to touch HH or his robe, hoping that he might heal them or make their prayers come true. But since they couldn't reach him, they would touch us, his guards.

The next morning, September 11, 2001, we were en route from Kyrgyzstan to Afghanistan, flying in HH's twin Gulfstreams. When we landed in Kabul, someone asked us, "Have you seen what happened in New York and DC?"

In shock and disbelief, we watched footage of the towers crumbling to the ground on the rickety TV in the guesthouse lobby. Commentators speculated that the terrorists were members of al-Qaeda and had been directed by Osama bin Laden. We knew that bin Laden was in Afghanistan, and he and al-Qaeda operated with the blessing of the Taliban government.

The very next day, CIA Special Activities Division (SAD) operatives started to arrive at the guesthouse where we were staying.

One of them said to me, "You guys don't want to stay in Kabul, because soon this place is going to be flattened."

A low-key intelligence man named Michael S. called me into his room and said, "Simon, we need to get this thing moving right away. Are you with us? What can you and your men do to help?"

I said, "My mates and I can do forward observation, we can direct fire, we're trained in counterinsurgency. Whatever you want. But first we have to return HH to Chantilly. If you can get us back in, we'll be happy to start working for you."

"You're hired."

That was a critical turning point for me and ex-soldiers like myself—the exact moment when the business turned from private security work to private military, and we returned to using our old skills and drills. It's never been the same since.

CHAPTER FIVE

AFGHANISTAN

I**T WAS** the second week of September 2001, and Michael S. had asked us to go to Herat in northwestern Afghanistan to start working with the Afghan Northern Alliance (NA).

The United States and its allies knew that if they wanted to dislodge the Taliban from power, it was imperative that they partner with the United Islamic Front—known in the West as the Northern Alliance—a coalition of northern tribes including Tajiks, Uzbeks, and Hazara that had opposed the Pashtun-dominated Taliban for years. Sadly, the NA's charismatic political and military leader Ahmad Shah Massoud, a longtime enemy of the Taliban and Osama bin Laden, had been killed by al-Qaeda operatives in a suicide bombing two days before the attacks on New York and Washington. With no central leader, the anti-Taliban alliance was dispirited and in disarray.

Our mission was to engender goodwill with the Tajik tribesmen, build relationships with the local NA leaders, and try to bring the various militias together into a single effective fighting unit so they could unseat the Taliban.

Initially, the team consisted of me, Justin, Paul C., Snowy, Topsy, Dolly, and Dinger—all of whom were ex–Brit mil and men I had worked with before. None of us spoke the local Herati language (a version of Persian), so we brought with us the same terps we had used when working with HH and paid them handsomely.

Getting to Herat wasn't easy. Since it was controlled by the Taliban, under the leadership of Khairullah Khairkhwa, and the city was already under siege, receiving daily barrages of mortar and rocket fire from the local Northern Alliance directed by local warlord Ismail Khan, we couldn't simply fly in.

Instead we flew first to Bishkek, Kyrgyzstan, on a Gulfstream IV, refueled, and pushed on to Tashkent, Uzbekistan, where we landed at an airport that looked like it had been taken over by the US military; C-130s, Black Hawks, and other planes lined the tarmac. The International Hotel, where we were put up, bustled with officers and officials from a whole mélange of US and UK agencies.

For the next three days, we received regular briefings from Michael S. on what was going on in the city of Herat and the surrounding province, including specifics on Taliban troop strength, positions, and weapons capabilities. Michael was the quintessential intelligence officer—a smart, engaging man in his fifties who was everyone's friend, but nobody really knew much about. Even in a war zone, he dressed in khaki slacks, loafers, and what looked like his grandfather's cardigan and was always calm even in the most stressful situations. I got the impression he was the guy every power player in and out of the US government called when facing a sticky situation.

From Tashkent my team and I flew by jet to Termez on the

Uzbekistan-Afghanistan border, then hopped on Black Hawk helos for a ride into the Kushk District, eighty miles east of Herat city.

There we met our host, a rakishly thin man named Abdul Raouf Khadem, who was a leader of the NA army in western Afghanistan and a lieutenant to warlords Ismail Khan, Dr. Ibrahim, and Fazl Karim Aimaq. Raouf's serious, hardened demeanor caved the minute he cracked a toothless grin. Wearing a thick blanket wrapped around his *salwar kameez* (lightweight pajamas) and carrying a loaded AK-47, he escorted us to battered pickups manned by several of his weary-looking fighters.

The ride seemed endless, over dirt and gravel roads pocked with craters and sometimes blocked with boulders. Throughout it all, our driver grinned as if to say, Sit back and enjoy the ride, guys, I know what I'm doing.

Finally, we reached the foothills of Herat—Afghanistan's third-largest city with a population of about eight hundred thousand, which stood a few clicks away from the Iranian border. Situated in the fertile valley of the Hari River, in ancient times Herat had been a prosperous trade route between the Middle East and Central and South Asia. Greek historian Herodotus had described this place as the bread basket of Central Asia three centuries before the birth of Christ. Alexander the Great had conquered the city and built a massive wall to protect it. Despite his efforts, Herat had been conquered many times—by the Arabs in the seventh century, by Genghis Khan's Mongol army in 1221, and by us Brits in the nineteenth century, during our century-long conflict with the Russians known as the Great Game.

In the 1960s US engineers had constructed a modern airport outside the city, which became a Soviet base in 1979 after the Soviets invaded Afghanistan. They met stiff resistance from local mujahideen under the command of warlord Ismail Khan. When they pulled out of the area in '83, they left behind a city in rubble. In 1995 the city had been captured by the Taliban, forcing Khan to flee, and had been nominally under its control ever since.

Now, for the first time in our careers, we were on our own. No boss, no uniforms, no Brit mil rules and structure. We had to make our own decisions and were relying on the street smarts we had picked up in East London and other working-class locales.

It was a tremendous adjustment, and one we had to make quickly. The local NA leaders we met with were fierce-looking dudes with long beards and ragged clothes, clutching AKs and Kalashnikovs. We started to let our beards and hair grow. We'd sit across from them on rugs in dark, airless huts, racking our brains for how to "build trust." First thing I did was remove my body armor. Then I'd put my weapons down, which was a violation of Brit mil General Order 2.

In the Brit mil it had always been *If you do this for me, I'll do this for you.* Now, I started by asking them: What can we do to help you?

They needed the basics. Their fighters were ill equipped and ill disciplined, cutting about in *salwar kameez,* sneakers or sandals, nifty little turbans, and well-worn AK-47s. Although they were hardened and seasoned individual fighters—every male baby born in Afghanistan seems to be given an AK before he gets a rattle—they had zero military tactical training.

We started teaching the guys dry drills and how to strip, assemble, and maintain their weapons so they didn't jam or malfunction at a critical point. We ran organized range instruction that progressed into fire and maneuvering training. And we showed them how to patrol, communicate, set up an ambush, and apply trauma medicine.

At first, it was like herding cats. On the positive side, the fighters were tough, tenacious, and hated the Taliban. They also had discipline, physical fitness, and a concept of how to fight together. In a matter of weeks, what at first seemed like an impossible task given the barriers of culture and language turned into an effective training course. We also set up a supply network through the US mil so newly trained fighters could get proper kits—namely socks, boots, battle dress uniforms (BDUs), jackets, web belts, weapons, and med kits.

Over the course of the following weeks and months, whenever Ismail Khan or his senior commanders came to visit, Raouf would display his newly trained and smartly equipped men like a proud parent at graduation.

Because of the fighting and primitive conditions, many of the locals needed medical care. As trained medics, Justin, Phil, and I rolled up our sleeves and got busy attending to infections, broken limbs, shrapnel wounds, and sore throats. I called the US Agency for International Development (USAID) coordinator in Kabul on our satellite phone and told him that we needed medicines and bandages. I also requested an engineer. An enterprising bloke named Gaz Marsden arrived on the next helicopter. With the help of the local tribesmen, Gaz erected a medical center in a week, which we outfitted with beds, IV bags, and sterilized areas that could be sectioned off.

We also spent a lot of time with the local children, handing out pencils and paper, showing them how to write their names in English. After Gaz finished the clinic, he built a proper schoolhouse with desks, chairs, and blackboards. Next we helped him build a little town hall with a makeshift kitchen, where the tribesmen and women could gather to sing, eat, and dance.

As the fighting in and around Herat heated up, I kept up a stream of requests to USAID—for Dora the Explorer backpacks for the kids, soccer balls, pencils, and paper.

We tried to avoid the mistakes the US military was making in other areas of the country. Like when they flew over towns in helicopters and dropped leaflets in English. Or, months later, when the US Corps of Engineers shipped gallons of Gatorade to towns in the south, where the villagers weren't used to drinking it and became violently ill.

Or the thousands of soccer balls printed with a map of Afghanistan and the words ALLAHU AKBAR that were distributed throughout the country. I actually had to explain to a US general that in Muslim Afghanistan it was a sign of disrespect to show the soles of your feet to anyone and a huge insult to print PRAISE GOD on something that you were expected to kick.

The war was progressing faster than anyone had predicted, as small teams of US CIA officers, PMCs like us, special forces soldiers working with local Northern Alliance units in various parts of country, and US and UK air support softened Taliban resistance. The first major city to fall, on November 9, was Mazar-e Sharif, to our east.

Two days later, supported by US special forces and Iranian commandos, Ismail Khan's militiamen forced the Taliban to flee Herat. The following night, Taliban troops left Kabul under the cover of darkness.

With Herat under Northern Alliance control, we were tasked with doing the same liaison building and military training with tribes closer to the Uzbekistan border, near the town of Termez. On November 27 as we finished meeting with local leaders in the town of Balkh, we learned via MBITR (multiband inter/intra team radio) that there had been an uprising of Taliban and al-Qaeda prisoners at Qala-i Jangi outside of Mazar-e Sharif.

We arrived in the late afternoon to a scene of tremendous carnage. Two days earlier, five hundred Taliban and al-Qaeda prisoners had rioted and taken over the prison, which looked like a massive medieval fortress surrounded by two sets of thick mud walls complete with ramparts and turrets. CIA officer Mike Spann and more than a dozen Northern Alliance guards had been killed in the initial fighting.

US-UK coalition special forces (SF) teams and planes had responded quickly. Unfortunately, one errant thousand-pound bomb destroyed the northeastern tower of the prison, badly injuring five US SF operators and two Brits from the SBS. The remaining SBS guys huddled around the gate to the inner compound and told us that most of prison was now secure, except for scores of prisoners who had retreated to a dungeon under one of the buildings. They continued fighting, even though the NA warlord who controlled the area, General Dostum, had ordered the dungeon flooded the night before.

Although the carnage in the inner courtyard was appalling—bodies strewn everywhere along with about a dozen dead horses that had lived in the prison stables—what really surprised me was the number of journalists milling about. We had a harder time hiding from their cameras than dodging the odd bullet.

Soon after we arrived, the siege ended, and ninety or so of the remaining prisoners were dragged out of the flooded dungeon. Among them was a wounded, gaunt American named John Walker Lindh, who would later be sentenced to twenty years in federal prison for conspiracy to supply services to the Taliban.

We had been traveling back and forth to Bagram Airfield outside of Kabul by helicopter, picking up materials and coordinating with Michael S. Week by week we saw the situation in and around the capital evolve. Michael and his boys had seamlessly taken control of the airport, and a firm called Global Security Resources flew in a thousand men to patrol it.

When Michael had hired my mates and me the day after 9/11, he asked us how much we wanted to be paid. At the time we were each making fifteen hundred dollars a week guarding Aga Khan IV.

I huddled with Justin and Phil and discussed it. My penny-pinching Scottish mate Phil, of cheap-suit fame, wanted me to ask for ten thousand dollars a week.

I said, "Guys, let's be reasonable. I'll ask for five."

So I went back to Michael S. and said, "Michael, we're going from private security to military. There will be a higher risk, and it will be a lot of work. Conditions are shit. And when you start bombing, we'll be on our own."

"How much do you want?"

I gave him my number—five thousand dollars per man a week.

"Fine," he said without blinking. "I'll pay you in cash at the end of every week."

At the end of each week, Michael would hand me a duffel bag filled with cash. Twelve blokes at five thousand dollars per man totaled sixty thousand dollars. Ten weeks into the Herat operation, and after that the fall of Kabul, the storage room in our secure Kabul guesthouse was filled with duffel bags of cash. None of us had left the country, so the money had piled up.

Justin asked, "What are we going to do with this?"

"Now that we're established," I answered, "I'm going to put in a regular leave structure. So guys can fly from here to Dubai and catch flights from there to London."

"Yeah, but how are we going to move the cash?" asked Justin. "We'll never get this amount of money through Terminal Four at Heathrow."

He had a point. Anyone who tried to move that amount of cash through British customs would be suspected of money laundering and detained. And we wouldn't be able to explain to British officials how we had earned it.

So I went down the street to the former Taliban guesthouse where Michael S. was staying and said, "Michael, we have a problem. How do we repatriate the funds we've been earning?"

"I knew you were going to ask that," Michael answered with a grin. "Have you ever heard of *hawala* banking? We use it all the time."

"No. What's that?"

"Well, this is how it works. I've got a guy here in Kabul. We'll call him Mo. You'll give him the money; he'll count it and ring his cousin Saleem, who works at a bank in Dubai. He'll say, I have a man here who has a million dollars. He's going to give it to me now and get on a plane tomorrow. When he gets to the bank, you give him one million dollars."

"Say that again."

"That's how they move money in this part of the world," Michael said.

"Let me get this right. I'm going to give one million of our money to a guy I've never met who's dressed in bedding and flip-flops, and he's going to ring his cousin, who I also haven't met, who we believe lives in Dubai and works at a bank. Then I'm going to get on a plane and leave this country, having left my money with Mo, and land in Dubai, and Saleem is going to give me the same amount of money in a new bank account?"

"Yes," Michael answered.

"That's fucking crazy."

"We do it all the time."

When I went back to our guesthouse and tried to sell it to the boys, they looked at me like I was bonkers.

Paul C. got in my face and shouted, "Are you fucking on drugs, mate? Who told you that?"

"Michael S."

"Well, Michael lies for a living."

I couldn't argue with that.

I said, "We have three choices. One, take it to Heathrow and have it confiscated. Two, leave it here and live like kings in Kabul. Or three, try this *hawala* banking thing."

The boys agreed to take a chance with Michael S.'s method. The following day I met with Michael and this young Afghan guy named Mo, who counted the money. He called someone in Dubai and spoke to him in Dari, which I couldn't understand. After that, I handed him the money, six hundred thousand dollars in total.

Michael slapped his hands together and said, "That's it. It's done. I'll get you some tickets to Dubai. How many do you need?"

"Three should do it."

Next day, Justin, Paul, and I flew to Dubai. Once we landed, we hailed a cab that took us directly to the Dubai Free Bank. There we met with a guy named Saleem, who spoke English and claimed to be Mo's cousin. He was friendly, super polite, and humble.

Saleem said, "I have your money for you, and this is what I recommend that you do. I've opened an account under the name of the British Men's Association in the Dubai Free Bank. If I were you, I would use this money to buy properties on the Palm, which is a man-made island that is now being constructed. Keep those properties for however long and sell them and put that money in an HBCC account, which is a more legitimate bank. Then you can move that money back into the UK."

Saleem's financial advice proved sound, and within months, the CIA–Department of Defense (DOD) pay system became a lot more structured with signed contracts, regular invoices, and checks sent to offshore accounts. It was yet another aspect of the PMC world that was changing right before our eyes.

There were several important reasons why. First and foremost, the United States and its allies were starting to spend massive amounts of money on the war against terrorism. According to a study conducted by the Centre for European Studies, of the $3.7 to $4.4 trillion that the United States would spend from 2001 to 2011 fighting wars in Afghanistan and Iraq, "Undeniably, the services supplied by contractors were a large proportion of the overall cost."

Second, Western powers had become reluctant to get entangled in the increasing number of local conflicts where no national interests were at stake, a trend that had started after the end of the Cold War. Third, the collapse of state structures in weak and failing states like Somalia, Haiti, and Sudan led to demands from incumbent regimes, dissidents, nongovernmental organizations (NGOs), and even multinational companies for private security and military services.

Also, since the 1980s there had been a shift toward the privatization of police and military forces in an effort to reduce public expenditures; many countries now privatized or outsourced prison security, immigration control, and airport security. In the military sector, most major powers in Europe and North America made substantial cuts in their defense budgets following the Cold War. So by 9/11 Western militaries were not only smaller in manpower but also substantially different in terms of organization and composition— concentrating on their core competencies and outsourcing other aspects of their operations to other providers.

I saw the change coming but had no idea how massive it would be. Ten years after the attacks on New York and Washington, private security and military contracting had blown up into a $100-billion-per-year global industry.

The Centre for European Studies concluded "the PSC [private security contractor] sector has become so important that in states as different as the US, the UK, India and Bulgaria, the number of PSC contractors is much greater than the number of employees in the respective state security agencies."

By 2012, the London-based PSC behemoth G4S would boast that it was the second-largest private employer in the world, operating in 120 countries, with over 625,000 employees. As the war in Iraq picked up steam, its annual revenues swelled from £3 billion in 2004 to £10 billion in 2010. G4S's closest rival, Securitas AB, based in Stockholm, Sweden, had around 300,000 workers spread out over 53 countries and an annual revenue in 2012 of $10 billion.

MPRI, which is a subsidiary of L-3 Communications, operates out of forty offices in the United States and other countries and specializes in military training. Its officials boast that it employs more generals (retired) than the US Army has in service.

Triple Canopy, founded by former US special forces operators and based in Chicago, rose to prominence in 2004 when it secured a US government contract in Iraq valued at $1.5 billion. That dwarfed the $293 million contact awarded to Aegis Defense Services to provide protection and assistance during the US government's restructuring of Iraq.

Jobs that had once been the exclusive purview of the green army were now being transferred to private contractors—including static guards, mobile security teams, air assets, recce teams, intelligence gathering, and quick reaction forces. Small companies that were once being run out of home offices took up plush suites in London and Washington, hiring former ambassadors, cabinet ministers, and military officers to serve as their CEOs, COOs, and board advisers.

Their leaders became a common sight in the corridors of Whitehall and the Pentagon as they advertised their services and lobbied for future contracts. Unlike the small private security companies of the seventies, eighties, and early nineties, these burgeoning behemoths were structured corporate entities, registered for the most part in the British Virgin or Cayman Islands. They maintained branch offices in Dubai, Kabul, and later Baghdad.

As the war on terror intensified, these companies became a vital part of the US combat machine. Their guards and operators made up a large part of the population of the US military forward operating bases (FOBs) and collocated operating bases (COBs) that were springing up throughout Afghanistan. PMCs like myself and my mates were issued DOD ID cards that availed us of all the perks— including single-man and two-man rooms in prefab trailers, hot and cold running water in the shower blocks, and hot meals four times a day in the DFACs (dining facilities). In our downtime we could wander over to an MWR (morale, welfare, and recreation) facility to use the well-equipped gym, check a book out of the library, play video games, or watch a movie. If we didn't like the food at the DFAC on a particular night, we could drive over to dine at the equivalent of Pizza Hut or McDonalds.

Gone were the days of washing your clothes in a bucket and hanging them out to dry like we did in Herat. Now we simply filled out a laundry list, handed the dirty items to the staff (also made up of private contractors), and collected them twenty-four hours later, washed, dried, and pressed.

If we were on an official DOD contract, we had access to the best equipment from the base armory. This usually included M4 automatic rifles, belt-fed M249 machine guns, Glock pistols, which we could customize any way we wanted. Special fore grips, stock pads, Picatinny rails, Mag-Lite holders, ACOG sights, short barrels, and bipods could be ordered from the armorer. Anything not in stock would be flown in.

Coming and going to and from theater also got a whole lot easier. You'd simply hand your leave rotation form with your home airport hub to the travel department, and it would organize your tickets. From Kabul, I'd usually hop on one of the regular and convenient KBR flights to Dubai. And from Dubai there were numerous commercial flights to wherever you were going.

Lesson number 7: After 9/11, jobs became lucrative and abundant, and the missions a lot more deadly than guarding some rich bloke, as my mates and I soon found out.

CHAPTER SIX

OSAMA BIN LADEN

AUGUST 2004, I was back in London guarding a Greek shipping family when I got a call from my friend Michael S. and his colleague Ted G.—another former high-ranking intelligence official. Both men were now working on top-secret government contracts. Ted, though taller than Michael and dressed slightly better, was just as soft-spoken and intelligent.

Ted said, "We've got a job working with Michael and myself hunting HVTs. Are you interested?"

I was in the mood for something more exciting, so I answered, "Yes."

"Can you put a team together? You'll be the lead on this. You'll need five additional men. All former Tier One operators. We've got three former Delta guys who can blend in with your guys and are ready to go."

The first two blokes I rang were Justin and Phil, who had both worked with me in Herat. In the interim, Justin and I had completed an assignment for Scimitar guarding diamonds for one of the largest gem merchants in the world.

The three of us met at a café on High Street, Kensington. I said, "I've got a job in Afghanistan. Two weeks. Looking for an HVT."

The guys nodded. Scottish Phil, still as penny pinching as ever, had been guarding Qatari and Saudi royals and grown bored with that. Rounding out the team were my super-smart friend Stumpy (Nick), who had been studying for a master's degree in criminology; Stevie O. (a super-thin black former SAS operator from Scotland); and my childhood mate Pete. Why Stumpy wanted to take a job like this surprised me.

Several weeks later, we were in Dubai sunning ourselves by the pool at the Jumeirah Beach Hotel—a rough-looking tatted-out lot that didn't blend in with the other tourists and businessmen. We had also picked up a couple of tails from Oman State Security at the airport. Dudes in immaculate white robes (called dishdashas) followed us wherever we went—bars, restaurants, even when Justin and Stevie went out to hang one on with some Russian hookers.

Ted and Michael S. showed up two days later, and things turned serious. They told us the firm running the job was called Unity Management (it later changed its name to Unity Resources). During the cab ride to its offices on Feather Road, Ted explained that we'd be meeting two of its execs, Gavin R., an American, and Roger W., an old-school guy from the SBS, cut from the same cloth as the infamous Tony Hunter-Choat.

In the lobby we met the three former Delta operators—Sam, Danny, and Mark. Dressed in jeans, T-shirts, and flip-flops, we rode an elevator up the sleek glass-and-steel Burj Tower to see Ted and the Unity guys, who all wore suits.

Danny was the only one of the Delta operators I had worked

with before—a surfer dude from California, laid back, friendly, and shredded. The other two made a strange but likable pair—Mark, very tall and fit, and Sam, older and built like a tank. Reminded me of the dwarf from *Lord of the Rings*. All three wore beards and tats.

The Unity gentlemen played their cards close to their vests. "It's a two-week job, high risk, Afghanistan. Searching for an HVT. Pay is two thousand dollars a day per man. All accommodations, transport, and food will be provided or reimbursed."

We signed a brief contract and filled out insurance forms and a K&R (kidnap and ransom) sheet with five personal proof-of-life questions to ask a potential kidnapper to make sure he was telling the truth. Questions like the name of your favorite dog, your mother's birthday, your favorite football team.

The next evening we boarded an RAF C-130 to Bagram Airfield wearing holiday gear, beards, and long hair. Several of the guys sported big sleeve tats, which were just coming into the culture and became the contractors' way of distinguishing themselves from the regular mil. Mine included my blood group—an o on my left shoulder, which I had gotten in Portsmouth at age eighteen—a scorpion on my right arm along with the Arabic proverb BE BEAUTIFUL AND SEE BEAUTIFUL THINGS. Inked on my right arm PEACE AND COURAGE, also in Arabic; on my back a Spartan helmet and the phrase MOLON LABE (Come and get them); and on my left chest a Celtic warrior.

Accompanying us on the flight were forty young Brit soldiers in uniform. They looked at us like we were exotic animals just let out of cages.

After we had chilled to tunes on iPods for three hours, the pilot executed his standard war-zone evasive maneuver, and we touched down with lights out at Bagram Airfield outside of Kabul. Two Land Cruisers waited for us on the tarmac and took us to a mini-compound at the far end of the base that housed MI6, the DIA (Defense Intelligence Agency), and the CIA. They would be our hosts for the next two days while we waited for a flight to our next destination, Jalalabad—or J-bad, as it was commonly called.

As the temperature dropped past freezing, we were shown to our individual CHUs (containerized housing units), basically weatherized-steel International Organization of Standardization (ISO) shipping containers outfitted with beds, fake-oak paneling, electric sockets, and maybe a desk. If you were lucky you got a "wet" CHU with a little bathroom. Ours were dry, which meant that if we woke in the middle of the night and had to take a piss, we had to walk three hundred meters to the loo or do it in a bottle and dump it in the trash in the a.m. I bottled mine. Fuck stumbling about in the dark...

We passed our time at the spook base eating, hitting the gym a couple times a day, Skyping with friends and family, and watching movies we had downloaded on hard drives.

In the Brit mil, we were given weeks, maybe months, to prepare for an op and had a staff of corporals and sergeant majors to help. Knowing that we would probably only be given mere days and would have to do everything ourselves, I grabbed Ted every time he was free and peppered him with questions. Where were we going specifically? Who would we be meeting with once in theater? What were the names of our tribal liaisons? What kind of kit would we be carrying? Would we have to buy it ourselves on the local market, or would it be provided by the American mil?

He wasn't ready to reveal much. So Justin, Phil, and I hashed out a list of everything we might possibly need for a two-week deployment—from vehicles to meals, ready to eat (MREs)—while the other guys fucked about.

We figured wherever we were going we'd be taking vehicles at least part of the way. Given the crap condition of the roads around Jalalabad, our biggest threats would probably come from IEDs and RTAs (road traffic accidents). So we'd need one med bag per man packed with tourniquets, big Israeli bandages, QuikClot, gauze, tape, and fluids. Each individual operator would carry an IFAK (individual first-aid kit) to use on himself and himself only. Inside of those we wanted smaller bandages, blowout patches, tape, and morphine surrets.

We also made a preliminary list of tactical equipment—eighty-mil mortars, M4s, mags, frag and smoke grenades, grenade launchers, pistols, et cetera. We didn't have mapping or infil (entry) and exfil (exit) plans with primary, secondary, and tertiary routes. All that critical preparation would have to wait.

Our second night in, Ted knocked on the door of my CHU and told me we were leaving for J-bad the next morning at 1100.

After a bouncy one-hour flight, we landed at the military airport, approximately three miles outside the city of Jalalabad and ninety-five miles of paved highway east of Kabul. The city boasted some two hundred thousand inhabitants and was known as a center of Pashtun culture, an agricultural and trading hub with nearby Pakistan, and a Taliban stronghold. Al-Qaeda and bin Laden had maintained a strong presence in the area, including several training camps, up until 2002.

We started our prep with a visit to the tactical operations center (TOC), which is the electronic nerve center of any forward base, equipped with all manner of tracking, radio, and communications gear. A year or so later, that TOC was named the CONOC (contractors' operation center), but its role remained the same—monitoring all the contracting teams on the ground using radios, sat phones, transponders on vehicles, and personal trackers that looked like little flashlights each operator wore on or inside his plate carriers. I learned straightaway that there were nine different contracting teams operating out of that Jalalabad TOC and performing missions similar to ours.

Though Ted still wouldn't reveal our specific target, he did tell me that we would get three B6 armored Toyota Land Cruisers with flat-run tires to launch our op from. So I sent Pete, Sam, and Stevie O. over to the vehicle bay to check them out.

Pete, Sam, and Stevie rolled up their sleeves and immediately started customizing the Land Cruisers into tactical vehicles, starting by ripping one rear seat out of each. In two vehicles, that space would accommodate a rear gunner with a belt-fed 5.56 machine gun. The area in the third—the ambulance truck—would hold a stretcher with a paracord strung from the ceiling for an IV bag.

They also removed any unnecessary paneling and welded brackets on the doors to hold extra ammo. The front doors were outfitted with brackets for smoke grenades, so we could quickly activate smoke-for-cover if we had to evacuate in a firefight.

They then loaded all three vehicles with pen flares, pink and orange flags to signal helicopters and friendly troops, comms, transponders, jacks, crowbars, shovels, and so on. It took them a day and a half to complete this work and summon Justin and me for a talk through. We designated the Land Cruisers "Alpha," "Bravo," and "Charlie," with Bravo serving as the ambulance.

While Pete and his guys were attending to the vehicles, Danny, Mark, and Phil pulled together the items for our personal kit. This involved several trips to the armorer—a guy we called Super Mario because he stood five foot nothing with a large mustache on a pair of legs. They presented him a list of eight times M4s, Glocks, RPGs (*ruchnoy protivotankovyi granatomyot*, handheld antitank grenade launchers), and sniper rifles. We preferred the L1M4 Brit mil standard but were given Russian PKMs instead. Mario explained that because the extremes in hot and cold fucked with metal, the PKMs were better suited to prevailing local conditions.

Once we were armed, our weapons never left our sides. We babied them—cleaning, disassembling, oiling, doing dry drills to make sure all the parts worked smoothly. At night in our individual CHUs, we kept them within reach because the base was getting hit on a daily basis, and security provided by the penny-pinching Global Security Resources wasn't worth shit.

The next morning, we were up at six. After breakfast and a workout, we sorted out our plate-carrier vests. They would provide our bread and butter in the field, and everybody organized theirs differently. Knife here, comms in this pocket, extra mags, med kit, protein bars, et cetera. We'd slip the vest on and jump up and down to make sure everything was tied in tight.

Then we organized our grab bags (or bug-out bags), stuffing in extra mags and grenades. Most of us had spent part of the previous night bombing (loading individual rounds into clips). Anticipation started to build.

Finally, at the end of day 2, we met with Ted, Michael, Roger W., and two guys from DIA to receive our formal brief.

Ted pushed a case file across the metal table. I opened it and stared at a mug shot of Osama bin Laden. The boys leaned in around me. Were we really going to get a chance to go after the King of Spades, according to the deck of HVTs that had been circulating among coalition military and intel operators since 2001?

Adrenaline surged into my system. Under the photos of OBL were pictures of his two top lieutenants and his five main bodyguards. Ted said bin Laden usually traveled with a cordon of twenty hardened fighters, so we should keep an eye out for them, too. He also might be accompanied by members of the 055 (or Fifty-Fifth Arab) Brigade—a group of foreign al-Qaeda fighters that had been integrated into the Taliban army.

Also in the file were the names and photographs of the local tribal leaders we would be working with—Hazrat Ali and Mohammad Zaman, the leading Northern Alliance chiefs in the area largely controlled by the Pashtun Taliban. The more prominent of the two, Hazrat Ali, was the leader of the small Pashai tribe that controlled a valley at the northern tip of Nangarhar Province. Born in 1964, he'd been fighting since he was a teenager, first opposing the Soviets and then the Taliban. In 2003, he was appointed chief of police of Jalalabad by President Hamid Karzai but was sacked nine months later for allegedly taking bribes from the Taliban and Iran.

Mohammad Zaman Ghamsharik was the leader of the Pashtun Khungari tribe that populated the mountain area of Tora Bora. Like Hazrat Ali, he had also fought against the Soviets and Taliban, and he was living in exile in Dijon, France, when the United States launched attacks against al-Qaeda and the Taliban in late 2001, at which point he quickly returned to Afghanistan to help the CIA–special forces team led by Gary Berntsen that was searching for bin Laden in Tora Bora.

Although Hazrat Ali and Mohammad Zaman had been paid millions by the US and UK governments to enlist their tribesmen in the fight against bin Laden and his al-Qaeda followers in 2001, both were accused of assisting bin Laden and accepting bribes from him to facilitate his escape into Pakistan.

Knowing this, I asked Ted if they could be trusted now.

He said, "We've used Hazrat Ali in the past, and he's let us down every time. We regard Mohammad Zaman as slightly better, but slippery, too."

I did a double take. "Excuse me, Ted," I said. "Could you repeat that? Did you say that Hazrat Ali has let you down every time, and he's the guy we're relying on?"

"Yes."

"Then why are you using him again?"

"Politics" was his one-word answer.

Inside the file was the specific location of where bin Laden was believed to be—somewhere above the hamlet of Gharo Chinech, which was roughly forty miles south of Jalalabad on desolate, steep terrain covered with cedar trees, boulders, and loose shale. It was the same area he and several thousand of his followers had retreated to after the fall of the Taliban in 2001. Our mission was to climb up there and get him, dead or alive.

"When was he last spotted there?" I asked.

"Last week," Ted answered.

"Can your source or sources be trusted?"

"We believe so. Yes."

The information was sketchy at best. If bin Laden had been seen a week ago, why hadn't the US mil or CIA sent a team in already?

Ted made it clear that as PMCs we wouldn't have an official US mil support team behind us. Nor were we likely to get air support if we got in a firefight. We'd be on our own, except for whatever assistance we might get from Hazrat Ali, Mohammad Zaman, and their militias.

We were given thirty minutes to study the information in the file, mark our maps, program our GPSs, and then throw everything into a burn bag by the door before we split.

Inside the file were the names of three supposedly safe villages under the control of Ali and Zaman on the way to Tora Bora. The first one was fifteen miles southeast and named Qalayahe Allah Naa. In that village we were supposed to meet Hazrat Ali. The subsequent two were Bakalay and Wazir. The latter sat at the foot of the mountains and was the last village accessible by SUV. Our radio call sign was designated as Sierra One Alpha.

From the briefing room, bare-knuckle fighter Justin and I walked directly to the mapping hut, which was run by technicians from the National Reconnaissance Office (NRO). They were responsible for launching, maintaining, and monitoring US spy satellites. I took the sat map Ted had given us, taken from ten thousand feet, and cut out the section I wanted them to focus on.

Using a computer program known as FalconView, the NRO guys zoomed in to one thousand feet, and magically foot trails and mountain paths appeared. Justin and I used a printout to track our primary, secondary, and tertiary routes. We also requested close-ups of the three villages or "safe havens" so we could mark the best entrance and egress points and the best places from which to mount a defense if we were attacked.

We marked each route with one-mile waypoints, named them 1, 2, 3, et cetera, and then asked the NRO technicians to generate fifteen sets of each map—one for each member of the team, one each for Ted and Michael, and the rest for the guys in the TOC.

Back in our team room, the other operators were waiting to hold a Chinese parliament. Their excitement was palpable, their questions numerous and pointed. One thing we had been told in the brief was that OBL had weak kidneys and therefore needed weekly dialysis.

Pete asked, "If that's true, how's he getting in and out of Tora Bora?"

Cheap-suit Phil asked, "If he's up there with so many men, how come they didn't show us recent photos of them taken by drones?"

"If they know he's been up there a week, why the bloody hell hasn't he been picked up already?" Pete added. "And why are we relying on tribal leaders who we already know can't be trusted?"

They were all good questions and the first ones I posed to Ted and Michael when I saw them again the next the morning. Their answers were vague and evasive. Legal restrictions on political assassinations (Executive Order 12333) made an official US mission against bin Laden difficult. (EO 12333 was amended later that year by President George W. Bush to allow for political assassination under extraordinary circumstances.) There were other teams in the area searching for other HVTs. Because of all the activity, the US and UK mils had no available Tier 1 assets. And Hazrat Ali and Mohammad Zaman were the most important and reliable tribal leaders in the Jalalabad–Tora Bora region.

A day away from mission launch, I went over our preliminary plan, then gave Ted and Michael a list of supplies we needed, including an extra medical kit and cases of water, Coke, and Gatorade.

"What the hell do you need so much Gatorade for?" Ted asked.

"The local militiamen love the stuff," I answered. "So when we pull up to a checkpoint and one of them is pointing an AK at my head, if I can hand him a Gatorade, and that Gatorade puts a smile on his face, it's worth taking."

Since none of us spoke Dari or Pashtu, we would be using three local terps, all in their early twenties, named Emal, Shah, and Jan. They would drive the three vehicles. I provided Ted and Michael with flat sheets with designated seating positions in Alpha, Bravo, and Charlie—an arrangement that wouldn't change. Why? So as not to confuse the guys in the TOC, who were given the same flat sheets with the blood types, phone numbers, and known allergies of every operator and terp in case someone required medevac.

As the TL (team leader), I would sit in the passenger seat of Alpha. Phil, the chief medic, would occupy the passenger seat of Bravo. Justin, as the 2IC (second in command), would run the comms from the passenger seat of Charlie.

We designated two medics (Phil and Justin), two rear gunners (Mark and Sam), and two dedicated marksmen (Stevie and Danny), who would find high points and lay down designated shots in case we had to evacuate the vehicles. The gun trucks, Alpha and Charlie, were equipped with gun ports on the rear and side-rear windows that were spring loaded and would lift right and out so the barrel of the 5.56-millimeter M249 could stick out.

Phil was responsible for packing each vehicle's medical bag with labels on each pocket indicating what was inside. He then inspected Bravo for spare fluids, made sure the ceiling paracord was properly hung, and folded and unfolded the stretcher to make sure it worked.

Because there was so much information to remember, I made trim sheets for each operator. One listed the TOC number (call sign Zero Bravo) and all the other call signs; others contained the medevac nine-line report, trauma management card, contact report, mine report, and rules of engagement.

The rules of engagement spelled out the graduated use of force (GUF) set by DOD. According to the GUF, if, for example, you were on the road in a combat zone and a vehicle sped up behind you, you weren't allowed to just blow it away. The first level of engagement required that you hang a pink flag from the back of the vehicle. Every local Afghan knew what that meant—Back the fuck off. If that didn't work, you could stick a pen flare through the rear gun port and fire into the road in front of the oncoming vehicle. If it still didn't stop, you could fire a warning round from your M4 into the ground. If it still kept coming, you could shoot two rounds into the engine block or the vehicle's tires. If you'd executed all those steps and the vehicle still didn't stop, you could shoot the driver.

I took all the flat sheets and shrunk them down to a quarter page, copied them, covered them with plastic, punched a hole in the corner of each, tied them together with a piece of paracord, and distributed one set each to all the operators.

Some guys clipped it to their vest. I preferred to stuff mine in a Velcro wallet along with my DOD ID card, Afghan visa, USF-I card, and hang it around my neck behind my plate carrier.

The night before we set out, I lay in my little CHU, listening to mortars thud in the distance and reviewing checklists of gear in my head. I had no time for e-mails home or other distractions. Anything forgotten—for example, extra batteries for the sat phone—could become critical if things got nasty.

CHAPTER SEVEN
TORA BORA

THE MORNING of October 17, 2004, the nine of us and our three terps were prepped, kitted out, and ready to roll. Just before I climbed into the Alpha vehicle, I turned to Ted and said, "We're taking the secondary route."

"Got it," he answered.

I did this to maintain operational security (OPSEC), because there were dozens of locals working on the base, cleaning rooms, including the TOC itself. This way if any of them were allied with OBL or the Taliban, they couldn't know our route ahead of time. I marked our secondary route, designated as "Blue," on the map with waypoints that I would call out to the TOC as we passed.

Armed guards pushed open the black-iron blast gate, and we exited slowly and started to slalom through a field of concrete T-walls that formed a perimeter around the camp. Fifty meters later, we passed through a second blast gate and picked up speed as we drove between one hundred meters of barbed-wire fence. The guards posted to our left and right transitioned from US mil to local Afghan police.

Now we had to cross a notorious danger zone that stretched three miles before we would reach the city. Through my Motorola, I reported to the team, "Speed sixty. Road surface good."

Our main concern at this point were IEDs, so I strained my eyes left and right, scanning the roadsides for rocks that were out of place, recently turned-over soil, stray pieces of litter, and dead dogs packed with explosives.

As we pushed northwest, I did a radio check with each vehicle, then Justin, in charge of comms, did a check with the TOC.

"Zero Bravo, this is Sierra One Alpha. I need an air, route, and transponder check over," Justin said.

Someone in the TOC made sure our transponder appeared on the large computer-generated map and that it was "pinging" green. Then he checked to see if there had been recent events on our route. Third, he ascertained from the radar map that there was air cover in the area.

Via radio, he responded, "Sierra One Alpha, this is Zero Bravo. Transponder green, route green, air cover green. Over."

That's exactly what we wanted to hear. If one any of those three indicators had come back negative, we would have turned around and headed back to base. The saying among operators was "Air red, back to bed."

When we reached mile 1, designated as waypoint Blue 1 on the map, I called it out to the TOC. We sped down the paved Touk Highway, which took us northwest into the city, past shops selling produce, burkas, and local clothes; parks; and mosques.

After we passed through town, we hung a left onto Kabul–J-bad Highway, Blue 6. The concrete huts to either side of us became sparse, and the landscape turned rural. We passed little stalls set up along the road selling bottles of water and bags of chips.

Since this was the main supply route into Pakistan and used to ferry supplies to Karachi to US bases, we passed several convoys resting along the side of the road after the long climb over the mountains. They posed a ripe target for Taliban ambushers and were attacked regularly. Groups of armed contractors from El Salvador and the Philippines stood guard with their M4s pointed skyward.

Justin in Charlie saw a car approaching behind us. His voice came over the radio, "All call signs, one fast mover, left side, two pax up."

Emal, the terp driver of Alpha, steered to the right while Mark, Sam, and I readied our weapons and watched the battered Nissan fly past. For whatever reason—the stress, constant danger, or thin line between life and death—people in Afghanistan tended to drive like maniacs. Serious accidents were common.

I called out, "All call signs, fast mover, clear."

Minutes after we turned onto Sapra Road and I called out the waypoint Blue 6, I spotted a column of black smoke rising over the fields ahead. In most cases white smoke indicated a brush fire. The black element usually resulted from the accelerant in an IED.

Peering through my binos, I saw a US mil convoy stopped on the far side of the road. As we slowed, Justin, who was in charge of comms with Zero Bravo, reported it to the TOC. Then Mark, rear gunner of Alpha, opened up the gun port in the roof and waved a pink flag. This told the US mil convoy that we were friendly PMCs.

The gruesome reality in this mostly Taliban-controlled area was that the preponderance of IED attacks were followed up by ambushes. So the members of the damaged convoy ahead had blocked all traffic in both directions and were on high alert. Seeing our pink flag, they waved us through. We proceeded slowly past a Humvee that had been ripped to shit. Two US Marine casualties lay smoldering along the shoulder.

A few more miles southwest, and we turned onto Sheikh Massin Road, Blue 7. A loop around some rocky hills deposited us in a valley and Qalayahe Allah Naa—the site of Hazrat Ali's compound, which was by far the largest and most modern in town. His guards checked us out, then opened the battered green-metal gate to let us in.

The entire compound was fifty meters square with a courtyard in the center, two low-lying buildings along the sides, and a large two-story villa directly in front of us. That's where we met Hazrat Ali, standing with three of his cousins and five of his top aides. They were all dressed in local garb—*salwar kameez,* long vests, boots or black leather sandals, called *chablee,* with thick socks, and woolen caps.

Hazrat Ali greeted us in English, a gap-tooth smile peeking through his thick black beard, "Welcome to my home, my village. We are here to help you."

He was friendly and totally in control. We sat in the main room of the villa, drinking sweet mint tea and eating honey bread. Speaking through our interpreter Emal because his aides didn't understand English, he asked questions like "What's it like living in America?" and "Where do you come from in England?"

His simple country-boy mannerisms hid a sly, calculating intelligence. We were conducting our mission with his permission, so we had to play the appreciative guests. It was all a game to some extent, and as a regional warlord who was getting millions of dollars a year from the US government and had survived the Soviet occupation along with six years of Taliban rule, he knew the rules much better than we did.

After our initial chat, which yielded no new information about bin Laden or what we could expect when we reached the mountains, he took us on a tour of Qalayahe Allah Naa. First a little schoolhouse, then the clinic, which was filled with some of Ali's tribesmen recently wounded in ongoing fighting with the Taliban. Phil, Justin, Pete, and I pulled on rubber gloves and went to work, applying sutures and re-dressing wounds. We did it not only as a friendly gesture but also to practice for the first aid we might have to administer during the mission ahead.

That night, after we dined with Hazrat Ali and his aides in his villa—lamb stew, rice, local bread, more mint tea—I showed him the photos in our intel pack and tried to get him to focus on the nitty-gritty. At this Hazrat turned more formal and guarded, answering through his right-hand man even though I was directing the questions to him. He said the pictures were old, which I already knew. When I asked him if his men had seen bin Laden in the location where we were going, he answered through his aide, "Yes, I believe bin Laden is in that area."

I opened a map and asked him to indicate the specific area where his men had seen the al-Qaeda leader. Hazrat Ali waved his hand over it and knitted his brow. His tribesmen had seen him, yes, but they weren't sure of the specific location. When I showed him the photos of the men who were believed to be bin Laden's top advisers, Ali said he didn't recognize any of them.

The harder I pressed for details, the more vague and evasive his answers grew. It was clear that he didn't want to be pinned down, and that though he was allowing our mission, he would only as-sist us to a point. All I could do was hope that Mohammad Zaman, whom we were scheduled to meet in the next village, would be more forthcoming.

We slept in three rooms along the right wall of the compound, on thick rugs stacked on a concrete floor. Pete arranged his body so that it blocked the door. All of us kept our weapons ready and our clothes on. The only things we took off were our boots, which we replaced with sneakers. In the event that we were hit in the middle of the night, we wanted to be able to move quickly.

Since our vehicles didn't fit inside the compound, we parked them outside and kept one man guarding them on a one-hour rotation. Each guy on duty sat in a different vehicle with the engine running—one, so he didn't freeze; and, two, because we didn't want the batteries to run out in the cold.

The next morning, we were up at six, did a mini-circuit of exercises to get the blood flowing, washed, and sat down to breakfast. Confronting us on pewter plates were the remnants of the lamb dinner from the night before mashed into a muddy-tasting stew. We had to eat it to appear polite but washed it down with as much mint tea as possible, hoping it would pass through our systems quickly without making us sick.

Outside, we inspected the vehicles again, restocked them with water and fuel, and I held what we called a bonnet (or front hood) brief, bringing everyone up to speed on what Hazrat Ali had told me the night before—which was very little. Today's mission was to proceed from RV (rendezvous point) Alpha 1 (Qalayahe Allah Naa) to RV Alpha 2 (Bakalay)—some twenty miles on the map and a several-hour drive over primitive gravel, mud, and loose-shale roads.

Hazrat Ali provided twenty men as an escort. Disheveled and haggard looking, they piled into two Toyota HiLux pickups and a flatbed truck. A few of them appeared jaundiced. Their weapons and kit were worn, scant, and out of date. Clearly, the millions a year in equipment and handouts Ali was getting from the US mil weren't reaching his troops. The only apparent signs of his own wealth were the size of his compound, the fact that it had been built with bricks and mortar instead of mud, three wives, and more than a dozen children.

Since we carried no demining equipment, I asked Hazrat Ali if his men had recently demined the road ahead. He answered no, but because the US mil sent teams up and down it all the time it was relatively safe. The Taliban, he said, planted IEDs between 2300 and 0300 so the US mil knew to demine it at 0400.

I hoped he was right as we pushed south on the mostly gravel Sheikh Medvi Road. As we started to climb and the terrain became less verdant and rockier, Hazrat Ali's men wanted our vehicles to ride in the middle, bookended by theirs. I had put them ahead of us for two reasons. One, if we encountered IEDs, they would get hit first. And, second, I wanted to keep an eye on them.

We weren't more than ten minutes out of Qalayahe Allah Naa when Justin came over the radio and growled, "Charlie wagon down. Rear tires gone."

Since he wasn't reporting contact, I assumed it was the result of the shitty road. We immediately slammed into our flat-tire drill, Alpha and Bravo both backing up and forming a defensive perimeter in front and in back of Charlie at thirty-degree angles, with us in front.

Once we were in position, I said into the radio, "Charlie, you're free to move."

As we operators in Alpha and Bravo readied our weapons and looked out for ambushes from the road that ran parallel to us, Jan (the terp-driver) got out of Charlie and removed the jack and blown tire. Meanwhile, Danny, in the gun seat, popped the roof out, grabbed the spare tire that was ratchet strapped on top, and handed it down to Justin.

I was nervous for a number of reasons. First, our militia escort had proceeded another hundred meters down the road, stopped there, and wasn't backing up to help us. Second, this was a notorious Taliban ambush site because of the parallel dirt road that led to contiguous hamlets and farming communities. Terry Taliban was known to lie in wait for stopped enemy vehicles and run up and down that parallel road blasting .50 cals from the back of their HiLuxes. We didn't have a .50 cal, only a less powerful belt-fed 5.56, which was effective up to three hundred meters. We also had our rear gunners up with M4s, which with good sights were accurate to a hundred meters.

As we scanned 360 expecting an attack any second, Justin and Jan quickly bolted on the spare tire and climbed back into Charlie. Relieved, we alerted the TOC and started moving forward again.

I said, "Speed good at fifty. Road surface gravel with potholes."

Twenty minutes later as we pushed past Blue 9 and turned on the Romeo-al Road, Blue 10, I heard a dull thump, felt the Alpha lurch forward, then heard dirt and metal rattling off the rear of the vehicle.

A split second later, Phil in Bravo yelled over the radio, "Contact! Contact! IED. Push, push, push!"

Adrenaline surged into my bloodstream again. Per Phil's instructions, we proceeded another two hundred meters, stopped, and established a safety cordon around Bravo at the same thirty-degree angles. While we were doing that, I reached into my grab bag and started laying extra mags out on the floor. I heard Mark in back getting the belt-fed ready.

Most IEDs were the size of Coke bottles and filled with explosives and nuts and bolts. Because our vehicles were B6 armor plated, I wasn't too worried that Bravo had been penetrated. But what I was very concerned about was the fact that most IED attacks were followed by ambushes, which were quick, intense, and violent.

I'd been in a few in the past and knew that in a short period of time you had to put down as much firepower as you could to hold back the enemy. Phil in Bravo did a sitrep to make sure nobody was injured, then craned his neck toward the instrument panel of Bravo to check that the oil and temp gauges weren't going through the roof.

Again, Hazrat Ali's militiamen sat in their vehicles one hundred meters down the road and did nothing. The explosion had ripped off the front bumper and grille. Luckily, everyone in Bravo was okay, and the vehicle was still running.

I made the decision to continue. We passed Blue 11 and turned onto Blue 12—a local loose-shale road with a long straightaway and a view of the spectacular white-capped mountains farther south. Ahead and off to the right, I spotted another black column of smoke and reached for the binos.

I called into the radio, "All call signs. Eyes up. Possible IED on the road ahead."

Justin alerted the TOC, and the TOC informed him that it was already aware that a US convoy consisting of one fuel truck and six Humvees had been hit and taken multiple casualties.

We were the only other vehicles on the road. Hazrat Ali's militiamen in their flatbed and two HiLuxes were moving fast ahead of us. Since they were radioless, I had no way of communicating with them and telling them to stop. Hoping to head off a possible blue-on-blue (friendly fire) incident, I told Emal to hit the gas and try to pass them.

Fortunately, the militiamen saw us approaching and slowed down. We steered around them and stopped in front of the convoy, where I got out and talked to the sergeant in charge—a big guy with a southern accent. He told me the first IED they rolled over had exploded but missed the convoy. So had the second. But when they passed over the third and fourth, they weren't as lucky. One hit the fuel truck, which was now a fireball. The other struck a

Humvee, resulting in two dead and several wounded. Helicopters and medevac were on their way.

Sadly, in this part of the country, coalition convoys were hit almost daily. And the more remote the roads became, the less effort the US mil made to demine them, which didn't make sense, since these roads were well traveled by convoys and teams like ours.

It was only 1500, but we were exhausted by the time we pulled into Bakalay and found Mohammad Zaman's compound. His was smaller than Ali's, and his inner circle larger.

Zaman was equally welcoming, shaking our hands and smiling constantly—an urbane, educated man with a short gray beard and hooded dark eyes. He struck me as someone who focused solely on how he could benefit from any situation, regardless of prior loyalties or any sense of right or wrong. As the Pashtun warlord alleged to be in control of the lucrative poppy trade in the region, he was known to locals as Mr. Ten Percent.

Zaman announced cheerfully that he would be personally escorting us to our jumping-off point into the mountains, Wazir. I wasn't sure if this was good news or bad. My first concern was reaching the TOC and letting them know that vehicle Bravo couldn't go farther because the hoses were shot.

The guys back at J-bad told us that they would try to source a replacement vehicle and get it to us in twenty-four hours, which would involve sending out another team. While Justin continued communicating with the TOC, I watched as one of Zaman's guys went to talk to Hazrat Ali's militiamen, who had stopped outside the gate. They exchanged heated words, then Ali's men climbed back into their vehicles and burned.

Two things were clear: One, Zaman and his men would take over from this point. And, two, the two tribal leaders, though allies, didn't trust each other.

Great. The farther we went, the more suspicion and uncertainty seemed to gather around our mission. Not knowing how long we would have to wait in Bakalay before we got the go-ahead to proceed, we sat down to a feast that night in Zaman's villa—roasted lamb, rice, honey bread, fruit, and tea…no surprises.

Zaman, our jolly, lizard-eyed host, never left our side for the next two days as we waited for the replacement vehicle. We spent that time busying ourselves in the little local clinic and helping to restock it with syringes, bandages, and IV drips.

Finally, the TOC sent word that it wasn't going to send a replacement vehicle because of the large number of IEDs and the fact that the roads wouldn't be cleared for two more days. Our choice was now to abandon the mission, to proceed to the foot of the mountain with only two vehicles, or to try to fix Bravo somehow. Phil, who had trained as a vehicle mechanic (VM), got excited the afternoon of day 2 when he located a tribesman who claimed to operate a small garage.

Instead of the replacement water hoses we needed, the eager young man produced two empty plastic water bottles, which clearly wouldn't do. There had been some confusion in the translation. Justin and I had a good laugh.

Now I made the decision to abandon Bravo, which involved stripping it of all sensitive equipment, including flap sheets, and comms. That night after supper, Justin and I sat down with Zaman and spread out the maps of Tora Bora.

As I had done with Ali, I asked him if his men had seen bin Laden in the area.

"Yes," he answered.

"When?" I asked.

"About two weeks ago."

"Which of your men saw him?"

"It wasn't one of my fighters. The information came from villagers who were passing from one part of Tora Bora to another. They saw him and reported this to my men."

This intel struck me as dubious at best. OBL had used the caves and foothills of the White Mountains (Safed Koh) as a base and hideout on and off since the early eighties, had employed many of the locals building houses and digging trenches, and was known to have many loyal followers in the area. So why would some of the tribesmen be informing on him now?

The specific location Zaman's men had seen OBL in was a hamlet northeast of where Ted and Ali's intel placed him. So I called Ted, who was still at J-bad, and asked him where he wanted us to look.

He said, "Go where Zaman says he is."

Having serious doubts that we could trust anything either Ali or Zaman had told us, I said, "Okay, Ted. We'll climb up there and spend forty-eight hours looking around."

"Fine," he answered. "But if when you get to Zaman's location, someone tells you that they've seen OBL somewhere else, what are you going to do?"

"That depends on our supplies," I answered. "We might have to fall back to RV3 [Wazir], rest, and resupply."

"Okay. Godspeed."

With our fear, anticipation, and distrust of the militiamen growing by the minute, none of us was sleeping well at night. I'd close my eyes, doze for twenty minutes, and wake up at the slightest sound of the wind buffeting the windows or someone moving outside.

The next morning, we got up early, had breakfast, and set out with

Zaman, three of his top advisers, and twenty of his men. Thankfully, we reached Wazir without incident.

This was the little village at the foot of the mountains where the combined CIA–special forces team and operators from Delta Force had launched their attacks against OBL in late 2001. It consisted of several dozen huts, a clinic, a one-room schoolhouse, and a small compound and TOC that served as Zaman's headquarters. From Wazir we slipped and slid five miles up a steep mountain road to an even-smaller hamlet called Gunde.

Because our Land Cruisers were heavy, Gunde was the farthest they could go. It was also in an area filled with mines and unexpected ordnance—most of which were cluster bombs dropped by the US coalition. The bomblets they produced looked like little metal balls. Kids had kicked them or picked them up, only to lose an arm or a leg. We saw several victims of the bomblets when we visited the dilapidated hut that served as the clinic.

The shame we felt contributed to our building sense of unease. That night we tossed and turned inside a farmhouse while Zaman sent his scouts out to check the area. They returned in the morning with no news and no reported sightings of OBL or his men.

"Is that good or bad?" Phil asked.

"Let's take it as a positive," I answered.

We bid goodbye to Zaman, removed all sensitive material from the Land Cruisers, locked them, and started climbing in patrol order with the guys strung out in five-meter intervals. That way a rocket or mortar strike wouldn't take us out all at once.

Before we set out, Sam, the diminutive former Delta operator, went down to his knees and said a prayer. Zaman's two top aides led the way. As the TL, I positioned myself in the rear so I could see everything happening in front of me. Every few meters, I'd turn and walk backward so I could see if anyone was following. Zaman's men, some of whom were in their fifties and sixties, created a protective cordon around us.

They were used to the terrain and acclimatized. We weren't. Although we had trained in mountain warfare, none of us had done any in years. We were also totally kitted out with Gore-Tex boots, body armor, and weighted down with roughly seventy pounds of gear each—including protein bars, extra mags, grenades, med kits, radios, and bladders of water.

Zaman's men carried their AKs, little satchels with tea sets and supplies, a bandolier with three extra mags, and wore slipperlike shoes with rubber soles, pajama pants, wool hats, and shawls.

Despite our fanatic CrossFit training, all nine of us were huffing and puffing within twenty minutes of slipping and climbing. The terrain was as beautiful as it was unforgiving—slashes of gray shale and loose beige limestone and clumps of thick Christmas-tree-shaped cedars, with the jagged White Mountains peaks in the distance.

I used my map and GPS to track the route we were supposed to follow, which was southeast from where Zaman's men were taking us, but in the same approximate direction. As we walked, I asked myself, *Are these sweet old men leading us into an ambush?*

As we entered farther into Taliban–al-Qaeda territory, we used our individual earpieces to keep in constant contact with one another.

"Simon, the last guy is now ten meters behind you," Justin reported.

"Roger that, mate."

"Zaman's OIC [officer in charge] is pushing over the next ridge."

"Roger."

The temperature dipped below zero, and the entire area grew

eerily quiet—interrupted by the otherworldly sound of wind whistling through trees. We were extremely aware of how noisy we sounded. And because we were climbing up gorges and narrow valleys, there was no place for the sound to go but up into the ears of our possible enemies.

Every thirty minutes, Justin did a radio check with the TOC. He discovered that the higher we climbed, the weaker the signal got. Two hours out of Gunde, the UHF crackled out completely. Now all we had was our sat phone, which operated on batteries that were notorious for losing power in frigid conditions.

As we pushed higher, single men armed with AKs appeared seemingly out of nowhere and greeted Zaman's men. *Who are these guys and what are they doing up here?* I asked myself. *Are they farmers from local villages or Taliban scouts?*

All the men in the area, including Zaman's fighters, wore the same dark eyelinerlike kohl around their eyes, which added another layer of weirdness and distrust.

Bare-knuckle fighter Justin kept up a steady stream of jokes to break the tension. "What kind of bloody mission is this, being in the middle of nowhere led by a group of cross-dressers? Did these blokes raid the makeup counter of some department store?"

The route from Gunde to Gharo Chinech covered about five miles and took us most of the day to climb. We were chin strapped by the time we arrived—eyes sunken and bloodshot, lips cracked, leg and back muscles aching. We were now in the approximate area OBL had recently been seen.

Through Emal, I asked a local farmer named Hamid for confirmation that bin Laden had been here.

Hamid didn't hesitate as he answered, "No, I haven't seen him here at all."

I was flummoxed and too drained to sort out the conflicting stories and motives. Refusing to rely on Zaman's men for security, I posted our own sentries at one-hour rotations and took the first watch myself. Meanwhile, the rest of the guys settled into the little mud farmhouse that Hamid had offered to us to sleep in.

Ducking in after my watch, thoroughly chilled and exhausted, I saw the rest of the guys leaning against the wall dry-checking their weapons in the candlelight.

Scottish Phil asked with a smirk, "What are we supposed to do now, Simon? Are we supposed to climb past the trees on that ridge and just run into bin Laden?"

"Your guess is as good as mine," I responded.

"Well, all of us think this job is fucking bonkers."

I couldn't disagree. In most HVT jobs you were given a position where the target had recently been seen. You'd infil the area, surveil the target's movements, and build a target package—where the target slept, where he went, and who was with him. Then you'd radio that intel back to HQ, and they'd tell you whether to capture him or take him out.

How could we put OBL under surveillance when we didn't know where he was, or if he was even here, in a region that covered at least a hundred square miles of mountains, cedar forests, shale cliffs, and caves?

"If he's fucking here, mate, don't you think he'll have scouts and sentries all over the place keeping an eye out for blokes like us?" Justin asked. "And what are we going to do if we run into him or Terry Taliban, and there's fifty guys with him against nine of us?"

"Excellent question, Justin. I really don't know."

CHAPTER EIGHT
GHARO CHINECH

WE SPENT the following day at Gharo Chinech—a hamlet of about a dozen mud huts—resting and putting out patrols that came back with no new intel. Through our terp Emal, I struck up a conversation with our host Hamid, who lived there with his wife and two children, growing vegetables and poppies.

The vegetables were for his family. He harvested the seeds from the poppies and sold them to Mohammad Zaman, whom he said was no more than a glorified drug dealer. According to Hamid, all the farmers in the area derived their incomes from poppies, and the trade was massive.

Knowing some of the guys on the Brit mil drug-eradication detail and having recently listened to Prime Minister Tony Blair sound off about its effectiveness on TV, I asked Hamid about it. He explained that he grew two fields of poppies—a modest one near his house and a larger one hidden in a valley farther west.

He and the other farmers would hear about the approaching coalition eradication team a week before it reached Gharo. And every year, the team would pay Hamid a certain amount of local currency in exchange for letting them burn the field near his house. But they never found the larger poppy field outside town. After they left, he'd harvest the seed pods from that field, which contained a milky sap that made up the crudest form of opium.

So much for the effectiveness of the coalition drug eradication effort. I later learned that opium poppy cultivation had actually increased since the US–UK occupation, reaching a record 7,054 tons in 2014, according to the UN Office on Drugs and Crime. That made Afghanistan the largest illicit opium producer in the world, supplying over 90 percent of the world's nonpharmaceutical-grade opiates.

The morning of the twenty-seventh, my teammates and I got up at 0600 and did a brief and weapons check. Then I sat with Emal and the guy running Zaman's militiamen and spread out the satellite maps.

"This is the area I want to look at," I said, pointing to a two-square-mile block of territory south of Gharo that ran up to the edge of the Safed Koh cave complex.

The caves had been naturally carved into the limestone and shored up with timber beams with ladders running from one to the other. OBL had sought shelter in some of them during the bombing of 2001. They weren't the super-modern reinforced caves outfitted with hydraulic lifts and electrical generators that had been described in the media, and which, by the way, didn't exist. If OBL was hiding in or near that cave complex now, we'd run into his sentries and recce patrols as we approached.

So we loaded up with weapons, ammo, water, and our med kits and set out southeast. It was slow going and difficult climbing. Around 1300 we found the first of four patches of scorched ground the size of a small car where someone had made a fire. They appeared to be about a week old. Around them we found empty shell casings and bullets—5.56s and 7.62s—indicating that an armed force had been in the area, rebombing (or reloading) their mags.

I marked the locations on the map, and we continued farther up the mountain until 1700, when it started to turn dark. That's when I gave the order to turn back. For the next three hours we stumbled down in the dark aided by our NVGs. The twenty of Zaman's blokes who had accompanied us walked in the pitch black.

Back at Gharo, I huddled with the guys and did a debrief. The route we had traced on the map and the route Zaman's men had taken us ran parallel. We wondered if maybe Zaman's men were deliberately guiding us away from OBL's position. But both routes went in the same approximate direction, southeast.

Gharo stood on the northeast side of the Tora Bora region. Another village called Sengani was located farther east. They were the last villages before the mountains that led into Pakistan.

I called Ted on the sat phone and gave him a sitrep, which included the fire signatures we had found. I told him that if we continued to push south we would be in the mountains.

"How far do you want us to go?" I asked. "Do you want us to keep climbing until we reach the Pakistani border, which is about six or seven days away?"

"That depends," Ted answered. "Have you received any incoming fire?"

"No. No, nothing like that. Only the odd guy coming out of the woods who looks like a farmer. And villagers in Gharo have told us emphatically that 'the sheikh' isn't there. Nor has he sent guys down to their village to purchase food."

Ted said, "Give me a couple of hours and I'll get back to you."

Two hours later, the sat phone lit up. It was Ted with instructions. "We'd like you to spend another twenty-four hours. Tomorrow do another arc farther west. If you don't see anything, we're of the same mind as you, that if OBL and his men were there a week ago, they're gone now."

"Roger."

I informed the guys, "Tomorrow if we don't see anything, we're popping smoke."

Justin felt that we had been sent on a wild-goose chase. "Ted and his guys probably knew from the start that there was little chance anything would come of this."

I felt the same, frankly, but reminded my teammates that this was pay and play. We were being paid to do a job, and it was our responsibility to complete it.

At 0200, I awoke to the sound of shelling from the west. It wasn't the percussive thud of mortars; more like the sharp crackle of Black Hawk 130 machine guns.

After a few tries, I reached Ted again on the sat phone.

He said, "The fire you hear is of no risk to you whatsoever. It's coming from an area near Mangai to the west, where Zaman and Ali's men are engaged in a dustup with the Taliban."

"Why are they shelling?" I asked.

"They're not shelling," Ted answered as calmly as if I had asked him about the weather. "What you're hearing is air support for Ali and Zaman's men."

We ate a quick breakfast, rechecked our weapons, then set out southwest on a path that ran parallel to the Pakistani border but five or six thousand feet below the mountain peak. We were at five thousand feet and climbing up steep terrain covered with loose shale and dirt.

Again we saw signs of a troop concentration, including fire signatures and animal bones. But we didn't spot anyone, and the fire signatures looked to be at least a week old.

Around 1700, as the sky started to darken, I stopped and said, "Okay, guys, let's make our way back."

We had descended for twenty minutes when a volley of AK fire cracked from the trees to our left. Then the whole mountain lit up with muzzle flashes and sparks from rounds.

Justin shouted through the radio, "Contact left and right!"

I hit the ground with my mouth open, froze, and tried to use my hearing to ascertain the direction and distance of the enemy.

Joining the volleys of AK fire were the whoosh of RPGs and the roar of PKM machine guns. We were pinned on our bellies facing west, with the mountain to our left and Gharo to our right, totally exposed to our attackers, who held the higher ground.

A phenomenal amount of fear coursed through my body and head. I tried to push it out of my mind and think straight. I knew for sure that I didn't want to rely on Zaman's fighters. Nor could I communicate with them via comms. I had to focus solely on the safety of my men.

I lifted my head, took a quick look around, and saw that the right was the most clear. I shouted into the Motorola to the rest of the team, "Right is clear. On 'Rapid,' peel right!"

I waited a few seconds, then gave the order, "Rapid!"

I told the team to put down as much brass as possible. Then as the rest of us laid down cover, Delta surfer dude Danny, who was the last in the line, stood and started to run toward me in a tactical peel. As he passed, he slapped me on the shoulder and said "Last man!" and continued running down the entire line, past Phil who was first.

Taking cover at the front, Danny shouted "Move!" which was the signal for me as the last man to stop firing at enemy positions eighty meters away and get up and start running.

The noise around us was deafening—AKs cracking, bullets ricocheting, rockets exploding. Suddenly two RPG rounds slammed smack in the middle of our line, and everything stopped. Dirt, rock, and shrapnel rained over us, and then there was a hush.

I shouted into the radio, "Sound off!"

All the guys shouted out, except for Stumpy and Danny. I was on my belly at the front of the line—the farthest down the mountain. The enemy had formed a rough U around us. I estimated that about thirty to fifty of them were trying to cut off our descent.

An eerie silence passed over us, then Phil called out, "Medic," and leapfrogged past Justin and Mark to the center of the line.

As our primary medic, he stopped at little Stumpy first. My witty, generous friend of more than ten years had been hit with a long sliver of shrapnel that entered near the armhole of his vest and severed his aorta. He had no pulse. Danny, the super-fit surfer, was lying on his side directly in front of Stumpy and had serious shrapnel wounds to his lower limbs and stomach.

Phil gave us a sitrep over the radio. Since I was the farthest down, Justin turned back and punched up the hill, breaking extra bandages out of his med kit as he went.

Working together, Justin and Phil placed one compression bandage over Danny's stomach, which quickly bled through. They put down a second, and then a third, which finally seemed to stem the bleeding.

Phil reported over the radio, "We need to get Danny down to Gharo so we can get some fluids in him."

My ears ringing from the rockets exploding in the dirt and rock around me, I shouted, "Say again, your last. Over."

"We need to get Danny down to Gharo, asap!"

Phil explained that he didn't want to give Danny morphine until he was settled and he could see exactly where he was putting it. Morphine was a drug you administered as a last resort. Because Danny was coming off an adrenaline high and had lost a lot of blood, a shot of morphine could lower his blood pressure further and kill him.

After ten tense minutes, the fire stopped, and the enemy remained quiet. So did we, which meant no more comms.

As I lay on my belly in the dark, shocked by the sudden loss of my friend Stumpy and trying to appraise our situation, Justin slowly squirmed down to my position on his belly.

Lying in the rock and mud, we formulated a plan. Scottish Phil would take the terp Khan and four of Zaman's men, who would form a human chair for Danny. Phil would run beside them holding the IV bag.

We stripped off Danny's and Stumpy's NVGs and handed them to two of the Afghans. They nodded and took off down the mountain carrying Danny feetfirst. Then Phil stopped them and insisted that they carry Danny the opposite way, headfirst, so that his legs would remain level with his heart, and he wouldn't lose as much blood.

In the chaos and horror, I had forgotten to give Phil the sat phone. Before I realized what I had done, our Motorolas were out of reach, and I had no way of communicating with Phil.

It was a real shitty feeling all around. We were outnumbered, and the eight blokes I had with me had been reduced to five in a heartbeat. Stumpy, who shouldn't have come in the first place, was dead; Danny badly injured; and cheap-ass but strong and dependable Phil was carrying him down the mountain. The twenty Afghan supports had shrunk to nine; four had gone with Phil, and another seven had run off at first contact.

As we lay on our bellies, Phil, Khan, the four Afghans, and Danny reached the outskirts of Gharo. Phil stopped in a patch of trees 150 meters from the little community and waited. He didn't know if the enemy had run ahead and set up in some of the mud huts.

So he instructed the locals to stay with Danny and approached slowly on his own, moving in a hunched walk, weapon ready, sweeping left, then right. After what felt like forty minutes, he arrived at the door of Hamid's farmhouse.

Phil knocked, backed away from the door, and dropped to his knees. Not knowing who was inside, he didn't want to remain upright and take two rounds in the chest.

Hamid opened the door and poked his head out. He saw Phil kneeling on the ground covered with blood.

Phil pointed inside the house and shouted, "Taliban? Taliban?"

The short, skinny farmer shook his head, whereupon Phil sprinted back to the trees and helped carry Danny to the farmhouse. As soon as they arrived, Hamid swung into action, fetching water, towels, and animal skins to keep Danny warm.

Phil couldn't summon medevac because he had no comms. All he had with him was his personal Motorola, which couldn't reach Gunde or J-bad. So he kept Khan and two of Zaman's fighters to provide security and sent the other two to Gunde to get help.

Meanwhile, Justin, Pete, Mark, Stevie, Sam, and I remained face-down in the freezing-cold shale and mud for almost three hours. With the enemy positioned above and to our left and right, we couldn't make a sound or lift our heads without becoming easy targets. The only element in our favor was the pitch-black, moonless night.

As we lay there, hundreds of thoughts careened through my brain. I figured the enemy had been following us from the first day we moved from Gunde to Gharo. They had remained at a safe distance until we were at the worst disadvantage and thoroughly exhausted. They were professional fighters, maybe Taliban, maybe OBL's Fifty-Fifth Brigade, maybe some of both.

Faces from grade school, silly stuff I had done as a kid, and bits of conversations drifted into my mind and faded. I thought about all the things I regretted, like stealing cars. And I wondered if I'd ever see my mum again.

I was sweating, even though the temperature had dipped below zero. And I could hear the enemy moving about. Were they surrounding us? Were they planning to press forward with their superior numbers and overwhelm us?

As the TL it was my responsibility to get the team back to safety. But how? I wasn't even sure where we were. All I knew was that we were about forty-five minutes away from the path marked Blue 17 that would take us north to Gharo.

The military commandments "Shoot," "Move," "Communicate" resounded in my head. If we didn't do one of them soon, we'd be fucked. Justin was trying to establish comms with the TOC and give them a TIC (troops in combat) report. But it was super difficult, as we were trying to stay quiet. I also knew that when we did deliver the TIC, we would go to the bottom of the list in terms of any kind of air support, because we weren't US, UK, or coalition mil. We were contractors and, therefore, on our own.

Squinting through my NVGs, I established that it was clear on the right. So I got on comms and whispered, "Stand by to move. We're going to push right."

Once again, we started to leapfrog positions and lay down cover. Every time I took a step, I couldn't believe I wasn't hit, because the amount of lead that flew toward us was staggering.

Still, the spirit of the guys was inspiring. All of us were shitting our pants, but every time one of my mates slapped me on the shoulder and passed, I'd see a big grin on his face.

Due to the lack of light, we did a lot of stumbling and falling. We also had to take turns carrying Stumpy, who we weren't going to leave behind. As I ran with him over my shoulder, blood poured down the back of my shirt.

We had managed to peel about 150 meters when lightning-fast Stevie, who was the last man, punched past me and stumbled.

As he went down, I heard him shout, "I'm hit! I'm down!"

The rest of us stopped, hit the ground again, and took cover behind the trunk of a cedar tree and two boulders. The seven Afghans who had sprinted past us down the hill scurried back to join us.

Justin and I attended to Stevie, who had been hit twice in the upper thigh and was covered with blood. We knew that if one of the bullets had nicked his femoral artery he'd bleed out quickly. But after we cut his pants leg away, we realized that most of the blood had come from Stumpy.

We slapped a couple Israeli bandages on the wounds, but they didn't stop the bleeding.

Justin looked up at me and whispered, "Fuck this, mate. Let's QuikClot it."

I broke the seal on a pack with my teeth, and together we started packing it into the wounds. The QuikClot was amazing—a synthetic derivative of volcanic rock filled with pores that capture and hold the water molecules that make up the majority of blood. It worked in seconds, accelerating the body's natural clotting process until the bleeding stopped.

Justin and I bandaged Stevie's thigh. While we worked on him, the black Scottish ex-parachuter—God bless him—kept smiling and asking, "Is everybody all right? Is everyone all right?"

Our concealment was decent, so we sat for thirty minutes rebombing mags and moving them from our grab bags to our vests. I worked the GPS to ascertain our position in relation to the path. The enemy still had the tactical advantage, and the sun was starting to rise.

We quickly downed protein bars, rehydrated, and then I gave the order to slowly peel right, which seemed to be our only safe direction, despite the uncomfortable feeling we were being herded that way by the enemy above.

It was very slow going this time because we were trying to stay quiet and Stevie was moving on his own—one, because he could, and, two, with Stumpy to carry or drag, we couldn't spare another man.

After forty minutes, we had to stop because Stevie was exhausted. The enemy started shooting again, this time in short clusters of well-placed shots that tore into the nearby trees and ground.

Pete rolled over to where I was lying and asked, "What the fuck do you think this is, mate?"

"Maybe the enemy's main fighting force is resting, and they sent a smaller patrol to follow us at a higher parallel and harass us."

I got on the comms and gave the order to lay down a barrage of suppressive fire and bound north as fast as possible. We started to peel, but it was chaotic because Zaman's men didn't understand the tactic, so they'd drop at various points and return fire past us as we ran.

It was dangerous, but I figured it was more important to keep moving. We continued, until Stevie planted his injured right leg down the hill, and his ankle gave way from the pressure, and he started to roll.

I ran up to him, scooped him under my shoulder, and asked, "What the fuck are you doing, Stevie?"

109

Pete behind me started to laugh. I did, too.

We were releasing some of the massive tension that gripped every particle of our beings. Our entire situation seemed hopeless and absurd.

As we hobbled with Stevie into a patch of trees and set him down, Justin shouted, "Last man!"

Pete then scurried to the back of the line to keep security while Justin and I carefully removed Stevie's boot and saw that his right ankle was broken.

"For fuck's sake, Stevie, you deliberately trying to make this as difficult as possible?" Justin joked.

We wrapped the ankle tightly and shimmied Stevie's boot back on, keeping the laces loose, as incoming started to pour in. We put down as much fire as we could to hold the enemy back and remained pinned for two hours, during which time two of Zaman's men were hit and died.

It was bloody obvious that our situation was growing more desperate by the second. We were running out of ammo, food, and water. And it seemed that no relief was coming.

I glanced at my watch and saw that it was 1330. We had been under attack for more than twenty hours and only managed to move about a third of a mile. At this rate, we'd all be dead by nightfall.

I started hoping for a miracle. Maybe the TOC would send a team in with Black Hawks. Maybe the nine Afghans who had run off in the initial contact would suddenly show up with 100 of their mates. Maybe the earth would open up and swallow the enemy. Maybe…

The three remaining militiamen who knelt in a cover of trees approximately four meters away from us never stopped talking. About what, I had no clue. I'd given up trying to keep them quiet or adhere to any standard of tactical awareness. Clearly, they were fighting according to a different set of rules determined by the big man upstairs. As they saw it, if your time was up, it was up, and there was nothing you could do about it.

Determined in that belief, the oldest of them—a wizened old man with kind eyes who had probably been fighting since he was a teenager—reached into his battered backpack, removed a pewter tea set, and walked to the open ground between our positions. Seemingly oblivious to the danger around him, he squatted down and started to build a fire and brew tea. He didn't stop even as enemy rounds started to ping off the rocks beside him.

Once he had brewed his tea, he poured two cups and calmly carried them to our position. Pete, Justin, Sam, Stevie, and I had been trying to keep small and remain quiet, but now we couldn't stop laughing. Tears streamed down our faces. Emal and Jan joined in.

The old man handed us cups of mint tea and returned to fetch more. It was an inspiring moment and a massive show of courage.

"What I wouldn't give for a bit of his dutch [courage] right now," tough-as-nails Justin said, nodding toward the old man.

Our spirits bolstered, and hot tea in our stomachs, we decided to make another push.

We completed two full bounds, dragging Stumpy and with Stevie limping on his own, until the enemy fire got so intense that we had to stop. We returned fire, caught our breath, and started to bound again.

This time as Pete ran past me, he was hit by a bullet, which caused him to lose his footing and tumble five meters down a sharp slope.

As my best mate spun past me, I heard him screaming in an East London accent, "Jesus fucking Christ!"

Half laughing, half filled with dread, I slid down on my ass to where Pete had stopped and found him lying there with a big grin on his face. "I can't believe it," he shouted. "Those bloody fucking cunts!" As he cursed, he was applying a bandage to the place above his left elbow where he had been shot.

Fortunately, the shot had passed clean through his arm below any major arteries. I tied a second Israeli bandage around the wound, then Pete picked up his M4 and started to return fire. Enemy bullets whizzed and ricocheted all around us. The incoming got so intense that we remained pinned behind a group of rocks and boulders for another hour and a half.

Now I had to monitor Pete, too, and change his bandage every half hour or so. Stevie, meanwhile, who was usually blacker than the ace of spades, looked pale and weak. Our two terps were practically hysterical, jabbering to themselves nonstop.

Out of desperation, I reached Ted on the sat phone and gave him a sitrep.

He told me that we weren't going to get any relief from the US mil and asked if we could get to Gharo.

I lost my shit and screamed back at him, "What the fuck do you think we're trying to do?"

"Yes. Yes, of course. I'll call Zaman now and give him your location. I'll tell him to push some of his troops up to you."

By this time we all knew that Zaman was a fucking liar, and any relief he promised wasn't coming.

All we wanted to do was get home. You could see it in the guys' eyes. They'd be joking one minute, taking the piss out of you, then stop and gaze off into the distance in a private moment. They were thinking about missed opportunities and other things they regretted. They might have been some of hardest men I'd ever met, but they were human.

Stevie had a young wife and two young girls back in Scotland. Pete was raising his own football team of six boys in Romford. I had talked all the guys into this job. Now we were getting caked.

What the fuck had I been thinking? The minute Ted told me we couldn't trust Zaman and Ali, I should have packed the job in right there.

We had been under attack almost a full twenty-four hours and had gone maybe a mile and a half. It was fucking madness. Would any of us get off this mountain alive?

After two more hours of being pinned, I gave everyone five minutes to get ready, then we start to peel again. We did one complete bound, before incoming started to rain around us.

I said into the Motorola, "Fuck it, mates! Let's keep going!"

We did another three bounds and started a fourth. I was in front of nimble, elflike Sam, and one of the remaining Afghans who flew past me was hit several times and went down. Sam rolled over to him and found him dead.

Mark, who was in first position, saw a drop-off ahead that he thought would provide good cover and shouted, "Baseline! Baseline! Baseline!"

We all dropped behind it and ducked while the enemy hosed us down from fifty meters with everything they had. The bullets and rockets came so heavy and thick that we couldn't return fire. All we could do was curl into little balls, make small, and pray.

After twenty minutes the barrage stopped. By that point the cordite in the air was so thick, we could barely breathe. We were mentally strung out, physically exhausted, hungry, thirsty, and down to four uninjured men and two Afghans. Our situation was fucking bleak, to put it mildly, and would soon get even worse.

CHAPTER NINE

BRIZE NORTON

FROM THE little hut farmhouse in Gharo, Phil heard the continued fighting farther up the mountain but had no way of communicating with J-bad. Thanks to his trauma medical training, he had managed to stabilize Danny.

Meanwhile, the two locals he had sent to Gunde raised another forty fighters and slowly made their way back to Gharo with a pickup truck. Once they arrived, they loaded Danny into the back of the pickup and rumbled down the mountain trail to Gunde. There, Phil hurried to the small TOC housed in a room in Zaman's compound and put a call into the TOC at J-bad.

He was told that the US mil had a total of eighteen PMC and military teams currently out in the field. A number of them were involved in TICs farther west of where we were pinned down. Since all available airpower was supporting those engagements, our team was on its own.

Fortunately, J-bad responded to the CASEVAC (casualty evacuation) report Phil delivered with more urgency. They quickly sent a helicopter and medevac team to Gunde to pick up Danny and Phil. Once the helo touched down in J-bad, Danny was wheeled to the med center (called the CASH) and taken into emergency surgery. He died five hours later of internal bleeding.

All a badly deflated Phil could do now was sit in the TOC and prod the guys there to give us any help they could.

By now it was late afternoon of the thirty-first. Dusk was approaching. From our cover under the ledge a mile or so above Gharo Chinech, we debated whether or not we should stay where we were or try to retreat down the mountain.

The batteries on our sat phone had died, and the extra ones we carried wrapped in foil had been drained by the extreme cold. So we had no comms.

Our team was down to two Afghans—the old man with the tea set and one other. We were constantly tending to two of our own wounded and had Nick's corpse to deal with. All of our bodies and minds were completely wasted.

God, please find us a way to get us off this mountain. Just throw us a bone. Please!

I figured that if we continued sitting where we were, the enemy would eventually encircle us and kill us all. What I didn't know was that the ledge we were on extended another mile west, which made any flanking maneuver on their part extremely treacherous.

Based on the knowledge I had, I decided our best tactic was to continue bounding. The boys agreed. So I gave the order to peel backward. The firing line consisted of me, Justin, Mark, Sam, Pete, and the two Afghans. Stevie was doing his best to hobble on a broken ankle and wounded leg, and we were taking turns dragging Stumpy. Our terps Emal and Jan stumbled along beside us.

I gave the guys numbers. The odd-numbered men would make small and give suppressive fire while the even numbers stood, turned and ran twenty meters, and took cover. Then the odds would stand and run past them twenty meters while the evens laid down fire.

The terrain below us was steep and slick, covered in spots with bits of loose shale and dirt. Our legs were so tired that they shook every time we put weight on them. So we all did a lot of slipping, tumbling, and falling. And as soon as we started to move, the incoming came at us fierce.

A group of the enemy had stopped at the ledge and was slamming us with RPGs, 5.56s, and PKMs nonstop. Rockets landed four and five at a time, producing shell shock and causing us to run faster. Blood trickled from my nose, and my eyes, lungs, and legs burned. My ears were numb. I ran oblivious to the dirt, rock, and shrapnel raining around me.

As Mark and Sam in the even group bounded past us, a rocket slammed the ground between them, lifting Sam off the ground and launching him ten feet. Mark somehow managed to stay on his feet and swerve around the column of dust and smoke. It looked like he had miraculously escaped undamaged, when another rocket tore into rock near his left side, and he tumbled down like a rag doll.

Pete and I ran to Mark's side. We found him rolling back and forth on his back with no sound coming out of his mouth. His right forearm looked like it had been pushed through a shredder, and both his legs were badly damaged.

We weren't in cover; nor was there time to move Mark. With bullets pinging and rockets exploding around us, I pulled two tourniquets out of Mark's vest and tied them around his left leg. I applied another two to his right, then ripped open a pack of QuikClot and started to slather it over his arm.

Pete meanwhile ran over to the group of boulders where little Sam had landed. That spot offered better cover.

Justin, seeing how exposed Mark and I were, ran over to help. He and I looped our arms under Mark and dragged him over to the group of boulders where Pete kneeled with Sam. When we got there, Pete turned to us and shook his head. Sam was dead.

Fuck. Things were going from bad to worse. Now Justin and I were the only remaining two on our team who weren't injured or gone.

The two Afghans joined us behind the little configuration of boulders and, together with Justin, put down suppressive fire. Meanwhile, Pete and I managed to stabilize Mark, dress his arm, and wrap it. Then we attended to his legs the best we could.

Enemy fire continued to pour in uninterrupted. As we sat pressed together, one of us noticed that Stumpy wasn't there. Justin told us that he had left Stumpy's body above when he ran down to help Mark and me.

"What the fuck do we do now?" Justin asked.

Pete said, "He's brown bread, mate. Just leave him."

Without thinking, I got up and started to run back up the hill. Justin and one of the Afghans followed. We found Stumpy and dragged him back to the concealed area.

Trying to catch my breath, I said, "Guys, I don't know what to do. I don't know if it's another mile or half mile back to Gharo or another two hundred meters. I mean, look at the fucking state we're in."

I was at the end of my rope. I had no idea if the enemy was in the process of sneaking around us or thought we were all dead. In desperation, I asked, "Does anyone have an idea?"

Pete spoke up and said, "Half the reason we took so many casualties is that we slowed ourselves by bringing Stumpy. We should have left him at the start."

I lost it, growling back, "Fuck you, mate. He's one of our best friends. How would you feel if it were you?"

"I wouldn't like it," Pete responded. "But these cunts are right on top of us, and taking him has slowed us down. Mark is bleeding out. Stevie is hobbling. We're right fucked!"

"Okay, then. What's your plan?"

Pete looked at our gaunt, hollowed-eyed faces, and answered, "We leave Stumpy and Sam, and we leg it back."

None of us liked the idea, but that's what we resolved to do. We had run out of food, and our water bladders and canteens were dry, so there was nothing left to drink or eat. We took a few minutes to rebomb. When I reached into my grab bag, I found two mags left. I had started with twenty-five.

Justin and I removed the bandages from Stevie's leg and re-dressed it. Blood was still leaking through. We patched up Mark as best we could, then waited until dark.

We stripped Sam and Stumpy's bodies of mags, comms, and maps, and pushed them as close into the wall of boulders as possible. Then we got up into crouches and started to bound.

We were all shitting ourselves with fear, and it was real slow going because we were trying to stay quiet. Justin, Pete, and I did something we had learned in basic training called cat walking. You'd put your heel down super soft, then roll your weight on the side of your foot, then carefully transfer it to the ball and toe.

Even though I was dehydrated, I sweated through my clothes. And my mind started playing tricks on me. I'd look left or right and think I saw men moving or faces in the trees.

We stopped constantly, because other guys were seeing things, too. I'd hear one of them whisper through the comms, "Contact right!" We'd all get down, make small, and wait.

You could hear a mouse's heartbeat at this point. That's how sensitive we were to movement and sound. Otherwise, our minds and bodies were shattered. Every time I looked over at Stevie, I saw him tumbling or rolling.

Amazing bloke. He'd been shot twice and broken his ankle but was still moving on his own. And he wasn't complaining.

As we descended slowly in the dark, I had the nagging feeling that we were walking in circles. I feared that when the sun came up, we'd find that we had only progressed a few meters.

Fortunately, I was wrong. Approximately four hours later, we staggered into Gharo Chinech, where the old Afghan fighter who had come with us down the mountain broke out his tea set and started brewing tea. Those of us who were still able to walk took up concealed positions and kept watch for the next four hours. We expected the enemy to descend on us at any second, but nothing happened.

We sat down to a meal of lamb stew prepared by Hamid's wife. What had tasted disgusting before was now as delicious as Mum's Sunday roast. Again, we took the dressings off Mark's leg and arm, Pete's arm, and Stevie's leg, cleaned their wounds as best we could, and re-dressed them.

One of our SUVs was still parked at Gunde. The other had been driven by Phil to Wazir and left there. So just before the sun came up, Pete and one of the old Afghan fighters climbed in the lone pickup at Gharo and drove down to Gunde. They returned five hours later with five pickups packed with thirty of Zaman's men.

Before we left the mountain, I wanted to push back and retrieve Sam and Nick. In fact, I made it very clear that I wasn't leaving without them.

So we rested, rebombed, filled our canteens with water, and set off carrying two body bags. The thirty Afghans formed a protective circle around us as we climbed. The amount of scorched earth and the number of trees felled from rocket rounds and bullet marks we saw were staggering. It was a miracle any of us had survived.

This time, we encountered no resistance. The enemy had turned into ghosts and vanished.

We loaded Sam and Stumpy into the body bags and did a tactical withdrawal. Again, we encountered no one.

Back at Gharo, we placed Sam and Stumpy's bodies in the pickups and blasted all the way to Wazir. At Wazir we radioed CASEVAC, and a helo arrived an hour later to ferry Stevie and Mark back to J-bad.

Hard-ass Pete insisted on staying with us, so the medic on the helo cut the dead skin away from his wound, punched in some butterfly sutures, jabbed him with penicillin, and sent him on his way.

When I called Ted to tell him that we had made it to Wazir and would soon be making our way back to J-bad, he asked me to do the courtesy of debriefing Zaman. But Zaman never appeared. Instead, Emal and I met with three of his aides.

As I sat with them, I wondered how the men on the mountain had found us so easily and if Zaman and his men had sold us out.

We followed the same route back, stopping at Bakalay and Qalayahe Allah Naa, and never setting eyes on Hazrat Ali again, either.

Once we reached J-bad, I sent everyone over to the med-bay to be treated, then sat with Ted, Michael, and the two guys from DIA and did a massive brief called an SIR (serious incident report). After a few minutes it started to turn into an interrogation with them firing pointed questions.

The adrenaline in my system had subsided and shock had set in. I was angry and depressed at the same time. Danny and Stumpy had been close friends. I'd first met Stumpy when we were both working for the SBS in Northern Ireland. We'd shared lots of laughs together and serious talks about life, women, and our futures when we roomed together while guarding the Qataris. I didn't know Sam as well, but he was a stand-up guy. Mark was in bad shape, and Stevie's leg was a bloody mess.

I said, "Gentlemen, this mission was set up to fail from the start. None of this should have happened. It was more of a publicity stunt than a serious op. We should never have been fucking sent there on the flimsy intel you had!"

As I spoke, all the emotion I had held at bay started to pour out of me.

Ted said, "Calm down, Simon. It's no one's fault."

"Easy for you to say," I growled back. "You don't understand. Now I've got to go on Skype and inform the next of kin. You're not going to fucking do that, are you Ted? It falls on me, and I'm fucking exhausted!"

I left the debrief, found my CHU, and lay down and slept, even though I hadn't eaten or showered and was filthy and hungry.

When I awoke seven hours later, I walked over to shower hut, found an empty stall, and turned the water on hot. As I watched the blood and dirt rinse off me and circle down the drain, my whole body started to shake.

I dressed and walked to the DFAC where I consumed a massive plate of eggs and met up with Justin and Pete. They told me that Mark was in stable condition and that he and Stevie would soon be flown to the US military hospital in Ramstein, Germany.

Hurrying over to the med center, I bid goodbye to my two mates and asked them not to tell anyone what had happened. "Blame it on an RTA," I said.

From there, I went back to my CHU, fired up my laptop, and stared at the Skype logo on the screen for two hours straight, trying to rehearse in my head what I was going to say.

I dialed Danny's house in Exmouth, southwest of London, where he lived with his English wife, Rose. I'd never actually met her but had heard him talking about her often.

Their computer rang and rang. I was hoping she wouldn't answer. But she did, and when she saw my image on the screen there were already tears rolling down my face.

"Simon, what happened?" she asked.

I tried, but couldn't get the words out. No military training had prepared me for a moment like this.

I cried, and Rose cried, too.

She said, "Thank you for calling. Thank you. Where is Danny now?"

I wiped the tears away and answered, "He's here with me in Jalalabad."

"How will he get home?" Rose asked.

"We'll fly from here to Kabul. Then from Kabul to Dubai, and Dubai to Brize Norton."

Brize Norton is a part-military, part-private-jet airport outside of London that's run by the Brit air force.

I said, "I'll make sure that you get a pass to get in."

The call with Rose gave me the confidence to ring Stumpy's girlfriend, Lisa. The talk with her was even more brutal. I was so overcome with emotion that I don't remember what I said, except that Stumpy had been a terrific friend, and I'd miss him. Since I hadn't recruited Sam, the job of informing his longtime girlfriend fell on Ted.

After we landed in Dubai, I called Rose and Lisa to let them know when we would be arriving at Brize Norton. Ted made the arrangements for them to get on the base.

It was an extremely depressing trip. Pete, Justin, and I had bitter tastes in our mouths, which turned even sourer when we landed. There was no honor guard at Brize Norton and no one to greet us. Just Lisa and Rose looking shattered standing beside two black hearses.

We loaded the body bags containing our mates into simple coffins, slid them in the back of the hearses, and Lisa and Rose drove off.

That was it. We left feeling completely used and abused. Since we were contractors, the men who had conceived of and launched our mission would have no one to answer to. There would be no official inquiries or stories in the newspaper. The lives of Stumpy, Danny, and Sam meant nothing to them. They would simply push the whole debacle under the carpet.

I had heard that there were nine or more other PMC teams like ours that were being run out of J-bad while we were there. God knows how many of them went through a similar experience.

I felt terrible for all the guys I had recruited, as well as Rose and Lisa and Stumpy's and Danny's families. Mark and Stevie had barely survived and would go through more than a year of surgeries and re-habilitation. We had gone to Tora Bora, gotten the shit kicked out of us, lost precious lives, and achieved nothing.

No "We're sorry, we screwed up." No "Thank you." Unity didn't even offer to pay for the funerals or compensate the families of the fallen men.

Since 2004, some PMC companies have improved and now cover funeral expenses and offer other forms of compensation to family members. But Unity isn't one of them. I've never worked for it again, and never will.

I returned to London depressed and bitter. The amount of trauma to my psyche was enormous. Over the subsequent weeks and months, there were days when I didn't even think of Tora Bora. Other days, my hands would start sweating, my body would shake uncontrollably, and I'd completely freak out.

A professional therapist told me that this was part of the healing process. My body and mind were letting go of the trauma. It would take months.

Lesson number 8: Part of you never comes back. You leave it there on the mountain with your sweat and piss, and the blood of your mates.

CHAPTER TEN
PAKISTANI DIVORCE CASE

AFTER THE horror of Tora Bora, it seemed like a good time to relax and refresh. And that's exactly what Pete and I thought we were doing. We were on the deck of a Greek freighter, the MSC *Nuria*, with a Scottish former marine mate of ours named Dave, chugging north along the coast of Somalia toward the Gulf of Aden and the Suez Canal.

Over the last several days, we'd spent hours sunning ourselves on the deck, reading, and trying to heal. But now, at three in the afternoon, the ship's distress signal suddenly started blasting in our ears.

"What the bloody hell is that about?" Dave asked.

"Beats the piss out of me. I'll go check with the captain."

"Don't bother," Pete shouted, pointing to boats approaching in the distance. "It's pirates!"

We scurried to our designated stations, charged the fire hoses, and grabbed the half-dozen flares we had on board. The three of us had taken what we thought would be a very mild security job, and now the ship we were guarding was about to be attacked. Because this was before international laws were changed to allow security men like ourselves to carry weapons, we were unarmed.

Through a pair of binoculars, Dave spotted two skiffs, approaching on either side of us, each carrying a half-dozen tribesmen. I instructed the Greek captain to ratchet up the speed another five knots and keep changing course. But the three-hundred-meter-long freighter, which was laden with machine and auto parts, wasn't a speedboat, and the pirate skiffs seemed to be three times faster and more maneuverable. Also, the guys on them were likely armed with rifles, knives, and pistols. Once they got on board and took the bridge, we'd be fucked.

One consequence of the 1991 civil war was that Somalia no longer had a coast guard and navy to patrol its coast, particularly around the island of Socotra and into the Gulf of Aden, where we were now. It was an area that once had been rich with high-value tuna, lobster, deepwater shrimp, white fish, and shark. Fishing trawlers from Taiwan, South Korea, France, Saudi Arabia, and Japan, which had previously not been permitted to fish there, moved in. They plied their trade with such avidity that, by the beginning of the twenty-first century, fishing stocks were severely depleted.

To make matters worse, large shipping companies and foreign criminal enterprises took advantage of the absence of government patrols to dump toxic waste in Somali waters.

The foreign fishermen moved on, and local Somali fishermen who had lived off the local catch for decades faced what they considered a terrible injustice. Angry with the foreign poachers and with no central government to appeal to, they turned to stealing cargo and hijacking vessels as an alternative source of income.

The Greek freighter Pete, Dave, and I were charged with protecting appeared to be their next victim, and we had very few deterrents. Upon boarding the ship in Sri Lanka three days ago we had rigged razor wire along the rail of the ship and the ladders and greased the sides of the boat. Now as the pirate skiffs closed in on us, we shot water out of the fire hoses and fired the few flares we had on board. But when we climbed out on the bridge wings that stuck out from the sides of the ship, we saw the pirates continuing to draw closer.

Pete called out, "Three hundred meters off. Two hundred. One hundred."

I said, "Let's recharge the hoses again."

"Fucking useless," Pete replied. "They've got guns."

Dave turned to me and shouted, "Come with me, Simon. I have a better plan."

I followed him into the crew mess area, where he unplugged the standard white GE refrigerator that stood in the corner.

"What the fuck are you going to do with that?" I asked.

"Help me lift it. You'll see."

As we started to carry it out, the Greek captain appeared and asked, "What are you doing with my fridge?"

"Out of our way."

Huffing and puffing, we carried the thing out to the bridge wing where Pete stood pointing to one of pirate skiffs pulling alongside the ship.

Dave and I had just hoisted the fridge up onto the rail when Pete shouted, "No, wait!"

He opened the door, removed a six-pack of Foster's, and set it near his feet on the deck.

Then he said, "Okay, carry on."

"Pete, what the fuck!"

When the skiff moved directly under us, we let the fridge go. I watched it tumble thirty feet and then plunge straight through the fiberglass bottom of the skiff, cutting it in half.

"Bull's-eye!" Dave shouted.

The pirates screamed, flailed their arms, and tread water until the other skiff came around to pick them up. Then they fucked off, and we returned to sunning ourselves on the forward deck.

So much for relaxing...

After that adventure, I hadn't been back in London more than a week when I received a call from another ex-regiment guy named David A. While serving as a major in the Royal Marines, David had been assigned to the Cabinet Office briefing rooms (COBR) in Whitehall (the historic building that houses the Ministry of Defense) where he developed a number of important contacts with government ministers and diplomats. He'd cleverly parlayed them into his own little company, securing the odd government contract and acting like a high-level fixer—akin to a very well-polished Ray Donovan.

I had done a few little jobs for him previously, including guarding gems in transit. Now he was asking me to meet him for tea at the Blakes Hotel in South Kensington to discuss a possible assignment. Built from a series of Victorian town houses, the super posh and very private Blakes had become a favorite meeting place for rock stars, celebrities, and Whitehall ministers. Afternoon tea was served in the sumptuous Chinese Room.

Tanned and dressed in my best suit, I sat across from David, who got straight to business. A colleague of his—a former defense minister from the Tory Party—had a lady friend who was in a predicament and needed help. This woman, Mary, he explained, came from a wealthy family that manufactured road-construction equipment.

She was in her midforties and had married a Pakistani business-man named Mohammed, and eventually filed for divorce.

It had all been quite amiable, according to Mary. No issues over money. She took their young daughter, Emma, and moved to one of their houses in West London, and he lived in another. Since Mo-hammed was a good father, they shared custody. Emma stayed with Mary Sunday night through Wednesday, and Mohammed had her Thursday through Sunday, and they swapped schedules every other week.

Everything had gone swimmingly until a recent Sunday when Mary went to Mohammed's house to pick Emma up and found no one there. She called and got no answer. She returned to Mo-hammed's front door and knocked again. Again, no one. She left messages on all his phones, then called the parents of Emma's friends to find out if playdates had been arranged or if Emma was attending a birthday party. The answer from everyone was no.

She called friends, her parents, even Mohammed's one family member—a cousin—who lived in West London. They hadn't heard from him, either. Her next call was to her lawyer, who phoned Mohammed's lawyer, who swore he knew nothing about his client's whereabouts or any plan he had to spirit Emma out of the country.

So Mary marched into the local police station in South Kensington and filed a report. Police officers asked her if her ex-husband had a history of violence or had ever abused Emma. Mary said no, he had always been a good father. They told her that since the two par-ents had joint custody and there was no provision in their divorce agreement that prevented one of them from taking Emma out of the country, there was nothing they could do.

A frustrated but determined Mary turned to her friends in the government, including the former Tory defense minister, who suggested she speak to David.

"She's a very nice woman," David explained, "and in a great deal of distress. You think you might be able to help her?"

I sipped my Oolong tea and answered, "Maybe. But I need to talk to her before I make a decision."

The next morning, I arrived at an old ewes cottage on a cobblestone street in South Kensington that served as David's office and met Mary, who was as described—intelligent, well educated, well mannered, and casually but expensively dressed.

I asked her to recount the whole drama, which she did without emotion. I took notes, wanting to make sure that her story made sense and matched up with the one she had told David. It did exactly.

I liked her immediately. At the end, I said, "Let me have a think on it, Mary. It won't take days."

If anything good had come out of the experience in Tora Bora, it had made me a softer, more empathetic human being. The suffering I went through made me value the simple beauty of life in ways I never had before. I wanted to use the skills I had acquired to help people in trouble and affect their lives in positive ways, if possible.

Here was a mother in distress. It seemed like a good place to start. So I called David to tell him I'd take the job and would need to meet Mary again to get more details.

She brought recent photos of Emma and Mohammed and was very well organized. I asked for complete descriptions of them both, including hair color, height, medical conditions, disabilities. Emma, who had been missing for two weeks now, looked to be a precious seven-year-old with her father's dark hair and complexion, combined with her mother's fine features.

I asked, "Where do you think that they went?"

"I strongly suspect that he took her to Pakistan," she answered, "but I don't know for sure."

"Do you think his family is helping him?"

"Maybe. I've met his parents, and they're very loving people."

"Did Emma ever mention any upcoming vacation with her daddy?" I asked.

"No."

I figured I would need a team of at least four to do proper surveillance. Pete had recently taken off to Dubai on another job. So I called my old bare-knuckle-boxer friend Justin, who had become an expert at locating people who didn't want to be found when he was in the COP (close observation platoon) from Northern Ireland. We agreed to meet at the Starbucks on High Street.

Gruff-mannered Justin ordered a double espresso and got down to brass tacks. "What's the rate of pay, mate?"

"Two thousand pounds a day, per man."

"For how long?"

"How long is a piece of string?" I asked back. "As long as it takes us to recover the girl."

I told Justin the little I had learned from Mary.

He said, "If the ex-husband is in Pakistan, he's gone back to where he feels the safest. That's what people in his situation do. I guarantee that he's sitting in his own village. All you have to do is ask Mary where he's from."

I didn't expect it would be that simple but called her nonetheless. She told me Mohammed had grown up in a suburb of Karachi called Surjani Town. His parents still lived there. She provided me with their address.

"Does he have a house there?" I asked.

"Not that I know of."

"Do you think Emma is in any danger?"

"No," she answered. "I don't think Mohammed would harm her in any way. But I simply can't go on without seeing her."

"I understand," I said. "Here's the plan. I'm going to need four people total. We'll fly to Karachi. Our first task is to locate Emma. Once we do that, we'll keep her under observation for two weeks so we can find the weak point in her daily routine."

"Okay."

"When it's time to grab her, I'm going to need you to come to Karachi, because I don't want four strangers approaching her, causing her to scream and run. With you there, she'll see Mommy and come with you without a problem. We'll get you in a car and drive you directly to the British consulate. Once you're in the gate and in UK jurisdiction, you'll be safe."

"That sounds perfectly reasonable," said Mary.

"Now, let's talk about costs. This operation is going to be expensive. Manpower alone will amount to two thousand per man a day. On top of that, we'll need plane tickets, hotel rooms, meals, and money to cover the costs of equipment, because we can't enter Pakistan with some of the things we'll need without raising suspicion."

"Money isn't an issue," she replied.

"We're also going to need to hire a private jet from Signature to sit on a private airstrip outside of Karachi and be ready if we need it. If something goes south, my team and I will have to get out of the country fast."

"Not a problem."

Ideally, I wanted a woman on the team, because I figured that two white guys in a car together driving around Karachi might look suspicious. But the woman I had in mind—Amanda I.—was doing another surveillance job in London for Control Risks. Justin recommended two of his former mates in COP, a guy we called Jonah and an Irish bloke, Jim.

A week later, the four of us landed in Karachi dressed like tourists and carrying cameras and checked into the Pearl Continental Hotel—a modern structure in the business center. We rented two standard rental cars—a Ford Fiesta and Toyota Corolla—and set out to take a look at the parents' house and surrounding area.

Surjani Town turned out to be a newer upper-middle-class suburb in northern Karachi just inside the M10 ring road, or beltway. The house itself was a two-story white-stucco structure with a high wall around it and a black metalwork gate. A smaller gate accessed the back parallel street.

Those two gates would be our trigger points. We took the maps we had brought with us and traced the fastest routes to the British consulate, Karachi Airport, and the nearest police station and hospital. Then we drove the routes at off-peak hours and during rush hour. The difference between the two was dramatic. A ten-minute drive to the local police station could easily take an hour during rush hour. And if traffic pushed you onto the M10, you were stuck.

Fourth day in, I sent Justin to a local electronics shop to buy four Motorola 500s and four chargers. Now with comms in hand, we drove back out to the house and tested them to ID any blackout points.

At night we'd return to the Pearl Continental to eat and maintain a low profile. I didn't want the guys going down to the bar, which was packed with expats, and striking up a conversation with someone or getting shit-faced.

We spent a week taking photos and building up a profile of the roads and area. At the beginning of week 2, we switched rental cars and started to surveil the grandparents' house—one car with two men parked twenty meters or so from the front gate, and the other at the same distance in back. The last thing we wanted was for Mohammed or one of his parents to pop out of a gate and spot us.

We alternated trigger points every hour—Justin and me in one car; Jonah and Jim in the other. It was the most boring work imaginable, sitting in a car in hot, humid Karachi, pissing in a bottle, and waiting for something to happen. We passed the time by taking the piss out of one another, cracking jokes, and profiling passersby. The first four days we saw no one enter or exit the house and started to wonder if we had the right place.

"No," David said when I called him that night. "It's his parents' address. I rechecked with Mary, and she's sure of it."

I gave the guys the next day off and switched cars again from Budget to Hertz. I knew we couldn't watch the house indefinitely without being spotted by one of the neighbors, who might call the police.

The following day, we again saw no one. The day after that Jim and Jonah saw a couple matching the description of Mohammed's parents exit the front gate and walk about a half mile to a little gathering of shops. Jim and Jonah followed on foot and took photos, which we e-mailed to David that night.

He showed them to Mary, who confirmed that they were Mohammed's parents. Now we knew we had the right house.

That night I worked out a schedule. Since we were working in a quiet neighborhood, I wanted to minimize the risk of being exposed. So instead of all four of us doing surveillance from 0700 to 2000 every day, from now on one car would show up at 0800 and work until 1800, and the other would be on duty from 1100 to 2000.

On the first day of our new schedule, Jim and Jonah were stationed near the trigger at the back gate. At 1500, they saw a man who matched Mohammed's description exit and head north to the same group of shops. They followed, Jim driving and Jonah walking on the opposite side of the street. This area wasn't frequented by tourists, so we knew we stuck out.

Mohammed entered a store, bought bottles of water, groceries, and cigarettes and returned to the house. Jonah and Jim didn't follow, since they knew where he was going.

The next day, Justin and I pulled the early shift. At 0800, the front gate opened and Mohammed drove out in an old blue Pakistani car. We were parked with our rental facing south. He drove north. Instead of making a U-turn and facing the danger of being spotted, we let him go. At 1800, just as we were leaving, he returned, got out of the car carrying a briefcase, and entered the house.

We took the next day off, and I traded cars again from Hertz to Thrifty, making sure to change colors and models.

The following day, Saturday, a new guy showed up at the house wearing pressed dress pants and an open shirt and carrying a black case. He stayed an hour. When he left, Jim and Jonah followed him to a modern office building where they established he was a doctor. They snapped photos of him, the building, and his nameplate in the lobby, which we e-mailed to David and Mary that night.

Mary had no idea who he was. While I had her on the phone, I asked if the boys could rent movies to watch in their rooms.

"Yes, of course," she answered. "Whatever you need."

I was super conscious of the bill we were running up. We had been on the job fifteen days, which meant that she was more than two hundred thousand dollars in already. And we still hadn't seen Emma.

Two days later, Jim and Jonah were parked near Trigger One at 0900 when Mohammed came out holding hands with a little girl who matched Emma's description. She wore sneakers and a little backpack. They walked ten meters, stopped, did a U-turn, and returned to the house.

Ten minutes later, they emerged again. This time the girl was carrying an additional bag. Mohammed put her in the backseat of his car, and pushed east on Lyari Basti Road, turned on Godhra Road, then onto a main street called Rashid Minhas, heading south. The morning traffic was so dense that Jim and Jonah followed only two cars behind them, instead of the usual four.

They trailed them into the city, past the M9 and left onto University Road, and into a school district that contained the Karachi University and a number of other schools.

Mohammed parked, took the girl by the hand, and walked her into the white two-story building. Ten minutes later, he emerged alone, got into his car, and drove north. Jim and Jonah decided not to follow him. Instead, they got out and recced the school and surrounding area, taking photos. They found a footpath that ran along the right side of the kindergarten and led to other schools in the complex. It passed the backyard of the kindergarten, which contained a little play area with swings, a sandpit, and slide. The only thing separating the yard from the path was a waist-high fence and a little wicker gate.

When Justin and I arrived at the grandparents' house, Jim and Jonah weren't there. From our car, we watched Mohammed pull up to the front of the house at 1300, park the car, and go into the house. When he emerged just before 1400 and got back in the car, we followed it to Abdul Hassan Road. While I sat in the parked rental, Justin got out to recce the area and ran into Jim and Jonah, who debriefed him on the events of the day.

That night we got David on the phone and told him the news, which he passed on to Mary. She confirmed that we had found

Emma. David and Mary were ecstatic. Naturally, they wanted to know what we would do next.

I said, "David, we have to build up a pattern of what she does during the day, so we can figure out the best time and place to take her."

"How long is that going to take?"

"I'm not sure...two weeks?" I answered.

"Two weeks? Really, that long? I'm going to have to run this past Mary."

"Tell her that we've got to do this the right way, because we're only going to get one chance."

Mary understood. Again, we changed our pattern. Instead of both cars going to the house, one would be stationed outside the house while the other went straight to Beacon House.

Father and daughter followed the same routine for two weeks. Twenty past eight Monday through Friday morning, he'd drive her to school. Two in the afternoon he'd pick her up.

Two things stood out. One, Mohammed seemed totally oblivious to being followed, which told me that he felt safe in his native country. And, two, Emma looked super happy to be with her dad. He might have been a dick of a husband, but he appeared to be a good father—which Mary had told me earlier.

We started to plot out the best way and time to snatch her. This wasn't the *A-Team,* so we weren't going to do anything stupid like trying to take her from her dad's car while it was stopped in traffic.

It seemed obvious that the best place to do this was at her school. So we started to build up a plan. The kindergarten class took three breaks—0930, 1130, and 1315. The first and third recess periods lasted roughly fifteen minutes. The middle one was twice as long.

The playground where the twenty or so kids played during those breaks was easy to access through the wicker gate along the path.

There seemed to be two or three adults (or teachers) running the class. During recess periods, they'd leave the doors open so the children could wander in and out. Usually, there was at least one teacher stationed in the yard watching the kids, but sometimes the teachers remained inside and one of them would occasionally pop her head out.

Emma seemed to enjoy the playtimes and stayed outside for the majority of them.

I discussed two scenarios with David and Mary over the phone. We could either try to grab Emma while she was playing in the yard, or Mary could walk in the front of the school, say she was picking up her daughter for a doctor's appointment, and leave with her.

The problem with the second course of action was that we didn't know what Mohammed had told the school authorities about his situation with Mary. For that and other reasons, the first option seemed best.

"What do you want to do?" Mary asked.

"I think you should fly to Karachi and stay at the Pearl Continental with us. We'll take you with us each day and wait for the best opportunity."

"Okay."

So that's what she did. Once she got settled, we met in my room. Referring to the maps and photos taped to the walls, I showed her the grandparents' house; the route they took to school; the kindergarten, path, and play area; and the route we planned to travel to the British consulate.

She seemed pleased. That's when I realized I had completely overlooked the matter of Emma's passport.

"Mary, do you have it with you?" I asked.

"No, he's got it."

I felt like a bloody idiot. "Then how's this going to work? In order to get Emma inside the consulate, you're going to have to show the guards at the gate a passport proving she's a British citizen. Same goes for when you try to get on a plane with her to leave the country."

"Don't worry," Mary replied. "I've already prepared for that."

"How?" I asked.

"Friends of mine have arranged for a consulate official to meet us at the gate. Once we're inside, they'll issue Emma a temporary passport and later escort us to the airport."

"Are you sure?" I asked. "Because if there isn't someone at the gate to meet you, we're screwed."

"Yes," she answered. "It's all arranged."

The following morning, Mary checked out of the Pearl Continental. We loaded her suitcases into the trunk of one of our cars and set off toward the school. I asked Mary to try to remain calm when she saw Emma.

She assured me that she would.

We sat in a car parked on the street near the school as Mohammed arrived with Emma. Mary, true to her word, remained as cool as a daisy. During the first play period at 0930, I walked with her down the path to the play area where Emma was standing next to a little plastic slide with a group of other children waiting her turn.

Seeing a teacher in the yard, I whispered to Mary, "Not now."

I didn't want Emma spotting her mom and shouting with excitement, so I quickly escorted Mary back to the car. We waited for the next recess at 1130. Again, we saw a teacher on the playground. The same thing happened at 1315.

So we returned to the Pearl Continental, where Mary checked in again. The next day was a Saturday. Instead of gadding about the city and blowing our covers, we spent a quiet weekend at the hotel.

During all the recesses on Monday, teachers remained on duty in the yard. Tuesday was the same.

Mary started to get stressed. Not only was she checking out of the hotel every morning and checking in again at night, she also had the frustration of seeing her daughter every day and not being able to do anything about it. I explained to her that this was how these jobs went. We would only get one chance to grab Emma and had to do it at the optimum time.

Wednesday morning at 0930, Justin got out to check the playground while I remained in the car with Mary. He returned a few minutes later and told us that the two teachers were sitting at a desk at the far end of the classroom and seemed to be occupied with paperwork. There were no adults watching the kids in the yard.

Mary got out and walked down the path with Justin while I remained behind the wheel of the car. They saw Emma standing near the sandpit. Justin nodded at Mary and then opened the little wicker gate. Mary took a step inside and called Emma's name.

Emma looked around as though she wasn't sure who was calling her. So Mary called her again. This time, Emma saw Mary and ran into her mother's arms.

Mary said simply, "Lovely to see you darling," turned and carried Emma out of the gate. Justin escorted them down the path, turned right, and continued along the sidewalk to where our car was parked. I got out and helped Mary and Emma into the backseat while Justin slid into the passenger seat.

I did a U-turn, and we were off. Jonah and Jim in the other rental pulled in behind us to act as a blocking car, if needed. We proceeded to Lyari Basti Road and continued toward the UK consulate.

While I drove, Mary explained to Emma that they were going to take a short trip to London to visit Mary's parents. The little girl seemed excited.

At one point she asked, "What's Daddy going to do?"

Mary was quick with her answer: "He'll probably join us later."

I stopped about a hundred meters from the consulate gates, and Jim and Jonah pulled in behind us. Justin went to the trunk to get Mary's two large suitcases while I started to escort mother and daughter to the entrance.

We walked slowly so as not attract attention. Mary stopped at the bulletproof-glass booth at the security gate, turned to me, and said, "Thank you very much."

"Are you sure you're going to be met?" I asked.

No sooner had I gotten the words out than a man in a suit hurried through the security gate, greeted Mary, and checked her passport. He then turned and escorted Mary and Emma inside.

I had given Mary my cell-phone number and instructed her to call me when she got through Immigration at the airport. Justin, Jonah, Jim, and I returned to the Pearl Continental, ate lunch, and waited.

At 1630 that afternoon Mary called and said, "Simon, we're at the airport. We're through departures and are waiting to take off."

"Terrific!"

I called David to tell him that Mary and Emma would soon be airborne and that we would spend the night in Karachi and leave in the morning. Then I called British Airways and booked four business-class tickets for the next day's 1300 flight.

A week later, I met Mary again at David's office in London. She seemed a bit disappointed that the rest of the guys weren't with me, because she wanted to thank them as well.

She was as gracious as ever. The whole operation had taken a little more than a month and cost her a pretty penny. She said that it was worth every cent.

Lesson number 9: There are advantages to being rich and having friends in high places.

I never heard from Mary again after that and have often wondered about the aftermath at the school and whether or not Mohammed reported the incident to the police or if Mary allowed him to see his Emma again. Given the kind of person she was, I imagine she did. But I don't know for sure.

Personal recovery jobs like those always leave me with similar questions.

Lesson number 10: As a hired contractor, you do what you think is right and try not to dwell on the moral ambiguities.

CHAPTER ELEVEN
IRAQ

THE EVENT that most radically added to the volume of PMC work was the US invasion of Iraq in March 2003 and subsequent occupation and reconstruction. The United States, the United Kingdom, and other coalition governments started doling out massive contracts to help secure and rebuild the country, and companies like Aegis, Control Risks, and Blackwater quickly opened up offices in Baghdad's Green Zone (which later became the International Zone) to take advantage.

In November 2003, the US Congress established the Iraq Relief and Reconstruction Fund (IRRF), which allocated $18.4 billion to rebuild Iraq's infrastructure after two wars and a long international embargo. That was on top of the $54.4 billion Congress had provided that year for Operation Iraqi Freedom, the $92.1 billion it set aside in 2004, the $58 billion in 2005, and so on. According to a US Congressional Budget Office study, from 2003 through 2007, US agencies awarded $85 billion in contracts for work "principally performed in the Iraq theater."

The money was huge. So was the number of firms that showed up to bid for contracts—181, according to a US Government Accounting Office report—eventually employing as many as 190,000 contractor and subcontractor personnel.

The big fish Blackwater quickly scooped up the lucrative State Department contract to protect its diplomats and other personnel working in-country. Control Risks Group won a contract doing similar work for the UK government. DynCorp netted a $50 million contract to run Abu Ghraib prison and train Iraqi police officers. Vinnell, a subsidiary of Northrop Grumman, was awarded $48 million to assist in training the New Iraqi Army.

There were many little fish as well, hired to do tasks like IT work, forensics, construction, running base kitchens, and translating. But the whale of all contracts went to the UK firm Aegis—a whopping $293 million to coordinate security for the US Army Corps of Engineers (USACE), which came to be known as Project Matrix.

Project Matrix became my primary source of employment starting in 2005, and Aegis ran a super-tight shop in terms of recruiting, vetting, training, and management. Upon arrival in Iraq, each member of the twenty-man induction class was given the same DOD badge issued to all US armed forces personnel, except under PAY GRADE ours said OTHER, and under BRANCH it read CONTRACTOR. This allowed us full access to all DOD facilities inside and outside the country. We also wore credit-card-sized US Forces–Iraq (USF-I) badges around our necks.

Even though all of us were former operators from elite US and UK regiments and units with years of experience, Aegis put us through a short training program that covered security in high-risk areas, so that all of us would be singing from the same sheet of music. The course ended with a rigorous fitness test—a hundred-meter fireman's carry, four-man timed stretcher carry, and a two-mile run in full gear that had to be completed in less than thirteen minutes. Anyone who didn't pass was sent packing.

Those of us chosen to serve as team medics were then put through an intense two-week trauma medicine course certified by the Royal College of Surgeons in Edinburgh. The first week was textbook study of all systems in the human body—circulatory, nervous, endocrine, and muscular. Crammed with that knowledge, we moved on to practical applications—how to save someone who had been blown up, lost a limb, had a stroke, a heart attack, et cetera.

Team leaders also had to complete an eleven-day condensed version of the junior and senior command courses in the Brit mil. There we learned fire and maneuver formations, control and cordon, how to develop an ops plan, how to brief a team, and how to look after everyone's welfare.

All of these courses were so well designed and effective that they became the benchmark in the PMC world. Going forward, any operator who worked on Project Matrix was highly sought after by other contract companies and could usually walk into another job with no questions asked.

Upon completion of the courses, we were each assigned to a team. For the purposes of administration, the US coalition split Iraq into three sectors—north, south, and central. The northern sector started at the town of Ramadi and included western Anbar Province, then extended north into Erbil, Mosul, and Kurdistan. The southern sector began at Kut and went south to Basra. The central sector included everything within ninety kilometers of Baghdad.

Each region was run through a central HQ and ops room, staffed by DOD personnel and contractors. Aegis mirrored the US coalition command with its own Reconstruction Operations Center with a director for each region, a deputy director, managers, regional security managers, and descending ranks.

According to the DOD project description, the services rendered by Aegis under Project Matrix included the following:

1. Provide static and mobile security teams for the Project and Contracting Office (PCO) and the USACE.
2. Conduct twenty-four-hour electronic tracking of all reconstruction security operations throughout Iraq.
3. Facilitate intelligence sharing between security forces and reconstruction contractors.
4. Provide continuous intel on threat assessment and the viability of road movement throughout the country.

In order to deliver these services, Aegis created three types of operational teams: PSD (personal security detail), SET (security escort team), and RLT (reconstruction liaison team), which was later renamed SRT (security reconnaissance team).

The role of the SETs was to escort PCO and USACE personnel outside the wire to their various reconstruction jobs—building roads, bridges, health-care facilities, and schools. Each SET was made up of eight or nine operators and two LNs (local nationals), who acted as terps. The LNs were fully vetted by the US Army and had also been put through a small-unit and firearms training course by Aegis.

At one point Aegis had as many as forty SETs and another dozen or so SRTs. Each team had a team leader and second in command and third in command (3IC). All personnel on the teams worked on a rotational basis—usually nine weeks in theater, and nine weeks off.

It was a huge undertaking. Stephen Armstrong, writing for the

Guardian, described the scale of Aegis's operation like this: "Spicer is effectively in charge of the second largest military force in Iraq—some 20,000 private soldiers."

Whether that number was real or inflated, the manpower was needed, because the country we were operating in was the definition of dysfunction. It had taken a sadistic, maniacal dictator to hold it together; now that he had been deposed, all the religious, ethnic, and personal hatreds that had been seething under the surface for years burst forth in an orgy of violence. Every day bombs went off, ripping apart schools, hospitals, markets, and mosques and bringing more tragedy. My friend Marvin, who had arrived in Iraq two months ahead of me, guarding reporters for Fox, BBC, and Sky News, warned me, "It's like the Wild West out here, mate. It's fucking madness."

He was right. My heart went out to Iraqi families who had to live in this environment.

It was so dangerous that none of us was allowed outside the wire without permission, and absolutely no one wandered out on foot. In the eyes of Sunni and Shiite insurgents, uniformed soldiers, contractors, Canadians, Brits, and Americans were all the same—we were all infidels, Mossad agents, or white devils. If the insurgents got their hands on you, you'd be killed, beheaded, blown apart, raped. Four Blackwater contractors learned that the hard way when they were overtaken by insurgents on a bridge over the Euphrates River and shot dead. Their bodies were then set on fire, mutilated, hung from the bridge, and dragged through the streets.

As members of SETs we were charged with protecting the people who were trying to rebuild the country from a similar fate. We did this by arming ourselves to the teeth and traveling in four armor-plated vehicles. The Alpha vehicle in front and Delta at the rear were lightweight B6-armored Toyota Land Cruisers modified with gun ports on the sides and back to accommodate belt-fed M249 machine guns. They served as gun trucks. Our clients, the USACE personnel we were assigned to protect, rode in two more comfortable and bulkier armored Ford Excursions, Bravo and Charlie.

Aegis ran its operation out of Camp Wolfe, named after navy commander Duane Wolfe, who had been killed by an IED outside Fallujah. Wolfe was the USACE's mini-base, part of the massive coalition base called Camp Victory, which occupied ten square kilometers of territory near the Baghdad International Airport, west of the city. The Camp Victory complex included other smaller bases named Camp Liberty, Camp Striker, Camp Slayer, and the al-Faw Palace— Saddam Hussein's sixty-nine-room former winter palace.

Camp Victory was a city unto itself, a male-dominated US suburb stuck in the seething shithole that was Baghdad and featuring all the comforts of home, including Pizza Hut, Subway, Cinnabon, Burger King, Taco Bell, and a whole range of other fast-food facilities. There were game rooms for playing Xbox, bowling alleys, basketball courts, fully equipped gyms, libraries, movie theaters, and five large DFACs with pastry bars, salad bars, a grill, deli, Mexican cantina, Chinese-food area, Ben & Jerry's, and dessert counter, all open 24/7. Guys living at Camp Victory didn't want for anything.

Since we were working under a DOD contract, we enjoyed full privileges at all US mil bases in Iraq. There were many of them strung throughout the country, run like smaller Camp Victorys and offering similar amenities.

This made for a weird dichotomy between the world inside the wire and the world outside, and between those individuals serving in Iraq who rarely ventured outside and operators like us who did so on a daily basis.

One of our Toyota Land Cruisers after a complex attack in Sadr City, Baghdad, Iraq.

Waiting for a CASEVAC extraction after a contact in Ramadi, Iraq. That's our medic hurrying in on the right.

Chris, aka Tex-Mex, taking cover during contact with insurgents just outside of Fallujah, Iraq.

Trying to herd cats! Premission deployment in Tallil, Iraq.

One of our team excursions after a small-arms-fire attack in Kabul, Afghanistan. You'll notice the armored glass under the conventional tinted glass.

Working with a Sky News crew in Mali, Africa.

Team training,
debuts, contact, and
casualty extraction
at Camp Victory,
Baghdad, Iraq.

Working a low-profile detail
in Ramadi, hence the Merc
tailing the SUV. We made it
to the end of this street, then
took a load of small-arms
fire from the side streets and
rooftops. Low-pro doesn't
always work!

Reilly showing off his
weapons-stripping-
and-assembly skills.

This how the locals live: streets overflowing with sewage and waste, right outside your "front door." Basra, Iraq.

Carrying out a recce and pulse check in a known-hostile neighborhood in southern Iraq. Spacing between SUVs is important so that we don't all get smashed at once. Any piece of rubble you see could be an IED.

The lads, Christmastime in Balad, about ninety miles north of Baghdad. Even Santa has a security detail in Iraq.

Team drills using one of the client vehicles, an armored Ford Excursion.

Pulse check, southern Iraq. The local car has pulled over to the side of the road to show a nonthreatening posture. Meanwhile, we have held back and trained our weapons on that car just in case. The green stuff is raw sewage, which now has a nice grassy covering!

This is actually a school, believe it or not, that the US Army Corps of Engineers helped to build in Tallil. Like so many projects, it remained empty until a local council member claimed it as his personal residence. Corruption is rife.

Checkpoint on the Iraq side of the Iraq-Syrian border, west of Ramadi. It looks high-tech, but isn't.

Everyday-ops kit includes plate carrier, chest rig, and belt with med kit (IFAK), comms, knife, weatherman's multitool, Mag-Lite, water bladder, map pouch, tourniquets, scarf to keep the dust and sand out of your face, and extra mags of 5.56mm and 9mm for the Glock pistol.

Game face/tired and ready to get home. Balad, Iraq

Iraq side of the Iraq-Syria border, carrying out training and hearts-and-minds ops. Notice the difference between how well equipped I am, and how he's not. Mind you, he has on nifty blue camo gear to blend into the desert environment. Go figure.

Pete on our villa rooftop overlooking the Tigris River in Baghdad. He never smiles.

Me and the guys, shortly after a dustup at a police checkpoint near the SWAT school outside Ramadi. What you're looking at is a police station. You'll notice the mattress and chairs on the roof for sunbathing and the abandoned weapons leaning against the top part of the building. Excellent weapons control.

Me and the guys, on the general's team at Camp Victory, Baghdad.

Taffy the photo geek who took this said, "Mr. Chase never smiles." Believe me, there's very little to smile about.

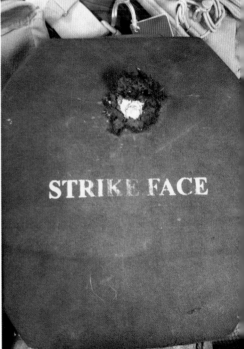

A very, very close shave indeed. Struck by an AK round at a police checkpoint on the road from Balad to Baghdad, after insurgents dressed as policemen ambushed the checkpoint with silenced pistols, then AKs.

In order to defend ourselves, we carried Glocks, M4 assault rifles, SOG knives, radios, penknives, Mag-Lites, and lots of ammo. All of it was issued by the US Army and in top condition. The only thing we provided were our own plate carriers, which came in assorted colors—khaki, olive drab, black—and could be modified by the individual operator. Mine carried six extra M4 mags, three 9mm Glock mags, and a small med kit. On the utility belt I carried three more M4 mags and three more Glock mags. We dressed in khaki fire-retardant flight suits with Nomex linings and carried grab bags loaded with another fourteen to sixteen mags.

All of this amounted to a shitload of firepower, but we needed it, because we ran into IED attacks and ambushes all the time. When things got ugly, our objective was to put down so much firepower in such a small window of time that it would act like a wall of lead to push the insurgents back and allow us to peel away.

Some runs were hellacious. Others were surreal and funny. The first SET I served on provided security to the general who audited reconstruction funds. It was his job to secure $17 billion in cash that had been flown in and was stored in warehouses around Baghdad. Armed and ready, we'd roll up to a sad-looking sheet-metal structure with two Iraqis sleeping on deck chairs outside. As we stood guard, the general would open the rusty padlock to reveal a stiflingly hot room stuffed floor to ceiling with pallets of shrink-wrapped hundred-dollar bills. In the early days, the cash was basically free to be taken by anyone with a vehicle and a key. Apparently, many had made the most of the opportunity.

Four hundred million of the fund was paid out to armed Iraqi organizations like the Sons of Iraq—a coalition of tribal sheikhs and former Iraqi military officers—to buy their loyalty and service, which included policing local communities, and stemming the growth of Sunni and Shiite insurgent groups. No receipt, no audit.

The route we traveled most frequently was the twelve-kilometer stretch between Camp Victory and the fortresslike Green Zone that had been constructed in the middle of Baghdad to house the US coalition HQ, Iraqi government, and various diplomatic quarters and embassies.

The road itself was a sweeping bend of lumpy concrete bordered by dust and palm trees known as Route Irish. It was also the mother of all insurgent shooting galleries. Journalists crowned it the world's most dangerous road. Those VIPs with sufficient clout got to make the journey between Camp Victory and the Green Zone via Black Hawk helicopter. But if the weather wasn't cooperating or there was no helo available or you didn't rank high enough, your only option was Route Irish—a fifteen-minute sphincter-clenching ride through hell.

Death waited behind every tree and overpass. It could come from a slowed car as we whipped past at ninety miles per hour or from cars parked along the road or from roadside stands as you entered the city. It could come from a bag of trash or the stomach of a dead dog stuffed with explosives and detonated electronically. Many expats lost limbs along this route or were scarred for life. Others died.

A typical day's client was General K. of the USACE, who because of his position was a high-profile target for various insurgent groups, including al-Qaeda in Iraq (AQI) and the Islamic State of Iraq (ISI). His predecessor had been blown to smithereens by a huge pressure plate IED on his way from the Green Zone to Camp Victory. It was our duty to ferry General K. safely along this same route.

I started the day with a mission brief and order of battle (ORBAT) for the other members of the team, then briefed General K. on the upcoming mission's Actions On—covering what would happen if we were attacked, shot at, hit an IED, had a flat tire, and so on.

We left the camp, rolled through the reinforced-cement security checks, and then sped out onto Route Irish. I reported the team call sign back to HQ, then instructed the drivers to bring the speed up to ninety miles per hour, super fast for two B6 armor-plated gun trucks and two Ford Excursions—one the client vehicle with me in it and the other a decoy vehicle.

All of us on the SET knew Irish like the back of our hand. The route was littered with overpasses and slip roads—all excellent ambush points and ideal locations for planting IEDs, explosive force penetrators (EFPs), and any other carnage-inducing devices the insurgents came up with. Sunset Boulevard it wasn't.

Every time you set out, you couldn't help asking yourself two questions: *Why am I still doing this?* And: *Is this the day we're going to be unlucky?*

On the day in question, we weren't out more than ten minutes before disaster struck. As we sped toward an overpass, our lead truck, Alpha, saw a slow-moving SUV start to roll down the slip road to our right, with the telltale signs of really bad news—battered, old, back heavy, two passengers. As we drew nearer, the SUV gathered speed and momentum, its weight pushing it forward.

I gave the command to put the top "gunners up" and engage the SUV, which seemed to present a clear threat. Within seconds we unleashed a fearsome amount of lead into the oncoming SUV, blowing out its tires, shattering the windshield, ripping apart the engine block, and killing the driver and passenger. But the vehicle kept rolling on a deadly trajectory that would send it right in the path of the client vehicle.

Bad news for me, because I rode in it. And even more bad news because it was our job to protect the client.

As seconds ticked by and the SUV rolled closer, we realized we were moving too fast to slam on the brakes and reverse. There was only one way to save the client, and our friends, Karl and Shaun, in the rear gun truck knew what that was. My two ex–Brit mil mates were a study in contrasts—Karl, a big teddy bear of a man in his early thirties with a one-year-old daughter he couldn't stop talking about, and Shaun, in his forties, short, scrawny, and super serious.

As General K. quickly crossed himself and started to mumble a prayer, heart-of-gold Karl came over the radio, calm as ever, and said, "Charlie, hit your brakes." We understood what the game plan was and also knew that we would never be seeing Karl and Shaun again.

We applied the brakes, and the lighter Land Cruiser gun truck Delta whipped around to our right side. Seconds later the SUV slammed into their truck, detonating the explosives inside and engulfing both vehicles in a ball of fire. The blast was so powerful that it ripped the SUV and gun truck to pieces. And the heat from it so intense it stripped the paint completely off the right side of our vehicle.

Our friends were dead, but the threat was neutralized, and our client was safe. What I felt at that moment is impossible to describe—intense rage, sadness, and disgust all rolled into one and multiplied by infinity. We had been trained, in an event like this, to stop farther up the road, call in medevac, send a sitrep to the operations room, and then form a secure cordon around the scene of the attack and wait for the quick-response force (QRF). So that's what we did, numbly, our bodies on autopilot.

The medics said they had never seen armor-plated vehicles burned to the point that all that remained was dust. We set about clearing the site and collecting our teammates. Tears ran down my cheeks as I helped shovel what was left of Karl and Shaun off the street and deposit their remains into body bags. How would we distinguish Shaun from Karl?

We couldn't. Instead, we loaded the body bags in our vehicles and rolled back to camp, where officials tagged each bag of ashes with a name, and that was that.

Even though we suffered a great and tragic loss, the mission was a success, because we had protected our client and returned him safely to Camp Victory.

If SETs were dangerous, RLTs (later renamed SRTs) were even worse. They were Aegis's version of special-forces units, tasked with doing recon and hearts-and-minds work in remote areas of the country. We called them pulse checks and considered them some of the most dangerous ops ever. Basically, RLTs acted as guinea pigs, sent into a region after a protest or march to test the mood of the people and the level of threat. Generally, nine operators and three LNs would drive three gun trucks into a town or an area to see how the locals would react. Some days nothing happened. Others times we'd laugh ourselves silly as hell rained down on us from all sides.

If we arrived in óne piece and the local leaders were willing, we'd sit down with them, drink tea, and ask them what they needed in terms of schools, housing, and health care. Back at base, I'd fill out a detailed report with names, descriptions of faces, what positions they occupied, and what the atmospherics were like.

The first RLT I ran was in Basra, Iraq's main port and second-largest city, with a population of 1.5 million. It had the reputation of being one of the hottest cities on the planet, with summer temps regularly topping 115 degrees Fahrenheit and considered by some to be the site of the biblical Garden of Eden.

It wasn't a Garden of Eden when I was stationed there in '06, because of the large number of attacks against coalition forces by the Iranian-backed Shia militia known as the Mahdi Army that wanted all Western forces out of Iraq. The scale of the violence directed against Brits and Americans in Shia-dominant Basra was so bad that the Iraqi prime minister Nuri al-Maliki had declared a state of emergency months before.

One blazing hot morning in July '06, I learned that our mission for the day was to join another RLT team and two SET teams on an inspection of the Basra police station and Children's Hospital, both newly rebuilt by the USACE. The SET teams would escort Colonel Dodd and a USACE civil engineer named Dr. Fox. Our job as RLTs was to act as advance scouts and provide support.

Because both the police station and Children's Hospital bordered a hostile area known as the Shia Flats, the deployment would include fourteen armored vehicles, twenty expats, and eight LNs. During the morning brief, my counterparts—JD in charge of SET 1; Craig heading SET 2; Gav, RLT 2—and I (RLT 1) covered all contingencies: weapons, comms (UHF and VHF Codans, MBITR, sat phones with each team for extra coverage), EVACs (evacuations), actions on, medical emergencies, mapping, and routes.

JD, Gav, and Craig were seasoned Iraq War vets. JD was a massive guy from northern England. Gav and Craig were serious "med heads," and Craig, in my opinion, was the best medic in the business.

We pored over maps of the city to determine our route while the other members of our teams went over the vehicles from top to bottom, triple-checking everything.

The SETs would move in their usual configuration of two client vehicles (Ford Excursions) in the middle with Toyota Land Cruiser gun trucks fore and aft. And each RLT would roll in a three–Toyota

Land Cruiser–gun–truck set—all armed with SAW M249 belt-fed 5.56 squad assault weapons.

We chose Red Route, which would take us from our FOB, through side roads, over a bridge, into a major intersection, and past the famed Twin Mosques. Fingers on triggers, nerves on high, we set out, with my RLT leading the way. Without incident, we arrived at the Children's Hospital, cleared and secured it, then radioed to the SET teams to enter with their clients.

Once that visit ended, we peeled away and executed the same procedure at the nearby police station. It appeared secure. We waited a twitchy forty-five minutes for the inspection to end, all the time alert to the whistle of incoming rockets and knowing that twenty-eight had been dumped on a coalition patrol not far from our location a few days ago.

In typical PMC fashion, we passed the time telling stupid jokes and discussing workouts, chicks we would smash in Thailand or Dubai, and what movies we had loaded onto our hard drives.

When JD gave the signal to clear, we all packed into our vehicles and headed back to the FOB. My Land Cruiser led the way in the forward lane with Craig's SET behind me. Gav's RLT and JD's SET followed in the oncoming lane in staggered dogleg formation—awkward, yes, but SOP (standard operating procedure) during that time in Iraq.

The intersection with Ahrair Road was clogged with cars and trucks, so I pulled over to let the other teams pass and to provide cover while they entered the two roundabouts (code-named Red 5 and Red 6) that would send them onto the main road back to base for tea. This was our highest-threat area, because of the epic traffic and adjoining roads. And sure enough, as we waited for SET 1 to pass, a covered truck sped out of an alley and cut right in front of the second Ford Excursion—the one that happened to be carrying Colonel Dodd and Dr. Fox.

The two clients had traveled in the first Excursion on the way out, which made me conclude that the Iraqi police had a hand in setting them up. Now several masked Iraqis were pushing a twin-array EFP (explosive force penetrator) out of the back of the truck onto the Excursion, which was trapped in traffic. Our worst fucking nightmare!

This EFP bad boy was copper back and housed in an oil drum. The copper disks inside were approximately fifteen inches in diameter, which made them four inches thicker than the armor on the Ford Excursion.

Before we could do anything to stop them, the insurgents ignited the passive infrared trigger and *ka-boom!*

A huge explosion tore through the busy intersection, and the whole world seemed to stop. Then several seconds later, it abruptly shifted into fast-forward, and the area filled with the sights and sounds of hell, and our various radios burst to life with contact reports. Through the clearing smoke, I saw locals who hadn't been wounded scrambling to flee the area—get off the X, as we called it—because they knew that the IED blast was only the beginning. Seconds later, PKM machine-gun fire echoed through the plaza and ripped toward us from the Shia Flats.

Adrenaline slammed into my bloodstream.

Over the radio JD screamed, "I have two Tier One casualties! Taking incoming on Excursion Two!"

The EFP had penetrated the left side of the Excursion, peppering the colonel's left side with copper shards and Dr. Fox's face, neck, and hands. It was carnage, but both men had been wearing armored vests and blast-proof eye protection, so it could have been much worse. The LN driver and vehicle commander (JD was riding in one of his team's Land Cruisers) had escaped relatively unscathed. But because the force of the blast had sealed the locks, the doors wouldn't open, and now the Excursion was taking heavy PKM 7.62 x 54mm machine-gun fire from about eight hundred meters away.

All the teams shifted into emergency mode, including SET 2, which smashed its way out of traffic and zigzagged out of the kill zone at 120 kph. It was my team's job to get JD, his clients, and men out.

Immediately, I reversed at speed toward SET 1, and as I did saw JD in the rearview mirror, trying to break into the Excursion as PKM rounds ricocheted off the street around him. Balls of steel. Our Land Cruiser hit a patch of oil from the damaged Excursion and skidded past JD, who shot me a *WTF!* look, before we smashed into the front of a local's car.

I revved forward, taking the local's front bumper with me, and positioned our vehicle along the contact side of the Excursion to give it maximum cover. More PKMs, maybe a half dozen, had joined in. Rounds were careening off our hood and slamming into our armored left side.

I grabbed my med bag in one hand, my M4 in the other, took a deep breath, jumped out, and sprinted like a rabbit to the rear of the Excursion. There I slammed into Craig who was arriving with his med bag—*bam!*

After seeking the little cover we could find near the rear bumper, regaining our breath, and returning fire, Craig and I tried to breach the side rear door and get inside, to no avail. Then like a scene out of a movie, JD ran up, grabbed the door handle, and yanked it with so much force that the handle came off in his hand and slammed him in the face, throwing him backward until his ass hit the pavement.

Even with the PKM rounds ricocheting all around us, Craig and I couldn't help but crack up. That further fueled JD's anger. He got up, gripped the top of the rear side door with his massive hands, and literally ripped it off its metal hinges. A total animal!

Craig and I jumped into the Excursion, which was a bloody mess, while JD crouched between the vehicles and returned fire. The good news was that Dr. Fox and the colonel were still alive. I did a quick assessment of the former, who was breathing, then cleared his throat of blood. In addition to shrapnel wounds, he had severe burns to his face and neck. The colonel appeared worse—fractured scapula and ribs, burn trauma to his face and neck, copper shrapnel punctures peppering his entire left side.

Craig and I grabbed the FFDs (first field dressings) that had been paracord strung to the ceiling and used them to stem the bleeding from the shrapnel wounds as the PKM rounds tore through the sides and roof.

Turning to Craig, I said, "Bro, we need to move before we're shot to shit!"

Just then, JD stuck his head in the door and shouted, "You fuckers gonna move or what?"

We'd practiced vehicle EVAC drills countless times before but hadn't anticipated the slipperiness produced by blood on the Excursion's rubber floor matting. I must have slipped ten times, and each time the M4 hanging on the old SA80 sling on my back slammed into Dr. Fox's face. Quick note to self: *Order a new sling and some carbina clips to hold the fucker in place. Also: rip out the rubber floor matting from the trucks.*

Three rounds in succession smashed into the door rim above Craig's head. Clearly we had to get the wounded clients out of the tight, slippery 120-degree space fast, or we would all be dead. But moving them was complicated because of their extensive injuries. I improvised, inching Fox like a caterpillar along the backseat toward the rear side door—bending his legs up, pushing him forward on his butt, straightening him, then repeating the process again.

Meanwhile, one of my LNs was trying to position another Land Cruiser on the right side of the Excursion so we could do a straight door-to-door transfer of the wounded, but because of the debris on the road and incoming, he was having trouble getting close enough.

Craig had the colonel laid out flat on the floor and was radioing for CASEVAC. "I've got two Tier One casualties. I need AIR-EVAC to my location ASAP. I need an answer in sixty seconds, or we're going to attempt to drive out of here. We're taking heavy incoming!"

Seconds later, I heard the response, "Negative at this time. You'll have to drive out!"

My guts twisted into a knot. Even more alarming I heard a loud *bra-ta-ta, bra-ta-ta,* the sound of a DShK .50-cal heavy machine gun—a nasty Soviet-made weapon that I knew could rip through the vehicle's armor and cut us to shreds. Craig and I froze for a moment and stared at each other in horror.

I asked the question that was on both our minds: "Does the Mahdi Army have a fucking DShK?"

His answer: "If they do, we're fucked!"

Then something unexpected happened. The PKM fire let up. I quickly scanned the intersection through the wrecked front windshield and saw that an Iraqi patrol had stopped on the other side of the roundabout. In the back of one of its vehicles sat a DShK, which now unleashed a ten-round burst toward a building in the Shia Flats.

That silenced everything for a moment. I had Dr. Fox bunched up midmove on the backseat when JD stuck his head in. "You need a hand with that?" he asked.

"Yeah, mate!"

He picked Fox up from under his armpits, pulled him out of the

Excursion, and carried him across the street to a Land Cruiser like a trussed up turkey. The medic inside the LC worked on Fox while Craig and I attended to Colonel Dodd, who had slipped into unconsciousness but was still breathing. Craig, being the expert medic he was, wrapped a chest seal around a wound under the colonel's body armor and stopped the bleeding, which saved his life.

While this was going on, Mahdi Army pickup trucks were frantically ferrying Shia gunmen to within thirty meters of our position. They opened up on us with AKs, PKMs, and small-arms fire. Soon the intensity of the incoming was so strong I couldn't hear myself think. Literally hundreds of rounds were striking the vehicles and ricocheting off the street, despite the fact that the Iraqi Army DShK was pounding back.

In the midst of this insanity, Craig, JD, and I carefully transferred Colonel Dodd to the other Excursion, then I legged it back to my team and gave the order to get off the X. The eight remaining vehicles hauled ass down Basra Road with pickups filled with insurgents following us and firing and my guys returning fire out the gun ports like the Wild fucking West. With spent shells flying and our truck filling up with cordite, I tried to account for everyone on my team and make sure we hadn't left anyone behind.

Just before we reached the bridge, I received an urgent message over the radio from Craig in the Excursion. "We've run out of O^2! Need it immediately! Over."

The problem was that the spare oxygen bottles were in an armored box strapped to our roof. I knew he needed it to keep Fox and Dodd alive.

So with rounds zinging past me and pinging off the sides of the truck, I got out and climbed up to get the tanks, only to discover that the box containing them was locked. I had instructed the LNs not to padlock it, but they had anyway. Quick note to self: *Get rid of the locks altogether.*

I tried smashing the lock off with the butt of my M4. When that didn't work, I climbed down, told the LN driver to cut the engine and hand me the keys, then hauled ass back up to the roof to undo the lock.

I ran to the nearby Excursion, handed JD the bottles, then jumped back into my Land Cruiser and we were off, flying over the dirt road at 120 kph, sweeping under the bridge, then circling round the back of the airbase and blasting into camp.

Somehow we made it. The time between contact and arriving at the Combat Support Hospital was twenty-eight minutes, but it had felt like an eternity. Approximately two thousand rounds had been fired at us, with dozens ending up trapped in the Excursion's door skins and roof. One 5.56 bullet had lodged in Craig's body armor. Miraculously, everyone survived.

For us it was just another day's work. Tomorrow we would get another mission brief and order of battle, and set out again.

Lesson number 11: That was Iraq—an open, festering, angry wound that shows no sign of healing anytime soon.

I wish I could tell you that all the billions of dollars the United States and its allies have poured into it and all the lives lost will lead to a brighter future. But if one exists, it's still a long way off.

CHAPTER TWELVE
HOLLYWOOD INTERVENTION

I WAS in Los Angeles doing protection work for a Greek shipping family in 2000 when it struck me that the weather was far better than London, the scenery lovely, and the beaches sublime. So I decided to buy a place in Malibu and start to put down roots.

A year later I met a beautiful woman named Mia and her young daughter, Olivia, who lived nearby. They quickly became the emotional center of my life. I phoned and Skyped with them daily when I was in the field and spent the majority of my time with them when I was home.

I kept my life in California simple and low-key. When I wasn't taking Mia out to a movie or dinner, or playing with Olivia or driving her to school, I was probably running along the beach or working out in the gym, trying to shed the stresses of the work.

Malibu seemed like a dream life—the perfect tonic after the violence and chaos of various war zones. I was living near the beach in almost year-round sunshine. My neighbors were beautiful, interesting people who drove fabulous cars and earned gobs of money making TV shows and movies. Slowly, I became friendly with some of them after running into them at the local coffee shop or gym.

I started to see that, beneath Hollywood's glittery surface, there were darker forces at work. I learned more about this when I was introduced to a guy in 2010 named Frank, who called himself an extreme interventionist. An intense, compact guy with an inspiring life story, Frank had grown up a street kid, became involved in dealing and using drugs, and had even served time in prison. Twenty years earlier while he was addicted to heroin, his girlfriend gave birth to their first child. Looking into the innocent face of his newborn daughter, Frank had an epiphany. He decided to clean himself up and dedicate his life to working with addicts like himself.

For the last decade he had helped hundreds of drugs addicts and alcoholics turn their lives around. He counseled people of all ages and economic means, but many of his clients were teenagers and young people in their early twenties who came from affluent local families—the sons and daughters of Hollywood A-listers, fabulously wealthy individuals, and politicians.

Children of affluence can be particularly vulnerable to addiction, Frank explained. They live in households where money is readily available and parenting is often deficient, disjointed, or psychologically toxic. Sometimes these kids get involved with members of gangs—including the Crips, Bloods, MS-13, Mexican EME, and the Chechens. Sometimes they end up in drug dens controlled by gang members. Their parents are then blackmailed to keep their kids' names and faces out of the press.

Part of what Frank did was to rescue people in circumstances like this through physical intervention. Working with a group of skilled private investigators, he would locate the young addicts, seize them, and whisk them off either to safe houses or to one of several sober-living facilities he managed, where compassionate counselors would help them cleanse their bodies and discover a new sense of purpose.

Frank's track record was outstanding. When I first met him in 2010, A&E Television was producing a series based on his life and work called *The Cleaner,* starring Benjamin Bratt. Frank served as one of the show's executive producers.

Sometimes when Frank was working on a difficult case, he would solicit my help. On other occasions, he'd ask me to talk to recovering addicts about what I did for a living and what I had learned about discipline—how it could help bring structure to your life.

One afternoon in 2011, I was at the gym in Malibu working out with my buddy Pete when Frank called.

"Sy," he said, "I have a client whose daughter is in trouble. Do you think you can give me a hand?"

"Sure. When?"

"Right now."

"Usual meeting place?"

"Yeah."

Without changing out of my grungy workout gear, I drove to the Starbucks in Studio City and sat with Frank at an outdoor table. His client, he said, was a famous African American movie star (whom I'll call Morris). Morris's twenty-one-year-old daughter (whom I'll call Nevada) had become addicted to drugs and was kicking around with a member of the Playboy Crips named KC. While keeping her high, he had gotten her to star in porn movies.

Nevada was now living in a Crip house run by KC's grandmother. In the tradition of other African American gang headquarters, she looked after the place and did all the cooking, while the gangbangers dealt drugs and ran their business.

For the past eighteen months, while Nevada had been running with the Playboy Crips, Frank had had her followed by private investigators. But since Nevada was over twenty-one and legally independent, her father couldn't intervene further without breaking the law. Nor could the LAPD take any action to rescue her, unless Nevada filed a complaint, which she was too out of it to do. Naturally, Morris was at his wit's end. He feared that if Nevada continued this way she would soon be dead.

"Is this something you can help me out with?" Frank asked.

"I think so," I answered. "But I have to meet her father first."

Frank drove me to an apartment he had bought in a new complex near the 101 Freeway, which he was using as an office. On the way there he told me that Morris was renting an apartment in the same complex while he shot a movie at Universal Studios, around the corner.

Morris greeted me warmly when we arrived at his apartment. "I'm so glad you're here," he said, ignoring my dirty attire. "Frank has told me a lot about you. I know you've just come back from Iraq and your time is valuable. I hope you can help."

"I'm sure I can," I said. "I just need to know the facts."

He invited me to have a seat at the dining room table and brought over a five-inch-thick binder that he set it in front of me. "I've had Nevada under surveillance for eighteen months," he said. "I've had guys watching her constantly. This is what they've found."

A quick glance revealed that the binder contained surveillance photos of his drugged-out daughter in the company of various Crip gangbangers.

I said, "Okay, I get the picture. Now I need to know where Nevada is being kept."

He nodded. "The house is in a little middle-class development near Ventura Boulevard and Van Nuys in Sherman Oaks," he said. "They're little cookie-cutter houses built in the sixties. It's the last place you'd expect to find a group of gangbangers."

"Cookie cutter is good," I responded. "That means the layout of all the houses are the same. Do you happen to know any of the other people who live on the street?"

"I've met a number of them," Morris answered. "They're all nice people and horrified that the Crips are living there. They know that house is being used to deal drugs, but they're too scared to complain. A lot of them say that the Crips haven't done anything that they could go to the police with."

"I understand."

"The neighbor to the right of the Crip house has been especially cooperative. His name is Donald. He lives there alone and has offered to help in any way he can."

"Can you get him on the phone?" I asked. "I'd like to speak with him."

"Now?" Morris asked.

"Yes."

If I was going to do this, I wanted to act quickly while his daughter was still alive. Donald, it turned out, was busy that afternoon and evening, but agreed to meet Frank and me at the Starbucks in Studio City in the morning.

He showed up in khakis and a striped golf shirt looking like a relaxed retiree. Right away he expressed his desire to help and showed us a plan of his house and a sketch of the neighborhood.

I said, "It looks from these drawings like you can see directly into the Crip house."

"That's correct," Donald answered. "There are no high walls or tall shrubs between us. When you stand in my bedroom window on the left side of my house, you can look straight into their yard and house."

"Excellent. With your permission I'd like to set up an urban OP there."

Donald didn't know what that meant, so I explained. Basically I wanted to create a setup similar to the ones we had used against the IRA, but minus the discomfort and rats.

"Is there a way for us to put remote cameras on the outside of your house without being obvious?" I asked.

Donald thought about it for a minute and answered, "Yes, because the chimney on that side of my house is in need of repair. I've had two contractors out there looking at it this week and giving me estimates."

"Perfect. Frank and I will knock on your door at four p.m. posing as the third set of contractors. I'll go up on a ladder and attach small cameras to the side of your house, which we'll be able to monitor from a laptop."

"Okay..." Donald looked a little nervous. I assured him that I had done this kind of thing many times, and it had always worked.

"After we attach the cameras, we'll come back at three a.m. and enter from the back alley. Leave the back door open. I'll give you a call on your cell to let you know it's us."

"Okay. Fine," Donald said.

"Let us in and we'll camp out in your house for the next forty-eight hours to get a picture of what's going on in the Crip house."

Morris offered to put Donald up at a luxury hotel while we were in his house. Donald accepted and chose the Pelican Hill Resort in Newport Beach.

Frank and I swung into action. First, we needed to look like contractors. We borrowed a pickup truck from a biker friend of Morris's and drove it to a nearby Home Depot, where we bought a couple of ladders, two pairs of overalls, and various construction materials to stick in the back.

Wearing the overalls, we rolled up in front of Donald's house at 4:00 p.m. I did a careful scan of the street as I got out. I was looking for low-riding gang cars with blacked-out windows but saw only normal SUVs, BMWs, Hondas, and a few Mercedes. The gang hang-out looked like a regular family house with a nicely trimmed lawn. Maybe it could use a fresh coat of paint and new screens on the windows, but otherwise it didn't stand out from the other houses on the block.

Donald let us in, and we sat for ten minutes as though we were talking about his chimney. Then Frank and I went back outside and moved the ladders in place. As I crossed along the right side of the gang house, I searched for the surveillance cameras, bars over the windows, and metal front doors that were standard on most crack dens. This house had none.

With the ladders in place, I returned to the pickup and opened the glove compartment to retrieve the thumb-sized cameras. I checked them first to make sure they were working, then slipped them into the pockets of my overalls.

Once the cameras were installed, we packed the ladders back in the truck and circled around to the alley that ran along the back of house, parallel to Ventura Boulevard. As we passed, I fired up the laptop to test that the cameras were working. All good.

Three in the morning I returned to Donald's place with Frank and one of his associates—an ex-LAPD detective named Ray. Usually after Frank snatched someone he moved them to a safe house on the opposite coast where they would stay for a month or two in isolation, attended to 24/7 by a sober companion and security guard while various counselors and doctors came and went. On these occasions, Ray often worked as one of the guards.

He wasn't what I'd call a tip-of-the-spear operator but was a real nice guy. All I really needed him to do was monitor the laptop.

Ray and I entered through the back door and passed through Donald's kitchen to the living room, where we set up the laptop. For the next two days, we monitored comings and goings from the gang house next door, keeping a log of who stayed in the house, when people arrived and left, what they were carrying, and if they were armed.

We carried on this way in two-hour shifts. One of us would stay glued to the monitor while the other ate, rested, watched TV, or did push-ups. As we approached forty-eight hours, I walked into the living room after a short nap.

Ray looked up from the laptop and said, "Sy, I think the house is empty."

"You mean they took Nevada away?"

"No. I think Nevada is the only one in the house."

"Really? Are you sure of that?"

He nodded. It was a possibility. This wouldn't be the only occasion during the last two days that the gangbangers had left her alone in the house for a short period of time when she was asleep or completely zonked out of her mind on drugs.

I said, "Okay. Let's do it, now."

I called Frank and told him the deal.

He called ten minutes later to say he was waiting farther down the alley with his lights off and the engine running—our getaway.

I slipped a lightweight stab vest made of a flexible metal fabric over my shirt, then deactivated the motion sensors at the back of Donald's house and exited out the back.

When I reached the alley, I hung a left and stood outside the gang house's back fence. I waited there a minute and took a breath to center myself before I tried the gate. It was locked.

I hopped over the fence, crouched near the ground, and waited for a few minutes. When I saw that no lights had come on inside the house, I crossed the backyard to the kitchen window. Standing on a water faucet sticking out of the wall, I reached up and pulled open the louvered window enough to squeeze through.

Because the gap was only six inches, I had to hoist myself up and twist my body to gain access. I was halfway in with my back facing the kitchen when I felt something slam against my back, causing me to lose my footing, fall, and crash onto the kitchen floor. A large knife remained stuck in the back of the vest but hadn't pierced my skin.

I had no time to attempt to remove it. Quickly trying to recover and orient myself, I rose to my feet and confronted a young gangbanger. It wasn't KC. He shouted—"Motherfucker!"—then lunged at me fist first. I had enough presence of mind to swipe his lead arm away, pivot, and grab him in a headlock. I squeezed until he lost consciousness, then lowered his body to the ground and stood quietly for a minute and listened, wondering if there was anyone else in the house.

All was silent except my pounding heart. I was familiar with the layout of the house and through the remote camera had learned the location of the bedroom where Nevada was staying. So I exited the kitchen in the dark and turned right.

I stopped in front of the first door and turned the knob. Through the shadows I made out the shape of Nevada, facedown on a double bed. I crossed to her and looked at her face. At first I wasn't sure she was breathing, but I quickly checked her vital signs and established that she was still alive.

Even when I lifted her off the bed, she didn't stir. She was in such a deep drug-induced stupor that I had to throw her over my shoulder and fireman-carry her out, not an easy task considering that she was tall and completely dead weight.

I maneuvered her through the narrow hallway into the kitchen, where I glanced at the gangbanger still lying on the floor unconscious. Turning left, I quickly carried her out the back to the gate to the alley, which was padlocked shut.

I wasn't tall enough to climb up and pull her over, so I lifted her up and pushed her over the six-foot-high fence and quickly climbed up after her. Fortunately, she landed in a green recycling bin that was half filled with leaves and other debris.

Nevada was still unconscious when I pulled her out. Frank saw us and quickly drove up. We loaded her into his Mercedes and sped off. From the car, Frank called some friends of his from the LAPD and claimed he was a neighbor reporting a ruckus at the gangbanger's house. That allowed the two teams of officers who arrived within ten minutes to do a "soft knock"—which meant they could knock on the door and query the residents inside without entering.

When no one answered, the officers had the right to do a "hard knock," which meant that they could kick the door in and search the house to ascertain if anyone was in danger. Conveniently, one of them found a bag of cocaine and other drug paraphernalia on the dining room table, giving them legal cause to search the rest of the house.

While the cops were going through the house, KC arrived home and was arrested. Subsequently, his grandmother and other Crip Playboys were taken into custody and charged as well. Once city officials established that the house had been bought with the proceeds of illegal drug sales, it was repossessed.

Our concern was Nevada. We were speeding her to a house Morris had rented in Newport Beach that faced the ocean. She remained there for the next ninety days, watched day and night by a companion and security guard. Frank supervised her recovery and rehabilitation. In the end, Nevada kicked her drug addiction and started to pull her life together.

Morris, who was thrilled to have his daughter back and healthy, offered to pay me for my efforts. I didn't want money. It was reward enough to help and give back in some small measure.

Over the years I've done a number of other jobs like that for Frank, and I continue to do them, especially when they involve a teenager or young person. Most people look at kids growing up in places like Malibu, Brentwood, and Hollywood and all they see is the luxury and glamour. But when you look closely, as I have, you often see kids in trouble, either through bad parenting or neglect.

Lesson number 12: Maybe it's better not to be so rich and fabulous and instead focus on nurturing a tight, loving family.

CHAPTER THIRTEEN

SYRIA

THERE AREN'T many things as invigorating as a swim in the Pacific Ocean on a hot afternoon. I often run along the edge of Zuma Beach, then up into the nature preserve of Little Dune, where I stand and watch the waves below. The very nature of my job, and the things I've seen and done, exact a psychic toll. But standing looking out on the ocean, I forget the horrors of warfare, even if only for a short time.

It was fall 2011, and I had just returned from a run and swim in the Pacific Ocean when I checked my cell phone and saw that Michael S. had called. Knowing the comms drill he wanted me to follow, I dressed, got in my car, and drove to a local Radio Shack, where I purchased a burner cell phone with cash. (Never use a credit card if you want to remain off the map, and go to a store you've never been to before.)

I spoke while I drove in the direction of Thousand Oaks, constantly checking the side and rearview mirrors to make sure I wasn't being followed.

"Michael, it's Simon. What's up?"

"I've got some friends in the Middle East who need advice. Can you help?"

"Yeah, no problem."

"Can you catch a flight this afternoon?"

I hesitated for a moment, because I'd recently returned from another stint in Iraq and was planning on spending time at home. Then again, in this business you never knew when the next phone call was going to come. Or your next paycheck. So I decided to at least see what Michael had to offer.

"Yes," I answered.

Turning into a shopping center, I pulled the SIM card out of the burner cell phone and snapped them both in half. The cell phone went into the trash in front of a takeout joint; the SIM card went into the garbage bin in front of Trader Joe's.

I met with Michael in DC the next morning at a suite in the Hay-Adams Hotel, a few hundred feet away from the White House. Rich in history and atmosphere, the old-world hotel has maintained strong ties to the intelligence community since it first opened its doors in 1928. Decorated with thick carpets, dark wood, and brass fittings, the rooms there have been the hatching place of numerous coups and covert actions, from Latin America to the Middle East. This visit was no different, the same Langley types milling about and intrigue in the air.

Michael introduced me to Anthony S.—a former US official with short brown hair who looked to be in his late forties. His suit appeared to have been slept in, and he wore the overworked and over-traveled look common to diplomats.

Wary of suited types, I gave Anthony a simple hello and let him take the floor. He explained that he was doing work for a State

Department registered charity called the Syrian Support Group (SSG), which had raised $600 million from Qatari and Saudi royals and wealthy Syrian American businessmen to help Syrian families displaced by the civil war. The Department of State couldn't be seen to be involved in the Syrian conflict—

I cut Anthony off there. "The State Department can't be seen helping displaced families that are being persecuted by their own government? That's a first," I said, not believing for a second that helping Syrian families was going to be the only role of the SSG.

I had followed events in Syria with interest. When anti-Assad demonstrations started in early 2011 as part of the Arab Spring, I thought they had little chance of succeeding. The authoritarian Assad regime, which represented the small Alawite Shiite elite, had been in power since the early seventies, first through Hafez al-Assad and then through his son Bashar.

As the oppressed Sunni majority continued to press for change, small groups of men took up arms. The Assad regime responded with customary brutality, and rebels were soon joined by thousands of Sunni defectors from the Syrian military.

In July, they had formed the Free Syrian Army (FSA), which currently boasted twenty thousand members. That's when the civil war really began.

I knew that the Assad regime had a brutal reputation for dealing with dissidents and enemies. Its military intelligence service, the Mukhabarat, was aggressive and deadly and trained and supported by Russia's foreign intelligence service, the SVR. So I wasn't surprised that when the FSA captured territory, the Assad military responded with cluster bombings, artillery, and rocket attacks on rebels and civilians.

I expected the United States and its European allies to do something, but nothing had happened so far.

Looking across at Michael and Anthony in the Hay-Adams, I asked, "What do you need from me?"

"We want you to find out how we can help the guys fighting the Assad regime," Anthony responded.

"Why isn't the agency or State doing this?" I asked, though I was pretty sure I knew the answer.

"The USG [US government] doesn't want to be openly involved at this point," Anthony answered. "They're getting a lot of political heat from the Chinese and Russians. The situation is further complicated by the number of jihadists streaming into Syria and taking up arms with the rebels."

"Specifically al-Nusra and the Islamic State of Iraq [ISI, later to become ISIS]," Michael added.

"Got it," I said, knowing that ISI's stated goal was to impose an Islamic government based on Sharia law in Sunni areas of Iraq, and al-Nusra was allied with the terrorist group al-Qaeda.

"Latest estimates put civilian casualties at tens of thousands, including women and children," Anthony continued. "We've received reports of mass graves, even genocide of Sunni villagers."

"We need to stop that," Michael stated emphatically.

I agreed. "So you want an assessment of conditions on the ground?"

"Yes," Michael answered. "We want to know what the rebels need in terms of operational support, equipment, and training."

"Fine," I said, "but I want to take someone else with me for support. I assume you want pictures."

"They would be helpful. Yes."

"When do you want us to leave?"

"Asap."

*　　　*　　　*

The next day I boarded a flight to Paris. My old Royal Marine mate Robbo met me outside of Charles de Gaulle Airport Customs & Immigration carrying a leather bag and looking as imposing as ever. No matter where he was in the world, or what he was doing, Robbo appeared to have just slipped off the cover of *GQ*—six foot two, perfect teeth, square jaw, a physique like Michelangelo's *David*, not to mention a comic's sense of timing and the gift of gab. He was a full-time chick magnet, always smiling, always joking, and it was hard to tell, as I would later find out, that all was not well in his world.

I briefed him as we walked together to the Turkish Airlines gate.

He said, in his thick Newcastle accent, "This job must be total arse if you called me."

"Total arse, mate," I replied with a smirk. "I'm surprised you even turned up."

Upon landing in Istanbul, I hailed a cab and asked the driver to take us to the Kir Evi Restaurant downtown.

"Perfect," Robbo said beside me. "I'm starved."

"You're always starved. Don't they have food in Newcastle?"

"Aye, we do. Just not enough for a machine like me."

When we arrived at the restaurant, instead of going in, I crossed the street to a waiting black sedan.

"What the fuck is this all about?" Robbo groaned, sliding in beside me.

"We're trying to shake any tail from Syrian intelligence. There will be sandwiches waiting on the next flight," I said as lights reflected off the Bosporus River to our right.

Twenty minutes later, the driver turned into the gates of a private airport and stopped in front a small airplane hangar. A Dassault Falcon 50 trijet sat waiting near the tarmac.

"That our ride?" Robbo asked.

"Looks like."

A forty-year-old American wearing a St. Louis Cardinals baseball cap, jeans, and a pistol in a holster came out of the hangar to greet us. He reminded me a bit of the actor George Peppard, minus the cigar.

"Hi, my name's Mike."

"Hi, Mike."

"My instructions are to drop you off in Aleppo and come back here and wait for you to call for pickup. In the back of the aircraft you'll find two duffel bags with the gear you requested. There's a sat phone in one of them preprogrammed with my number under 'Bird One.' Any questions?"

"Where are the sandwiches?" Robbo chirped, looking around.

During the flight, we went through the kit, which included the usual fare—med pack, comms, spare batteries, and a vest with pockets to slip in hard and soft armor—very handy for operators in hostile zones. You could also add pouches to the back and sides of it. I filled mine with spare mags for my pistol and rifle, a knife, Leatherman, radio, zip ties, GPS, tourniquet, and an extra pouch for odds and sods. Fully loaded, the vest weighed nearly fifty pounds. In addition, I carried a belt kit with my pistol, more mags, and other whizbang gadgets to sustain me for a few days on the move.

We settled in and read through the files Michael had sent us. Not overly informative—just a few paragraphs on the people we would be meeting, the region, what was needed for the visit, and the FSA. I learned that the Free Syrian Army had been formed by a group of seven defected Syrian armed forces (SAF) officers and somewhere between two thousand and eight thousand soldiers at the outset of the Syrian civil war on July 29, 2011. Around 90 percent of them were Sunni Muslims. They held pockets of territory throughout the country, especially in the northwest (including the cities of Idlib and

Aleppo) and central regions, and maintained a command center in the Hatay Province of southern Turkey near the Syrian border.

Two hours later, we landed on a barren airstrip outside of Syria's largest city, Aleppo. Outside the window I saw a ragtag group of fifty soldiers standing around pickups with .50-cal machine guns mounted in back. I took a deep breath and stepped off the plane, wearing an armored vest and with my M5 slung over my shoulder, finger resting above the trigger guard, just in case.

A stoop-shouldered man in his sixties shuffled forward to greet us. The interpreter by his side, named Dana, who turned out to be his nephew, introduced the man as General Amir Ahmed Sabir of the FSA.

I placed my hand over my heart and said in Arabic, *"Salam Ali kum."* Peace be with you.

"Wa ali kum salam," the general replied. And peace be with you. He pointed to the Arabic saying tattooed on my right arm and recited, *"Kum jameelan tera ajood tameelan."* Be beautiful and see beautiful things.

I nodded.

He smiled back, crinkling the skin around his wise, tired-looking eyes, then barked an order over his shoulder, sending the men piling into the four pickup trucks. As the Dassault Falcon 50 revved up behind me, I noticed one young fighter who couldn't have been more than fifteen kneel down and zip up a *Transformers* backpack filled with ammo. He slung it over his shoulder and ran to one of the trucks.

The image jolted me back to my home near the Pacific Ocean and the stark, shocking contrast between children back there and here. In Malibu, kids had soft, smiling faces. I imagined one with this same backpack, filled with books, hopping out of his parents' luxury SUV.

Here the kids were hollow eyed and hardened beyond their years. Instead of books and games, their backpacks were loaded with instruments of death. Sometimes, it didn't seem possible that both worlds, so different, could exist on the same planet.

The driver of the pickup we rode in wove around deep craters in the dirt road—remnants of an earlier shelling. We passed through a number of villages as we pushed west on the M5—the main road out of Aleppo—toward our destination, a Sunni tribal area made up of several small towns and villages known as Kaoukab. To our left and right stood primitive mud structures pockmarked with bullet holes. The roofs of some had caved in.

Robbo's camera never stopped clicking, and as he snapped he kept muttering "Fuck me" under his breath. Just when I thought we'd seen the worst image of devastation, another greeted us from around the corner.

This time it was the sad eyes of a girl of four or five standing by the road and clutching a battered teddy bear with one arm. The other ended at the wrist, a bloody stump covered with dirty bandages.

I felt something clutch in my chest as her mother ran out of a nearby shack to pull her away. I was still processing that encounter as the trucks braked to a sudden stop and fighters leaped out holding shovels and shouting.

"What's going on?" I asked Dana.

He pointed to a slew of football-sized bomblets from a Soviet-era cluster bomb on the road ahead. "We have to clear the road."

"Tell everyone to clear back!" I shouted, knowing how sensitive and lethal the bomblets were.

Dana looked at me with confusion. I realized that there weren't any bomb-disposal units to call in. This was what civil war looked like. Fighters carefully slid their shovels under the soil beneath the bomblets to lift them and carry them away.

Dana explained that the Assad regime, knowing that the only way villagers in the area could travel to and from school and work was via these dirt tracks, had deliberately seeded them with bomblets and mines. A sickening tactic.

"How many of your soldiers died before they figured that technique out?" Robbo asked from the seat behind me.

It was a good question. Suddenly, a dull explosion tore through the air, and blood sprayed across the windshield, followed by the sound of lethal shrapnel ripping into the sides of the vehicle.

I pulled myself up from the seat, checked to see that Robbo was okay, and ran out to attend to the wounded, my ears ringing, my mouth and throat clogged with dust. Next thing I remember, I was running with a wounded man in my arms, my hands covered with blood, my heart racing. The legs below both his knees were missing.

Robbo ran by my side with the wounded fifteen-year-old soldier in his arms—the one I'd seen with the *Transformers* backpack. Men shouted urgently. They pointed to a cement structure. We entered and hurried down concrete steps into the main room of a makeshift hospital. Several doctors were attending to a collection of old people, children, and amputees lying on dirty mattresses strewn on the dirt floor.

The rot of bacterial infection and decomposition hit my nostrils as the doctors scurried about looking for a place for us to lay the wounded fighters. Robbo and I leaned on the wall, half in shock, watching as the doctors worked on the wounded with primitive, unsterilized equipment.

Dana stopped near my shoulder and asked in heavily accented English, "What do you think of our medical facilities?"

All I could do was look back at him. I didn't want to say "pathetic" or "barbaric"—the two words that came to mind.

He said, "The general wants to see you now."

I wiped the blood off my hands and followed him to a building on the far edge of the village. Kaoukab was made up of a series of towns all linked by dirt roads. We were in the main village and administrative center. As in most Middle Eastern countries I'd visited, the farther away you got from the big cities with their fancy new villas and glass towers, the lower you slipped down the poverty line to mud-brick homes and subsistence farms.

Coming from the luxury of Southern California, I never ceased to be humbled by places like this. I often wondered how the people who inhabited them managed to exist. On the spiderweb of crater-ridden dirt tracks that linked the gathering of huts, the only form of transport was by foot, horse-drawn cart, or maybe sharing a ride in a beat-up old car with some neighbors. Every half mile or so you might pass a little shop offering nothing but a few cans of fruit, rugs, bottles of water, and some local produce. Even though the stores had only a handful of visitors per week, the owners would stand in them each day proudly, smiling and keen to serve you.

We entered and passed through bare concrete rooms to a larger one sparsely decorated with a rug and a few family photos on the wall. Around a tea urn in the middle of the room sat General Sabir and a dozen village elders on the rug, behind plates of goat meat, rice, dried fruit, and honey bread.

The general indicated a place beside him for me to sit.

Dana, behind me, whispered, "You can remove your things if you like."

I assumed he was referring to my body armor, which I wasn't ready to take off. The men ate in silence as I sipped the tea, which cleared the dust from my mouth and throat.

After several minutes, General Sabir turned to me and asked in Arabic, "Why did you come here?"

"To help," I answered.

He looked deep into my eyes and nodded. "We need help," he said plaintively. "We need the help of America. Every day we are lucky to drive back Assad's forces. But the next day they return, stronger in numbers. The weapons we have are useless against their tanks and planes."

"I understand."

He extended his arm and pointed to the dozen faces staring at me with weary eyes and said, "As you can see, we are simple people, Mr. Chase. Farmers, carpenters. We don't know how to fight. It is only a matter of time before all that is here is lost."

His sincerity moved me. He hadn't mentioned a word about overthrowing the Assad government. He and his men were focused on the survival of their families.

Outside the sun set over fields of wheat and barley. I watched from a balcony as Robbo showed off his soccer skills to a group of boys in the little town square. Villagers with gaunt faces stood in groups talking among themselves.

A rumbling in the distance sent a shiver up my spine. I saw Robbo place a pair of NVGs on his head and sweep the fields of vegetation left to right. I was reaching in my pack for mine when I heard him shout, "RPG! Take cover."

A rocket sailed over his head and slammed into the street near the children. *Blam!*

Chaos followed. Children screamed; men shouted and reached for their weapons. People ran for cover amid the falling dust. What sounded like a mortar round exploded to my right.

I hurried outside and to the corner of a house where Robbo stood peering through his NVGs.

"What do you see?"

He pointed to the field beyond the village. "North side. Forty to fifty men, small arms and technical."

I saw Dana standing nearby and shouted, "We need to set up fire teams on the north side!" Machine-gun fire rang out in the distance, and another mortar shell exploded to my right.

Dana looked back at me in shock.

"We need to set up fire teams immediately!"

He either couldn't hear me or didn't understand what I was saying. Machine-gun rounds slammed into the mud walls of the house in front of us. I waved toward two fighters who were crouched nearby and ran with them to a structure at the north edge of the village. Robbo grabbed two more men and followed.

Upon reaching a hut at the north perimeter, I climbed to the flat roof and motioned for the men to follow. Bullets ripped into the earth and walls, and mortar shells exploded nearby. A foot-high mud-brick lip surrounded the mud roof. I pushed the men down to the flat surface and pointed to where I wanted them to direct their fire.

With bullets ricocheting off the wall in front of them, they sprayed volleys from their AKs wildly across the field, then paused to pray. I bellied down beside them, aimed at the Assad soldiers advancing across the field with the half-moon behind them, and dropped three in succession. The fighters beside me nodded.

I instructed them to reload and follow my example—accurate, controlled bursts on located targets. They got it, and started to inflict damage.

In the noise and confusion, I couldn't make out what fighters on the street were shouting. Then a rocket slammed into the house below us, and the whole damn thing shook like it was about to collapse.

I got ready to jump, spit the cordite and dust out of the side of my mouth, and then rolled along the north side of the roof to where another group of fighters had assembled. These three men, all teenagers, looked terrified. I took aim at targets on the field and dropped them, one by one. They seemed to get the idea.

Meanwhile, Robbo was on the street with four other fighters, moving forward from house to house. I saw him stop, take cover, and shove a magazine into his weapon as a barrage of bullets punched into the wall in front of him.

Hearing a groan behind him, he turned to see that one of the FSA fighters had been hit in the chest. The others started to back away in panic.

"Stay low," he shouted, gesturing with his left hand.

Rolling to the fallen fighter, he checked his pulse. Dead.

He rolled back into position, ran and crouched behind a wall, and peered through his NVGs. Expertly and calmly he released bursts that cut down some of the advancing Syrian troops.

Two other fighters joined him. But Robbo knew that they didn't have enough firepower to stop the advance or the .50-cal cannon the Syrians a hundred meters ahead were rolling into position.

With bullets peppering the wall, he looked for an answer. Six feet behind him he saw the bandaged teenager with the *Transformers* backpack. It was still loaded with ammo and explosives. As the fighters around him watched, Robbo ripped two grenades from the nearest one's bandolier, pulled the pins, popping the armed levers, dropped them in the backpack, and launched it over the wall at the advancing Syrian troops.

I was on the roof firing when I saw the entire sky in front of me light up. A split second later a tremendous explosion lifted me off the deck. As I hit the concrete chest-first, a huge fireball ripped into the sky. Dust and bits of rock, mud, and body parts rained onto my back.

"Robbo?" I shouted.

No answer.

I instructed the fighters on the roof to maintain their position and keep firing, then ran down the steps to the street. I sprinted from doorway to doorway, weapon ready, looking for Robbo. Near a collapsed wall to my left I saw two fighters on their knees trying to free someone from a mound of dirt, field cover, and bricks.

"Robbo?"

I heard him coughing under the mess of debris.

"Hold on, mate!"

Desperately, we cleared the debris off him and sat him up. Then I checked him for wounds. He turned his head away and spit out a chunk of mud. "Fuck this!"

A grim smile returned to his face. The sporadic firing from the fields stopped. In the eerie calm that followed, I looked through the NVGs and saw the Syrians leaving in their trucks. Sixty meters ahead I spotted a smoldering crater littered with Syrian dead.

I instructed a few fighters to guard the north perimeter, then Robbo and I headed back to the center of the village. We passed men and women attending to wounded fighters and others covering the dead. With every footstep, the rush of adrenaline subsided to reveal weariness and sadness.

I knew it was only a matter of days until the Syrians returned. Next time they would bring more soldiers and heavier artillery and maybe wipe out the entire village.

When I found Dana, I said, "You need to perimeter up the entire village and set up sentries. All four corners. Three-hundred-and-sixty-degree cover. Tell General Sabir."

The next morning I called Chuck on the sat phone to tell him we were ready to exfil. Two hours later, he touched down on the same airstrip where we had landed. General Sabir hugged me hard to his chest as two dozen of his armed fighters looked on from the back of a truck.

Deeply touched by the hopeless look in his eyes, I said, "I'll be back."

The general removed the shemagh he wore and wrapped it around my shoulders.

"Isha' Allah," he said placing his hand over his heart. Go with Allah. *"Isha' Allah."*

Robbo and I left knowing that without proper training and support, General Sabir and his men would soon be dead.

Three days later I met with Michael S., Anthony, and two men who said they worked for the US government in a suite at the Hay-Adams Hotel in DC. Michael read the report I had tapped out on my iPad while the officials flipped through the photos we brought back.

When he finished, Michael said, "I think we're good. There's evidence of genocide here. Real atrocities. This should be enough to green-light this thing."

"Not so fast, Michael," said one of the government suits. "Without evidence of chemical weapons we'll never be able to sell this on the Hill. We also have the issue of foreign fighters."

I told him that we hadn't seen any foreign fighters in Kaoukab.

They thanked me for my work, and that was it. With a heavy heart I flew back to California. Soon after I landed at LAX, I checked my cell phone and saw that I had a message from Michael.

I called him immediately and informed him we were talking on an unsecure line.

Michael chose his words carefully. "The guys think it's worth a second visit. What they're looking for is physical evidence and photographic proof."

"What guys?"

"The guys in the room."

"Got it. You know any freelance photographers who are already in-country?" I asked, thinking that we could contact one and tell him or her what we needed.

"Probably," Michael answered. "But everything needs to be authenticated. They're not going to take the word of some wartime paparazzi trying to make a buck."

"So you need me and my mate to go back?"

"Correct."

"When?"

"Asap. Wheels up."

I turned around with my bag in hand and booked a flight to London. On the way, I contacted Robbo, who stood waiting for me when I deplaned in Heathrow. Twenty hours later, we were standing beside General Sabir again on the dirt landing strip outside of Aleppo.

CHAPTER FOURTEEN

BULGARIA

GENERAL SABIR was happy to see us but asked why we hadn't brought weapons and supplies. I explained through Dana that Washington needed evidence that Assad was using chemical weapons against his own people first.

The general said, "If we had oil like Iraq you wouldn't need this evidence."

I knew exactly where he was coming from and appreciated his frustration. If Syria possessed massive oil reserves like Iraq, coalition forces would have come streaming into the country to aid the FSA long ago. This process was going to be more painstaking.

"General," I explained, "I'm one man. I'm trying to help. If this evidence exists, can you help me find it?"

A day later, Dana took Robbo and me to a northeastern suburb of the city of Aleppo called al-Maara, which was largely under FSA control but under constant bombardment from the Syrian military. Aleppo, I knew, was about two hundred miles west of Damascus and the largest city in Syria, with a population of over 2 million. Before the war it had been the country's main commercial and manufacturing center, producing textiles, chemicals, and pharmaceuticals.

Aleppo had been a major battleground in the civil war since February, when battalions of FSA captured several districts in the southern and northeastern parts of the city. We had arrived in the midst of what was later described as the "mother of battles" as rebels tried to press into the center of the city and the Assad regime responded with massive bombardments and airstrikes, including barrel bombs dropped from helicopters that had destroyed entire neighborhoods and killed thousands of civilians. Hundreds of thousands of others had been forced to evacuate.

The destruction we saw around us—blocks of houses in ruins, the burned-out carcasses of cars, trucks, and buses, cratered streets filled with refuse, and desperate-looking armed men standing smoking and pointing at the sky—was shocking.

We were out of our Toyota pickup no more than two minutes when we heard a high whistling howl and watched the men scurry for cover.

"Incoming!" Robbo shouted.

Dana waved at us to follow him to the collapsed side of what looked to be an apartment tower and steps that led to a basement bunker. As the artillery round exploded, the cinder-block walls shook on either side of us. More mortar rounds exploded, and we entered a sandbag-reinforced room lit by exposed electric bulbs.

Huddled in the corners were groups of mainly women and children, and a few men. Their faces reflected fear and abandonment. Signs of malnutrition and dehydration were also evident, and Dana explained that getting food and water to these beleaguered people had become increasingly difficult. Assad's forces had adopted a new tactic. If they couldn't shell them out of their homes, they'd starve them.

Sitting among them was a pale, skinny Westerner with a tattered oxford shirt cuffed at the elbows and a camera bag over his shoulder.

I introduced myself as more explosions thudded outside. He said his name was Ryan O. and he was a freelance journalist-photographer from Cambridge.

"What are you doing here?" he asked, lighting a cigarette.

"My mate Robbo and I are fact finding."

"You with the CIA? MI Five?"

"No, the Syrian Support Group."

"What's that?"

"We're looking for evidence of chemical weapons use," I offered.

"Well, you've come to the right place."

He removed one of the cameras from his bag and showed us a series of horrific photos of men, women, and children lying in contorted death poses, caked with white powder.

"Where were these taken?" I asked.

"Right here, at the end of the street," Ryan answered. "You can use them...for a price."

"The people I work for need me to get my own eyes on it. Can you take me to the site?"

"No chance. Assad's troops have moved in," Ryan answered. "It's filled with snipers."

"Can you at least point me in the right direction?"

"Sure, I can. For a price."

As soon as the shelling stopped, the four of us—Robbo, Dana, Ryan, and myself—piled into the Toyota pickup. It always amazed me that every time I saw a group of armed men in a war-torn corner of the Middle East or Africa they seemed to be flying around in a

Toyota HiLux. Where did they all come from? Who was the enterprising dealer making the sales? Some very rich bugger by now, that's for sure.

Dana directed the driver to take us downtown. While Robbo snapped pictures of white phosphorous burn signatures on the sides of buildings, I kept a lookout for snipers. Up ahead I spotted two pickups flying black flags blocking the road. Yep, HiLuxes.

"Who the fuck are they?" I asked.

In hindsight, it was a stupid question. No matter where I went in the world, foreign fighters looked like what they were: foreign fighters—eighteen-to-forty-year-old males outfitted hurriedly at the sports clothing and bedding sections of Target topped off with a moody set of shades.

"Foreign fighters," Ryan confirmed. "We'd better back up and get out."

This was going to be difficult, first, because the road had deep gullies and severe drop-offs on either side, which would require a slow reverse. Second, any indication that we were trying to avoid these guys could lead to further problems.

Several of the heavily armed men with long black beards waved at us to stop. They'd constructed an improvised checkpoint out of old tires, pieces of granite, and lengths of wood, backed up by the trusty HiLuxes. We'd seen similar sights before in Iraq, which was where most of these guys hailed from.

They were members of al-Nusra Brigade—a mix of foreign fighters from other Arab countries and even England and France—which had originally wreaked havoc in Iraq, where they were known as al-Qaeda in Iraq. They now swarmed into Syria, ostensibly to help the FSA in its fight against the Assad regime. But as we came to find out, many of them later blended into ISIS—an organization with a different agenda: namely, to establish an Islamic state in the Sunni-dominated stretches of Iraq and Syria.

Today they're notorious for beheading Westerners and for their brutality toward the other tribes and factions in the Syrian civil war. Back in late 2011, they were allies of men like General Sabir—though better trained and equipped and more experienced in insurgency-style warfare and small-unit tactics, thanks to their time in Iraq. They operated in groups of twenty to thirty fighters and proved a very agile, mobile force, effective in resisting Assad's mechanized units.

I turned to Ryan and asked, "When did these fuckers start showing up?"

"The jihadists? More and more appear every day. A couple weeks ago this Saudi cat rolled in. Al-Nasr something."

"Sanafi al-Nasr?" I asked.

"Yeah, that's him. Since he's been here, things have gotten real nasty."

I'd heard that Sanafi had been dispatched by al-Qaeda boss Ayman al-Zawahiri to organize and lead al-Qaeda-allied groups in Syria. AQ clearly saw an opportunity to take advantage of the chaos to further their terrorist agenda.

Robbo and I were well aware of how al-Nusra had treated Westerners like us in Iraq. If they got their hands on us, we were either going to get a hall pass or a prime-time spot on Al Jazeera wearing orange boilersuits. We readied our weapons. There were two dozen of them and four of us.

"Now what?" I asked.

Dana said, "I'm going to go speak to them."

"Is that smart?" Robbo asked.

Dana was already out of the vehicle with his hands over his

head, advancing toward the bearded men, who didn't appear happy to see us.

I flipped off the safety and kept my finger near the trigger guard of my M4—ready to engage, stomach turning queasy, adrenaline surging into my veins.

"Look," Robbo said, pointing his chin toward Dana, who had turned and was on his way back. Simultaneously, the jihadists were climbing into their trucks and appeared to be backing them up to let us through.

"How'd that go?" I asked when Dana returned.

"Okay" was all he answered, even though he appeared thoroughly rattled.

The tension mounted as we passed—the jihadists' suspicious eyes boring into us, us staring back. Then as we sat silently, the driver wound through the rubble for another mile until we came to what had once been the end of the Silk Road that stretched into Central Asia and Mesopotamia, and the entrance to the ancient sector of one of the oldest cities in the world—first settled in the sixth millennium b.c. Sadly, many of the city's historic buildings had already been destroyed.

We crawled at a snail's pace across the crater-filled streets. Houses with three walls and no rooftops leered hauntingly from all angles.

Ryan pointed to a narrow street that rose in a sharp incline ahead. "The place I took the pics is up there."

We were in a sniper's paradise—a narrow hundred-yard stretch uphill flanked by buildings and trees on both sides. To make matters worse, our driver refused to go any farther. If we were going to get pictorial evidence, we'd have to set out on foot.

Robbo and I rechecked our kits—M4s, Glocks, ammo, IFAKs, cameras, and spare batteries. You would think we were preparing to deploy on a two-day patrol. Ryan wisely chose to stay with the truck. Dana, though not wearing a protective vest, wanted to come with us. Standing beside Robbo with nothing but an AK-47 and a small vest with pouches, he looked a little underequipped.

"Probably not a good idea," I warned.

"You are the guests of the general, and it's my duty to look after you," Dana countered. "Besides, if a bullet is meant to find me, then by Allah's will it is so."

I wasn't in the mood to argue. And I'd seen enough of Aleppo to know that I didn't want to stay around a minute longer than I had to.

"Okay, Dana. You stick with me."

The three of us dashed ahead, took cover behind the entrance of what had once been a pharmacy, and carefully eyeballed each side of the quiet street. Nothing moved—no breeze, no dogs barking, no people stirring. Only eerie silence. Waiting a minute and seeing nothing suspicious, I nodded back at Robbo, then made a beeline for a building ahead while he covered my six.

From a crouch, I scanned the buildings carefully and waited. After a minute, I signaled to Robbo and Dana, who quickly joined me. We proceeded like this diagonally and thirty to forty feet at a time up the hill.

I reached the top first. As I hid behind a wall, catching my breath, I was hit with the unmistakable stench of putrefying human bodies.

Glancing to my right, I saw Robbo pointing to a large trench that had been carved into the cobblestone street ten feet ahead of us and slightly to the left.

"What?"

It was stuffed full of the corpses of men, women, and children covered with a ghostly white powder.

"Fuck me," I gasped, covering my mouth.

"White phosphorous." Robbo groaned. "Disgusting."

He started snapping pictures of the grotesque bodies as outrage grew inside me. *How could a leader of a country do this to his own people, including women and children? Why is the rest of the world standing by and allowing this to fucking happen?*

As I was thinking this, something hit the ground by my foot, kicking up a cloud of dust. I was so transfixed by the horrible sight in front of me that the danger didn't register until Robbo slammed me to the ground and screamed, "Contact!"

"What?"

"Assad forces, top window of the building fifty meters to the right!" he shouted.

The wind knocked out of me, I had to fight the urge to gasp for breath and inhale the white powder that had kicked up. Choking and trying to get my bearings, I pushed myself up. Robbo and Dana climbed in the trench beside me.

"You were lucky, mate. Keep low, make small."

"Fuck!"

We were on our bellies near the lip of the trench, trying to forget the bodies beneath us, scanning the windows of the building across the street for the shooter. Without warning gunshots rang from several directions. We ducked. Bullets tore into the street around us, ricocheting and throwing dust and debris in our faces.

We responded with precise, calculated shots—fixing our sights on specific targets in the building, delivering lethal hits, covering each other when one of us had to change mags. As I fired, Robbo collected samples of the powder, scraping it into plastic ziplock bags with a knife.

Suddenly a rocket round sailed over our heads from behind and slammed into the Syrian troops in the building in front of us. *Wham!*

"What the fuck was that?"

Wondering where it had come from, I turned and saw a group of foreign fighters taking up positions behind us.

They started pounding the buildings ahead with RPGs and mortars. The Syrians in front responded, and the battle was on. Problem was, we were stuck right in the middle.

"Prepare to move!" I shouted over the deafening roar.

Our means of escape was to our left and down. I looked at Robbo. He nodded back. We knew the drill and had been through it together many times in Iraq and Afghanistan.

"You're coming with me!" he shouted in Dana's panic-stricken face.

I continued lying on my stomach, returning fire. With bullets sailing over our heads and tearing into the pavement around us, Robbo shouted, "Moving!"

He rolled left over the berm, sprinted twenty feet, and dropped behind the carcass of a burned-out truck with Dana following on his heels.

I expended the bullets in the mag, reloaded, then did the same, rolling left and sprinting, hitting the ground, taking precise aim at targets, and screaming at Robbo to "Move!" again.

"Moving!" Robbo responded.

He got up and zigzagged down the street diagonally another twenty feet, M4 in his right hand, dragging Dana with his left. I aimed and fired, then ran again, heart pounding, sweat dripping down my pants legs into my boots.

"Moving!" Robbo shouted again. The racket behind us and to our right seemed to have reached a fever pitch.

I had eyes on an enemy target when I heard Robbo's scream. "I'm hit! I'm hit!"

I turned left and saw him lying in the street near another burned-out car, holding his left leg. Dana ran out from behind the car, grabbed Robbo by the left arm, and started to drag him to cover.

Then Dana was hit, too. I saw his shoulder jerk back and his AK fly in the air.

Fuck!

In a wild frenzy, I launched myself toward them, skidding across the asphalt, dropping beside them, and returning fire. I dragged Robbo behind the destroyed car, then went back for Dana.

Robbo was bleeding from his left thigh. Grimacing, he'd propped himself against the back bumper of the vehicle and picked up his weapon.

"I can't run, but I can shoot!" he growled.

"Let's go!"

I half dragged, half carried them down the hill, one by one, twenty feet at a stretch, half aware that the firing had eased up.

Two-thirds of the way down, Ryan ran up to help me. Eventually we made our way to the bottom of the hill and the waiting pickup. Breathing hard, my back and arms aching, I loaded Dana and Robbo into the bed and pushed Ryan toward the cab. "Go! Go! Tell the driver. Let's get the fuck out of here!"

Suddenly a tremendous volley of automatic-weapons fire echoed from the top of the hill, followed by shouts of *"Allahu akbar!"* Turning toward the sound, I saw victorious foreign jihadists crowding the street, firing their guns in the air in celebration. Several of them were pushing captured Syrian soldiers to the ground.

We didn't stick around to see what grizzly fate awaited them. We were off, tearing in the opposite direction, as I applied Israeli bandages to the bullet wounds in Robbo's leg and Dana's shoulder.

We made it back to the village, where locals carried Robbo and Dana into the underground "hospital." It wasn't ideal, but better than nothing. The doctors there had become expert at patching gun wounds with little to no equipment.

Sometime later I was sitting in a dark room shaking from head to toe, my arms and hands covered with blood. I remember studying them as though they belonged to someone else, my mind drifting back to the trench and the bodies covered in white. I realized that no amount of military training could prepare someone for a sight like that.

I waited for the adrenaline to wear off and the shakes to cleanse my body, pushing the images to the back of my mind to be dealt with sometime later. Someone was knocking on my door. It was one of Sabir's men summoning me to see the general.

He wanted to thank me for saving Dana, who he said was being treated by a doctor and going to be okay. Robbo had been stabilized, too.

I returned to the room, washed off the blood and grit, and looked at my weary face in the mirror, hardly recognizing myself and amazed at how much the lack of bathing, extreme summer heat, no food, and my mate's blood crusted on my face had changed my appearance in such a short time.

Several days later I was back in Washington meeting with Michael, Anthony, and the same two government officials. As they looked through the pictures, one of them turned to me and asked, "Did you take these yourself?"

Part of me was still in that trench in Aleppo, the smell of death burning my nostrils. "We did. Yes. And we got this off the dead civilians."

I lay two of the ziplock Baggies with the white residue on the coffee table between us. The officials recoiled.

Michael, seated beside me on the sofa, said, "Relax, men, it's harmless."

In a separate folder I was carrying photos Ryan and Robbo had taken of the al-Nusra jihadists. Now I spread them on the table. Anthony and the two suits leaned forward to take a closer look.

"We saw these guys this time," I started. "Foreign fighters from the al-Nusra Brigade."

No one said anything, so I continued, "Clearly, if we don't step up, a vacuum will form, which these guys will be happy to fill. And in a few years you'll have another Taliban-type state, this time on Europe's doorstep."

That night I met Michael in the lounge area of the Hay-Adams bar. He sat across from me and ordered a double scotch. I drank my usual sparkling water with a lime twist. Not quite the James Bond shaken, not stirred, martini.

"I've spoken at length with Anthony and the others. We're looking at other options," Michael offered.

"What does that mean?" I asked, expecting to be disappointed.

"It means that I'll be in touch soon."

I hoped so, because I knew it would be hard to live with what I'd seen and know that no help was coming to General Sabir and his people. No matter how many hours I spent at the gym or at the beach, the haunting visions of Syria wouldn't disappear.

I didn't have to wait long in bureaucratic terms. Around four weeks later, I got a call from Michael instructing me to meet him at his cabin in Utah. I deleted the message and booked a flight.

There, surrounded by tranquil nature, he laid out the plan: purchase weapons, ship them to the FSA in Syria, and then train the rebels in counterinsurgency warfare and FIBUA (fighting in built-up areas)—a skill I had acquired as a member of the Brit mil in Northern Ireland.

Michael said, "Let me be very clear: there can't be any US footprint on any of this—the weapons, the transfer, the training....Any of it. You understand?"

"Zero footprint," I answered.

"The first step is to secure the weapons," he continued. "I suggest you fly to London and meet with Darren F."

"Darren F.?" I said. "I haven't heard that name in years."

Darren was a former British intelligence official with high contacts in Kurdistan and Iraq. During the height of the Iraq War, he operated as an ad hoc ambassador to the new al-Maliki government. Any foreigner who wanted to open an oil, consulting, or security business in Kurdistan had to go through him. A character straight out of a John le Carré novel, Darren F. was known to other expats as Lawrence of Kurdistan.

"He can help you source the weapons the rebels need," Michael said. "He can also supply you with contacts on the shipping front, because that's going to be complicated. I trust you and Darren will be able to sort it out."

It was a difficult assignment, but one I was happy to take on. I called home to tell Mia I would be delayed for about a week, then caught a flight to Heathrow. She was used to these phone calls by now but didn't like them. Balancing personal life and business had always been difficult for me and was growing harder with the pull of Syria.

From Heathrow, I took a cab directly to the Hilton Hotel on Park Lane, where I would stay for the next few days and confab with Darren F. The quintessential gentleman spy, highly intelligent and fluent in several languages, he'd used his time in the Middle East to broaden his political and business contacts and married into an aristocratic British family.

He informed me that he had a friend with contacts in Kurdistan and Iraq who could help secure the necessary end-user certificates to get the arms into Syria.

I stuck a pin in that aspect of the mission for the time being. First, I needed to secure weapons. The fact that I was shopping for hundreds of AK-47s, AKMs, PKMs, and RPG-7s severely narrowed the list of private suppliers.

Darren F., who traveled in rare, shadowy circles, took me to see an expert—Major General Axton S., former head of British special forces, who now worked as a consultant for various countries on geopolitics and military strategy. His office was in a town house in an affluent section of London. He greeted us wearing a Savile Row suit, spoke with an upper-crust accent, and exuded distinction and intelligence. He was a lot like Darren, only shorter and stiffer.

From all appearances, you'd have thought he was dealing in Rembrandts and Picassos rather than RPGs and AK-47s.

General Axton S. told us there were two sources of the kinds of weapons we needed (weapons that couldn't be traced back to the USG): Bulgaria and Libya. The Libyan stash contained NATO arms the Brits had left behind after the war against strongman Muammar Qaddafi. They were now in the possession of the terrorist group al-Qaeda in the Islamic Maghreb (AQIM).

Figuring the Libyan option would never meet with approval in DC, I decided to pursue the Bulgarian connection.

"Very good," General Axton S. said. "I'll go ahead and arrange a meeting with the individual you need to see in Sofia."

He was referring to the capital of Bulgaria and warned us ahead of time that we would be dealing with sketchy characters. "Keep your wits about you," he warned.

"It sounds like these are people you don't trust," I said.

"I don't. No, Simon. Absolutely not."

Since we would be handling a great deal of money, it was clear that we needed the best wing man we could find—quick witted, quick fisted, and a deadly shooter.

Robbo was still mending, so I called my mate Pete, who was possibly the hardest man I knew, and said, "I need your help, slim. You available?"

"Anything for you, mate. What is it?"

"Not on the phone. There'll be a ticket waiting for you at the Delta Airlines desk at Heathrow."

"Time frame?"

"Now to ENDEX." Exercise termination.

The three of us (Darren, Pete, and myself) flew to Sofia. Though I hadn't set foot in the country before, I had been the victim of one of its business schemes. When Bulgaria joined the European Union (EU) in 2007, I was one of the poor fools who invested in a luxury ski lodge in the Balkan Mountains. Twelve months later I learned that the sizable deposit I had put down on a deluxe three-bedroom ski chalet had vanished when the contracting company ran out of cash.

Despite my earlier experience, I found Sofia to be one of the most charming and affordable cities in Europe, where a night in a four-star hotel cost less than a hundred dollars, and a dinner for two with wine ran about forty dollars. But we weren't there to visit the eighteen-hundred-year-old Roman ruins or the magnificent Eastern Orthodox St. Alexander Nevsky Cathedral. We were in Sofia to see Boris, a former member of the Bulgaria secret police and now a member of a local Mafia, which made its money from drug and sex trafficking, cigarette smuggling, and extortion.

He proposed we get together that night in a bar on the outskirts of town. Knowing that it was never wise to go into a meet blind, Pete and I spent the afternoon recceing the area, taking note of egress points, points of entry, possible ambush sites, and bottlenecks. Once we knew how to get the hell out of there if we needed to, we agreed to sit down.

That evening we entered the smoke-filled dive bar and saw that it was filled with only men—most of whom looked unfriendly and dangerous. A football match played on the TV over the bar.

When I asked the overweight bartender for Boris, he nodded toward a well-dressed man sitting at a table by himself in the corner.

Ruddy-faced Darren and I sat across from him and immediately started to discuss business as Pete perched on a stool by the door keeping an eye on the various characters in the room.

Boris cut a suave figure from head to toe—clearly a man who had done well for himself since entering the "private sector." He spoke English with an accent and had a smooth manner, which only made him seem more ominous. He struck me as someone who was used to getting his way.

General Axton S. had assured me that Boris possessed thousands of AK-47s, PKMs, ammunition, and MANPADS (man-portable air-defense systems) through his contacts in the Eastern Bloc arms trade. Most of the equipment he was selling was left over from the Soviet era. When the wall came down, so did the fences around the various government armories.

I told Boris that we were looking for hundreds of units of each particular weapon.

He confirmed that he could supply them but added, "Your request is not simple, gentlemen. Such a large quantity of arms requires time and money. Lots of money."

"We have money," I offered.

Boris sized me up. He said, "I will need to see proof of funds. You understand, of course?"

"Of course. And we would need to see proof of consignment," I replied. "Specifically a case of each item so we can test the quality."

"Yes." He glanced across the room to three burly men sitting at a table sipping bottles of beer. "Tomorrow my man will contact you with a time and place. You will bring the money, and I will bring proof of consignment."

He wanted $50,000 up front and another $150,000 once he had assembled all the arms.

It was a lot of cash to carry around, but doable given the agency contacts Darren had in-country.

None of us trusted the man we now referred to as "Boris the sneaky fucking Bulgarian." So once again Pete and I recced the meeting site, then discussed an actions-on plan if things went south.

I said, "Pete, you'll be our eyes on. You enter the street about ten minutes before, walk it through, and give us a sitrep. If the atmospherics are off, we pop smoke and bail."

Pointing to an intersection on the map, I added, "Exfil the street and we'll pick you up at RV Alpha."

"If we ditch to the airport, what do we do with the toys, comms, and cash?" Pete asked.

"We leave the car at the airport. General Axton S.'s people will collect it later and sterilize the car."

*   *   *

The following day, the three of us pulled into the street where we were scheduled to meet. We sat at the entrance awhile, taking in the surroundings. Then Pete deployed, and we proceeded a little farther while he recced the street.

From halfway down the block, Pete spotted Boris standing with several suspicious characters in long overcoats at the end of the road, our only point of exit. Sensing that bad news waited ahead, Pete stopped and appeared to look in a shopwindow. What he was really doing was using the reflection in the glass to scan the street for further threats.

He found them.

"Simon, Pete," I heard in my earpiece.

"Send, mate."

"I've got three pax and Boris at the end of block and two old bills with tattoos on their heads heading toward me. Over."

I shared a look with Darren, who didn't appear his usual chipper self.

"Enough of this nonsense," Darren groaned. "Pick him up. This isn't going to turn out well."

I agreed that we were about to be royally set up and radioed Pete to meet us at the rendezvous spot. As I spoke, the two nasty-looking dudes with the shaved, tattooed heads crossed the street and started closing in on him.

I shifted the car into reverse while Pete bent down as if to tie his shoe. One of the Bulgarians who was now standing over him produced a pistol. Pete, who was not a man to fuck with, came up abruptly and slammed the tattooed man in the throat. As the Bulgarian fell backward, Pete used his handgun to pump two rounds into the second man's legs.

From our position at the rendezvous spot, I heard shots, then saw Pete tearing around the corner. Breathless and eyes popping out of his skull, he got in and we took off, back to the safe house, where we returned the money to our contact.

An hour or so later, we were on our way to London. From London, I flew to Washington and reported to Michael.

I said, "Option one is not going to work. What do you want to do now?"

CHAPTER FIFTEEN

LIBYA

I **RETURNED** to California with General Sabir and his fighters in my thoughts. Throughout the first months of 2012, I watched the carnage in Syria on TV with a heavy heart. Each week civilian casualties mounted, and more refugees poured into Kurdistan and Turkey, while the United States and its allies stood by and did nothing.

My frustration grew week by week. Whatever I tried to lose myself in—paddle surfing, going to the movies with my girlfriend, working out in the gym—the images of the dead women and children flashed in my head. I'd awake some nights in a sweat from nightmares of bombed hospitals and schools.

On a Tuesday morning I was sitting in Olivia's judo class watching her and the other nine-year-olds practice throws when I got an e-mail from Michael S. saying "Check your e-mail" and referring me to the Hotmail account I had created specifically for this purpose. I opened it and read "Option 2 is good." Then quickly pressed Delete.

*　　　*　　　*

Again I traveled to Utah to meet with Michael, who now told me we were going to deal with groups connected with AQIM, which surprised me. I pointed out that a year ago I had been fighting a lot of the same jihadists in Iraq. He didn't like dealing with these groups any more than I did, he said, but after what had gone down with Boris the Bulgarian there were no other options.

Given the extreme sensitivity of the operation, a zero footprint was again required.

My first question: "Are you sure they will sell the weapons to us?"

"Yes," Michael answered. "They're willing to do business with us because their friends in the al-Nusra Brigade are some of the FSA's best fighters, and they and other anti-Assad groups are working together toward the same goal."

I wasn't sure how I felt about that.

"This can be a win-win for us," Michael S. said enthusiastically. "We get the MANPADS, Stingers, and other weapons out of the hands of those fuckers in Libya, and help the FSA."

Frankly, I had big reservations about cooperating with known terrorists. But they were trumped by my desire to help General Sabir and the FSA.

The plan called for me to go to Benghazi, Libya, secure a base of operations under the name of a private company, start negotiating and buying weapons, and ship them to Kurdistan for transport into Syria. This was all unexplored territory to someone like myself, who had previously served almost exclusively as boots on the ground.

Obviously, I was going to need help putting this together. So the following day I flew to London. Minutes after I landed at Heathrow, I received a text from Darren F.: "Contact me on the other means when you reach your final destination."

Lovable rogue that he was, Darren sometimes got a little too caught up in the cloak-and-dagger stuff. What he meant by "other means" and "final destination," I had no idea. I checked into a boutique hotel in Knightsbridge, confident that he would contact me before too long with more specifics.

I wasn't in my room twenty minutes when the phone rang. Darren had found me—of course. He asked to meet in the swanky Caramel Room downstairs for afternoon tea, known as Prêt-à-Portea, with cakes and pastries decorated to look like the latest fashion designs.

It was a real odd place to discuss arms deals, but intimate and private, and anyone looking out of place would be easy to spot.

Darren breezed in like someone off the pages of a spy thriller, suited, Tory tied, and with a mischievous grin on his face. As we sipped tea, we caught up about what we'd both been up to since we'd seen each other last and old colleagues and friends. Darren sprinkled casual talk so liberally with acronyms that it was hard to follow what he was saying. No doubt this was by design. He also had the unpleasant habit of constantly glancing over his shoulder.

One thing I did make out clearly was his suggestion that we "pop over to the club and see Colin."

"Whatever you think is best."

Colin, I assumed, was his friend Colin A., a former British special forces operator who maintained close connections to the ruling Barzani clan of Kurdistan.

Darren and I finished our tea and then hailed a cab to the notorious Berkeley Club. After checking in at the security desk, we made our way to the first-floor dining room, where a waiter escorted us over to Colin, who was sitting by the window eating a piece of Dover sole. He was a likable rogue of about sixty—well dressed and well spoken. I was starting to get the impression that these were the gents who really ran the world.

Without wasting time on banalities, Colin laid out a plan and made it sound as easy and pleasant as an afternoon stroll. I would fly to Northern Iraq and open a joint-venture security company with a local, trusted company called Amada Bash. Amada Bash would then obtain a security contract with an oil company working in Kurdistan. This would be easy enough, Colin explained, because the oil company issuing the contract would be one of his subsidiaries.

Once that was done, I would staff my new company with several hundred Peshmerga troops under the command of former general Ibrahim Sameer Anwar, a close associate of the ruling Barzani clan and top officials in the Ministry of Interior (MOI). Conveniently, the MOI was charged with vetting and licensing foreign security companies and their operations in the region. In the general's employ was a young man named Asso Anwar, who happened to be the son of Kurdistan's director of special security—their version of the CIA. Colin suggested that I hire him as my assistant to avoid problems and red tape.

"After that, it's rather simple," he explained. "All you have to do is obtain a firearms license for your company and import the weapons and equipment under the legally obtained end-user certificate."

What we wouldn't be telling anyone, of course, was that once we got the weapons into Kurdistan, we were going to load them on flatbed trucks and drive them across the border into Syria.

"What about the border guards when we reach Syria?" I asked.

"Two things that work best in the region, Simon, are cash and family," Darren answered. "One or the other, and everything is doable. You have both and, well now, you're really in business."

"He's perfectly right," Colin added as he polished off a glass of Bordeaux.

My head was swimming. I'd never attempted anything like this before. As simple as it sounded in the plush luxury of a London club, I suspected it would be quite different on the ground.

Darren brushed off my skepticism with the wave of his hand. "Don't worry, old boy, we've done this a thousand times."

We left Colin with his brandy and shot across town to Mayfair to visit again with General Axton S., who, in addition to his expertise in where to secure private stocks of munitions, was also very knowledgeable about North Africa, specifically Libya, and the art of moving questionable goods across borders and through checkpoints.

Axton S. listened to my plan with great interest. His questions were analytical and thorough: Who would be involved? When were we planning to do this? Where would we deliver the arms to in Syria? What were we hoping to achieve?

As Darren and I chirped on for more than an hour, General Axton S. steepled his fingers and stared hard across the table, deep in thought. I had the feeling that he was already putting a plan together. At least, I hoped so.

At the end, Darren popped off to his next meeting, no doubt at another club with an evening cocktail, and I hailed a cab back to my hotel. As I sat in the backseat, my mind kept drifting back to the meeting at the Berkeley Club. I wondered about the guests at the other tables and if their conversations had been similar to ours. And I asked myself if the general public had any idea how much of the world's governance and future was decided by sixty-year-old former military men and businessmen in handmade suits over a bottle of wine and plate of Dover sole.

I had just reached my room when Michael S. called from DC to say that he and the other members of the Syrian Support Group had recently been in touch with Ryan—the freelance photographer I'd run into in Syria. Ryan had just returned from another trip to the war zone and claimed to have more photographic evidence of the Assad regime's use of chemical weapons. Michael asked if I could meet with him, look through the photos, and purchase any that I thought relevant.

Jet-lagged and exhausted, I returned to the elegant chocolate-colored Caramel Room, sat with Ryan, and scrolled through photos on his laptop. Bracing, horrible images flashed before my eyes. I was so tired at this point that their human implications didn't fully register. Besides, the project to arm the rebels had already been green-lit, so I didn't see why they were needed. Still, I bought four of them at two thousand dollars a pop.

The next day, I was back on the plane to California for a week of lounging, gym, hanging with my girlfriend, Mia, and her daughter, Olivia, and pretending I was a normal person with a regular life. In the meantime, Michael and Ted (who had entered the picture) were working with accountants and lawyers to revive a UK-based security company I had set up years ago called Sion Resources. Somehow (and I didn't ask how) they were able to generate three years of accounts so the company could pass muster at the tax office.

Once that was taken care of, I opened a branch company in California that was 51 percent owned by Sion Resources in London and 49 percent owned by a US national named Craig P. Then Sion Resources started to funnel money into Sion Resources LLC's US bank account—conveniently established at the HSBC branch in Van Nuys—and Craig and I started to purchase office equipment, including computers and desks that would never be used. Their sole purpose was to show that Sion Resources LLC was a legitimate company.

Now I was ready to board a plane with Michael and fly from LA to Paris; Paris to Amman, Jordan; Amman to Erbil. He and I were met at the airport by the young, friendly, and diminutive Asso Anwar, whose father was the chief of police, special projects.

Asso, I learned during the drive to the Rotana Hotel, was well traveled and experienced in wheeling and dealing despite his young age. He spoke excellent English, thanks to five years living in the UK, where he worked as a bus driver and ran a kebab stand. Every summer he would drive via Turkey, Romania, and the Czech Republic into Germany, where he would buy used BMWs. Then he'd return them to Kurdistan and sell the cars at a profit.

Erbil surprised me. Instead of resembling a dirty shithole like Baghdad with broken-up streets and decaying buildings from the seventies, the capital of Kurdistan had the polish and sparkle of a mini-Dubai—a polyglot city of ancient Islamic architecture, modern glass towers, nicely appointed public parks, and paved roads. It was also one of the most ancient cities in the world, founded around 6000 b.c.

The Barzani family had ruled the city and surrounding Iraqi Kurdistan region since the fall of the Ottoman Empire. Masoud Barzani was the current president and leader of the ruling Kurdistan Democratic Party and the government of Kurdistan, which had operated as an autonomous entity within Iraq since 1992. It was home to the world's sixth-largest oil reserve, which accounted for its wealth and the West's interest.

The new, modern Rotana Hotel featured the amenities that appeal to discreet business travelers—spacious, comfortable, clean rooms, attentive service, and excellent food. I wasn't there for the spa treatments. Instead, Michael and I spent the first couple of days driving around Erbil with Asso in a beat-up BMW, familiarizing ourselves with the city.

Asso clearly wanted to be helpful, and everywhere we went people seemed to know him. Out of respect and curiosity, I asked to meet his father.

He quickly arranged a meeting at the Ministry of the Interior. On the appointed day, we were escorted to what looked like a large banquet room. At the far end beside a large desk stood a little man wearing a suit several sizes too big for him, his many assistants lined up along the wall behind him.

"That's my father," Asso whispered proudly as we approached.

"Does he need a pair of binoculars to see people when they enter?" I whispered back.

His father stood, and I shook his hand and thanked him for welcoming us. These small signs of respect were important. I was a visitor in his country, arranging something that I knew was sketchy, and I wanted as few hiccups as possible.

Next I met with General Ibrahim Sameer Anwar, the former Peshmerga officer, who would head our local joint-venture security company. Though retired, he still wore a uniform and drove in a four-car motorcade. He had enemies in some of the rival clans and the emerging ISIS.

General Sameer invited us to dinner. Like Asso's father, he didn't speak a word of English, so the very alert and eager Asso did all the translating.

With General Sameer's okay and Asso's assistance, I began the process of establishing a local company. The first step was to secure a villa to use as headquarters and staff it to look like a fully operational private security company.

Michael S. returned to the luxury of Dubai while I spent the next five days driving around Erbil with Asso and his uncle, who was a real-estate agent, looking for properties. I located one in an affluent section of Allesan Street in close proximity to residences belonging to the security and housing ministers. The owner wanted twenty-five thousand dollars for a six-month lease. With Michael's okay, I leased it for the entire year.

Next, I hired contractors to redecorate the inside and turn it into functioning offices. That required extensive rewiring, moving walls, and repainting. The downstairs was converted into offices, a kitchen, dining room, living room, and a little gym in back. Upstairs accommodated four good-sized bedrooms.

They all had to be furnished and outfitted with desks, chairs, computers, lamps, flat-screen TVs, beds, dressers, et cetera, which I did with the help of Asso, his brother, who owned a truck, and a second young assistant named Harish. Since we were a security company that would ostensibly store weapons, we also needed to build a gun cage in the basement with two padlocks and gun racks, all according to MOI regulations.

Soon after work commenced on the gun cage, I heard a tremendous racket of metal saws and sledgehammers from the basement. Twenty minutes later, Asso came running into my office looking distressed.

"Mr. Chase," he announced breathlessly, "there's a problem. The Asayish is here. Someone on the street heard all the noise and called them."

The Asayish were the universally feared secret police. Since my arrival in Erbil, I had heard numerous stories about them picking up people who were never heard from again.

I asked, "Asso, do you know these guys?"

"No," he answered, nervously.

"Tell them I'll be down in twenty minutes."

I called Michael in Dubai, who had given the go ahead to build the gun cage and, I assumed, had secured the proper permits and permissions.

With the Asayish waiting downstairs, I said, "You told me you had all this squared away. What should I do now?"

"You're a big boy, Simon," Michael answered. "Sort it out."

I wanted to reach through the line and wring him by the neck. Instead, I put on my friendliest smile and went down to the kitchen to face the Asayish. They looked grim and unhappy.

"How can I help you, gentlemen?" I asked.

Several of them pointed at me and started talking harshly to Asso at the same time. They were speaking in Kurmanji—a variation of Persian—which I didn't understand.

"What are they saying?" I asked Asso.

"They're saying that you're building an illegal gun cage, which means that you have automatic weapons. They want to know where the weapons are. They say they're going to have to take you in."

I took a deep breath. No way was I going to let myself get carted off by these fellows. "Tell them that we'll stop working. There will be no gun cage. Get them out of here, Asso, then call your dad."

The Asayish promised to return in three hours. If the cage or any of the construction equipment was still here when they got back, I would be arrested.

While the contractors carted the stuff off, Asso called his father, who told the Asayish that I was a friend. We were allowed to build our gun cage. Problem solved.

The following afternoon, Asso entered my office and said, "This isn't a proper security company, Mr. Chase, because you're not hiring anyone."

At the time we were paying him five thousand dollars a month, which was a lot of money in Erbil. Although he had proven himself completely trustworthy and indispensable, I still hadn't told him the real reason we were establishing the company.

It was the moment of truth. Asso could easily have had me thrown out of the country if he wanted to. I explained the real purpose of the company, which was to smuggle arms to the Syrian rebels.

I said, "I know I've put you in a difficult position, but I couldn't help it. If you want more money, I'll get it for you."

He said, "No, Mr. Chase. Unlike most Westerners who come here to do business, you've treated me with respect. I support what you're doing and will help you in any way I can."

One of my principal concerns was my own security in an increasingly unstable Erbil. In recent weeks, there had been a marked uptick in attacks on Westerners. Hoping to buy a handgun I could keep in the villa for self-protection, I turned again to Asso. He told me that our other young assistant, Harish, knew a gun shop in town.

The next day, the three of us piled into the used BMW I had purchased from Asso to serve as our company car. With Harish at the wheel, we passed through the center of town and entered the outskirts.

"Where are we going, Harish?"

"Gun shop, Mr. Chase. Right ahead."

From the outskirts, he continued on a narrow road that led into the hills. I was starting to get nervous, because it was hard to imagine a gun shop anywhere nearby.

"How much farther?" I asked. "Where the fuck are we?"

"Very close now, Mr. Chase. Almost there."

The car climbed over a small redoubt and circled around a hill into a craterlike valley that contained a field of at least a hundred tents.

"Gun shop!" Harish said, smiling.

It was more like a giant gun bazaar in the middle of nowhere and seemed to be filled with militiamen mujahideen—members of ISIS, no doubt—stocking up on ammo and weapons. The makeshift parking lot was packed with banged-up HiLuxes and SUVs perforated with bullet holes. I tried to keep a low profile as we walked in but got lots of dirty looks.

"Asso, let's get this over with fast."

"Yes. Yes."

Harish led us to one of the blue tents, where a bearded man stood before a table that contained a hodge-podge of AKs and other automatic rifles. The two of them started chirping away. Meanwhile, guys with long beards started elbowing one another and pointing at me as the only Westerner at the bazaar.

"Let's speed this up, Asso," I whispered. "Tell him I want to buy two new Glocks and some ammunition."

The vendor nodded, went out the back, and returned with two plastic cases. I popped one open and studied the Glock inside. It was covered with grease.

"New?" I asked.

The vendor nodded.

"How much?"

"Three thousand dollars each."

It was a hell of a lot of money. Back in LA I could buy a new Glock on the black market for three hundred dollars. A new one purchased from a legitimate gun store would retail for twice that.

I racked back the top slide and heard a rasping sound. Turning to

Harish, I said, "Tell him this isn't new. That sound you just heard is sand and other shit caught in the top slide and barrel."

Harish translated, and the vendor threw up his hands, hurried out the back of the tent, and returned with two other cases. The Glocks this time were new and in good working condition. I counted out the money, grabbed the Glocks and ammo, and quickly returned to our BMW.

On the ride back to Erbil, I called Michael on my cell to tell him that I'd purchased the handguns.

"Good," he said. "But I hope you made sure to get a printed receipt, because we need records of everything."

"Michael, to get a printed receipt, the place would have to have a cash register and electricity. This place didn't even have proper walls. It was a fucking tent in the desert."

This time he laughed.

With the gun cage completed, we were ready to receive the MOI inspectors. They arrived one day and checked to make sure everything was connected and in working order—the phones, computers, e-mail, fax. Then they examined all our paperwork, including prospective contracts.

Finally, after two months of scurrying about, we had an official government-approved security company. Now we had to test whether our plan to smuggle guns—which we would obtain from AQIM in Libya—across the border into Syria would work. Asso and I met with General Sameer to discuss the plan. He outlined two routes into Syria. The first one went west into Mosul, then crossed into Syria at Tel Kotchek. The second one took you through Baskoy into Turkey and onto the D400 highway to Kilis, which was only fifty miles north of Aleppo. The second route required traveling through three countries but spent a much shorter time in Syria.

I wanted to test the primary route. But General Sameer, who knew the guards at the borders and was in charge of the transport, chose the second. Asso, Harish, and I made another trip to the arms bazaar, bought a crate of twenty AK-47s and a crate of ammo, and handed them over to General Sameer. His men packed them into a battered minivan, assigned his cousin as the driver, gave him two Peshmerga guards, and they were off.

I didn't hear anything for a week. Done with my work in Erbil for the time being, I returned to DC, where I checked with Asso several times a day.

"Where are they? What have they encountered?" I asked.

"I haven't heard anything."

It was frustrating. Normally, if I ran a team of former US or UK mil guys, I'd receive sitreps every hour. They'd tell me about all the obstacles—IEDs, recalcitrant guards, bribes that had to be paid, and resistance they encountered in Syria. But the locals were handling the transfer and wanted to show us they could take care of it. To their minds, everything depended on the will of Allah. If Allah willed it, it would happen. If not, we were out of luck.

I was back in LA, ferrying Olivia to one of her lessons, when Asso called via Skype on my cell.

"The shipment made it to Aleppo," he said.

"Great news. Did they have any problem with IEDs on the road?"

"I don't know."

"Any problems at any of the border checkpoints?"

"I don't know."

"Any resistance when they reached Syria?"

"I don't know."

"Any explanation as to why it took so long?"

"No."

*   *   *

While I was in Erbil and DC, General Axton S. had traveled to Benghazi to secure a compound there. My next task was to hire a team to manage the purchase of weapons from a Libyan militia group. I called on cage fighter and best mate Pete; Revis, or Salvador Slim (a Salvadorian-born ex–Navy SEAL); Matt "Cowboy" Marshall and Cory Aimes (both former US Marine scouts); Reilly (ex–Brit mil and father of two); Scottish John; Moxie (a former Royal Engineer who spoke fluent Arabic); and Craig "Underpants" Underwood (a laugh-a-minute practical joker who doted on his boy back home).

Reilly, the oldest of the crew at forty-two, was referred to by guys in the trade as "Operator as Fuck," because he was experienced as fuck—always prepared and totally unflappable. Cowboy, at the other extreme, was a deadly funny biker from Tennessee and very highly strung.

Robbo, who was in the last stages of recovery from his gunshot wound in Aleppo, would join us shortly, against doctor's orders.

It was a strong team, and I'd worked with them all before. We met at a Lebanese café on King's Road, where I laid everything out.

The boys had the usual questions. How are we getting paid? What's the insurance cover? Will we be covered under the DBA (Defense Billing Act)?

This was always a practical concern. Operators wanted to know that, if they were injured or disabled on the job, they or their families would receive medical coverage and disability payments.

The answer was that even though this was a "deniable job," it did fall under the DBA. So it wasn't really deniable. We filled out the appropriate paperwork and waited two weeks for our visas to be approved.

Then we flew to Tripoli on a Commonwealth Airlines flight with our basic kits and plate carriers. Next day we went to the US embassy compound where we equipped ourselves with the M4s, two belt-fed M249s, Glocks, ammo, and med bags that were always our bread and butter.

The next morning, we boarded an unmarked jet for Benghazi, where three local nationals driving two armored SUVs and a HiLux met us. They introduced themselves as Tayah, Ahmed (who we called Fatty), and Jamal. Tayah became my terp-driver. Fatty Ahmed also spoke fluent English and was a total character, always outfitted in PT gear and talking about his recent very rigorous workout, even though he looked as though he'd never seen the inside of a gym.

They drove us to the compound that had been leased to the tune of eleven thousand dollars a month by General Axton S. from a local businessman who was now residing in London. We turned off one of the ring roads into a gated seven-bedroom house on the northeast edge of the city, five minutes from the very large and ancient Atiq Mosque. It was furnished like a luxury hotel and came with two chefs and three maids.

Nice digs, which we now secured and kitted out for our purposes. First, we hired contractors to build two towers in each corner of the front wall and manned them 24/7 with local guards hired by Aegis. Then we equipped the SUVs and HiLux with tracking devices programmed to FalconView. On the wall of the ops room on the first floor we secured three flat-screens connected to computers to track the vehicles wherever they went. We also set up UHF and VHF radios and a sat phone.

In order to accommodate rotating team members in what we assumed would be an ongoing operation, we purchased two CHUs and had them stacked on top of each other along the side of the main house. Moxie, as chief engineer, welded a little gate around them and set a ladder up to the second CHU, and from the top of the higher CHU to the roof of the main villa. That way if we were bumped in the middle of the night, we could escape to the main roof and pull up the ladders.

Underpants asked the important question: "What happens when we're all trapped on the villa roof?"

"Fight the enemy off the best we can and hope to get rescued."

Benghazi, we learned, was a notoriously unstable city with no effective central government, policed by a coalition of militia units loosely cobbled into a single force known as the February 17 Martyrs Brigade. More Arab in ethnic makeup than the Libyan capital Tripoli, Benghazi boasted 650,000 people living in a verdant crescent along the Mediterranean coast. The Ancient Greeks, who founded the colony called Euesperides in 525 b.c., attributed the lushness of the area to fertility and the mythological gardens of Hesperides.

As with other beautiful things and places, it had been long fought over by the Spartans, Carthaginians, Romans, and Ottomans. Italy invaded the city in 1911 and made it a colony. After being overrun by the Germans and British in World War II, it was rebuilt as a gleaming showpiece of modern Libya, paid for with its newfound oil wealth. In February 2011, Benghazi was rocked by anti–Colonel Qaddafi protests that marked the beginning of the Libyan Civil War. It was the first city to fall to the rebels and had remained a rebel militia stronghold since, reluctant to fold easily into the new national government.

Against this backdrop of violence, beauty, and disorder, my mates and I set up shop and got ready to do business with a very unlikely client—Ayid Ghali, leader of the local militia group Ansar al-Sharia, which was part of al-Qaeda in the Islamic Maghreb.

CHAPTER SIXTEEN

BENGHAZI

WITH OUR Benghazi compound up and running, we were ready to launch the arms-purchase part of the operation. I called Michael S., who arranged a meeting with local Ansar al-Sharia leader Ayid Ghali. Ansar al-Sharia translated into English meant "partisans of Islamic Law." Their spiritual leader Mohamed al-Zahawi advocated the implementation of strict Sharia law across Libya. Our role was to serve as the tactical team tasked with making sure that the purchase and transfers of weapons from these Islamic radicals and AQIM supporters went smoothly. It was a tall order given the fact that we would be doing business with guys who openly hated Westerners.

Ayid Ghali controlled a large stash of UK and US weapons that had been left behind after the Libyan Civil War—a mixture of M4s, RPKs, AK-47s, RPGs, and MANPADS. MANPADS were shoulder-launched surface-to-air missiles capable of shooting down low-flying aircraft and helicopters—not the kind of weapons you want in the hands of terrorists. Which was why other contracting teams in

Benghazi, like Aegis, were working to get them out of the hands of the various militia groups in the area—particularly those allied with al-Qaeda.

Aegis was one of at least nine private contractors operating in and around the area. Others doing projects for the US and UK governments included Hart, BSL, Control Risks, Blue Mountain, Janusian, and Secure Risks. Some, like Blue Mountain, were tasked with supplying local security guards to various US and UK compounds, including that of the US Diplomatic Mission. Others were doing tribal liaison and recon work. It was all very shadowy and need to know.

The picture on the militia side of the security situation was even more complex and volatile. There were remnants of Qaddafi's Libyan army, which still operated under the leadership of generals like Khalifa Haftar, the Libyan Revolutionary Operation team (another offshoot of Qaddafi's army), National Security Directorate forces, al-Saiqa Forces, the Anti-Crime Unit of the Ministry of Interior, the Petroleum Facilities Guard, the Libya Shield, al-Aqsa Martyrs Brigade, al-Zintan Brigade, al-Sawi, Ansar al-Sharia Brigade, and the February 17 Martyrs Brigade—which was the largest and more or less controlled Benghazi.

The various groups sometimes cooperated, sometimes battled, and sometimes overlapped. Loyalties shifted as quickly and easily as the desert sand. And a lot of why they did what they did had to do with family connections.

One hot hazy morning the ten of us sat in our compound on Ah-Medash Sharid Street and held a brief. Our destination today was Ghali's main compound, approximately fifty miles northeast of the city. What we'd find there was unknown.

First, we had to go to Benina Airport to fetch our US liaison and the cash. We set out in four armored SUVs, armed and alert. We passed ramshackle strip malls, heavily guarded gated compounds, fabric stores, and roadside stands selling tomatoes and oranges. Guarding the front gate of the airport were militiamen from the Libya Shield and February 17 Martyrs Brigade. Salvador Slim and Cowboy got out to keep them company and make sure we weren't ambushed. Large amounts of US dollars in a lawless setting tend to bring out the worst in armed men.

The other two vehicles rolled past the modest mustard-colored terminal building, which had somehow escaped unscathed from the recent fighting, past a row of black-and-white cabs, and onto the tarmac, where we checked our comms and waited. Five minutes later, I heard the roar of a jet engine and looked up to see a Gulfstream III do a loop in the sky and level out for landing.

My nerves started to spike, as the Gulfstream rolled in front of us and idled. The forward ladder extracted, and the pilot came down with a "Howdy, gents" and a big smile. His copilot, who looked like a local, followed and continued to the tail of the plane, where he dropped the lower hatch and hauled out four large black duffels.

Pete and Scots John hurried over to load them into the SUVs while I greeted our liaison Kevin, a young, clean-cut guy wearing a blazer, chinos, blue shirt, club tie, and desert boots.

Together we retreated to the little VIP lounge in the terminal, where I gave him a quick safety brief and tried to put his nerves at ease. I don't think I succeeded. The look on his face said he was convinced we were going to be bumped by al-Sharia, tortured, and beheaded. He told me this would be a cash drop to try to establish trust, and we wouldn't be taking away weapons.

"Good, mate. All good."

He slid into the lead SUV with me, Fatty Ahmed, and Scots John, and we were off, pushing northeast at a good clip over a paved two-lane highway. The land around us had been baked brown like flat Middle Eastern bread. We passed the odd bongo truck, local bus stuffed with passengers, and produce stand. Approximately thirty minutes later we arrived in al-Marj without incident—a dusty little town made up of a half-dozen streets.

The compound itself was on a dirt track off the main road. We stopped twenty meters from the main gate and had a look around. The area seemed tame—children playing, women walking with bags of goods. No signs of imminent danger.

Our vehicles crept forward. Six guys in olive-drab uniforms emerged from the front gate clutching radios and holding up their arms. They circled our vehicles and peered inside. Then one of them reported to someone inside, the gate opened fully, and we were told to enter.

We rolled into thirty meters of open space, got out, and did a five-and-twenty check—a 360 look-around at five meters, and another 360 at twenty. There were lots of militiamen milling about. I counted over sixty. If they planned to jump us and take the money, it would be over fast.

Parked to one side of the compound along the wall were several military jeeps and an armored personnel carrier. None of the shabby HiLuxes with .50 cals welded in back. This was proper military equipment. We also saw two Russian-made DShKM antiaircraft guns.

The militiamen carried new AKs and M4s, wore proper uniforms, and looked like a disciplined military unit. I updated Robbo (who had joined us by now) in the ops room at Zero Alpha (our villa) every five minutes. If anything went south, he knew to alert the other security teams in Benghazi to organize a QRF. Robbo also kept Andy Edwards (a former signals regiment lad we'd brought in to set up our comms in Erbil) up to speed, so both teams knew what was going on.

Except for a little shoving and posturing from the militiamen, everything at the al-Marj compound seemed copacetic. Still, we were twitchy as we unloaded the duffels and waited. A short guy with beady eyes dressed in a nice shirt and pants came out with four guards and greeted us. He said his name was Gassan.

He turned and gestured for us to follow—Kevin, me, Scots John, Fatty Ahmed, and Pete, in that order. We'd chosen Ahmed over the other terps for this visit, because he was from a tribe that was related to Ghali's, which we hoped would work in our favor. Scots John stood six foot two, had the chiseled torso of a CrossFit fanatic, and was very quiet and at one with himself—the kind of Zen-calm, capable operator I wanted by my side at a time like this.

The rest of the guys waited by the vehicles to make sure they weren't interfered with. Last thing we wanted was a militiaman planting a bomb in one and the whole lot of 'em going up *Casino*-style when we fired the ignition.

Trying to appear unruffled, we followed Gassan past some outer buildings to the back of the main villa, passing more militiamen lounging about and drinking tea. They seemed more relaxed the closer we got to the front door, which was big, wooden, and ornate.

We entered an elegant foyer with carpets on a white marble floor. The walls had also been painted white and decorated with blue filigree. Gassan nodded and walked off. We waited silently with the guards while Kevin smiled nervously and pulled at his shirt collar.

Gassan returned five minutes later and escorted us to the back of the house and into what looked like a boardroom, with a big wooden twelve-seat table sitting at the center of the marble floor. A short, thickly built man wearing a gray suit with an open blue shirt stepped forward to greet us.

Al-Ghali looked more like a businessman than a wild-eyed insurgent—late thirties, round face, clear, intelligent eyes, short beard, well groomed. He was cordial, spoke perfect English, and seemed like a guy who had been living the good life. So far, so good.

"I'm al-Ghali," he said in a deep voice. "Welcome."

He gestured to dishes of olives and dates and cups of tea on the table. I felt that if he got a call from his superiors to cut our heads off, he happily would. But today he was acting like a cool-headed, reasonable businessman, which was good, but somewhat unsettling.

I introduced myself and then presented my associates: "This is Kevin, and these are my associates Pete and John."

Ghali showed us places at the table. As soon as we sat, Kevin explained that he had brought the funds that had been negotiated through back channels. I knew nothing about how that had worked, as the whole operation ran on a need-to-know basis. Fine with me.

This was the cue for me to text Cowboy, who arrived a few minutes later with Pete carrying the duffels. They set them on the floor and left. Neither Ghali nor Gassan got up to look inside them or count the cash. It was their way of acknowledging that they trusted us.

We started to discuss the structure of how things would work. Basically, when we were ready to receive a shipment of weapons, we would notify Gassan and tell him what we needed. He would then tell us where to meet him and how much the shipment would cost. Then Kevin or his associate Samuel would fly in with the funds.

Small shipments we'd pick up ourselves and drive to a private airstrip at the main airport. From there they would be flown to Erbil.

It was straightforward, really, and odd as fuck. We were dealing with an avowed enemy, and yet I had a feeling we could trust him. Talk about strange bedfellows.

As we climbed back into the SUVs, Robbo asked, "How did it go?"

"It went well, mate. It was easy, wasn't it, Kevin?"

"I wish everything in life were that simple," he answered, wiping the sweat off his brow.

As we drove away, I had a sick feeling in the pit of my stomach. This was going to be a really awkward, dangerous dance, with enemies acting like friends until one of them objected to the music, and the knives came out. I tried to tuck that image in a faraway corner of my mind, but it kept drifting back to the surface.

In the morning, we did a quick safety check and popped Kevin over to the airport for a flight to London. Back at Zero Alpha, we waited for the order from Michael S. and Ted. It came three days later—300 rifles, 7.52 ammo, and as many MANPADS as Ghali was willing to sell. Fatty Ahmed in his workout rig acted as the go-between, and a day later we rolled out to al-Marj again in three SUVs and two local bongo trucks that we had hired for the day.

Ghali wasn't there to greet us this time. Instead, we dealt with Gassan, who was super friendly. Actually, we were the ones who behaved a little standoffish, more out of discomfort than anything else. The crates sat waiting. We didn't open them or count the weapons inside as a gesture of mutual trust.

The jihadists were so accommodating that they provided an armed escort to the airport, which came in handy when we reached the security gate. Because Ghali's guys knew the militiamen who were manning it, there were no inspections of our cargo or bribes paid. The barrier was raised, and we were waved through.

We peeled right around the terminal to a Russian-made Antonov

An-70 medium-range transport plane, which was idling on the runway. A former US Air Force pilot named Greg greeted us and lowered the back cargo bay. There was no forklift available, so Ghali's fighters helped us load the weapons inside in the blazing afternoon heat.

As soon as the wheels on the Antonov went up, I telephoned our ops room in Erbil. One of the three ex-mil guys I had hired to man it answered right away.

I said, "Andy, wheels up. ETA nineteen twenty hours."

"Message received. We'll be there to meet it."

I returned to the villa, where I handed over command to Robbo, then packed my bag. Early the next morning, I left with Pete on a commercial Emirates Airlines flight that took me to Khartoum. There we boarded an Egypt Airlines flight to Cairo, and from Cairo we caught another flight to Erbil.

Thirty-six hours later, I greeted Asso and Andy in the terminal. They informed me that the weapons had already arrived and been taken to General Sameer's compound, where they were counted, inspected, loaded on flatbed trucks, and shipped across the border into Syria.

"They're there already?" I asked, surprised.

"That's correct," Andy answered, explaining that comms with Dana in Syria were complicated because they had to depend on Skype.

"You don't have radio comms up and running?"

"Not yet," he answered. "Also, the arms didn't go to Aleppo; they went to al-Hasakah instead."

"Why's that?"

"Dana says the rebels have been pushed into the outer suburb of Aleppo and don't have a stronghold anymore. Al-Hasakah seemed like a better bet. It's in the northeastern part of Syria, very close to the border, and controlled by al-Nusra."

I was a bit pissed off. "Why didn't you wait for me? I wanted to do the first transit myself."

They blamed General Sameer who, they said, was in a hurry to get the weapons across the border. All I could do now was try to catch up. Because we still needed to train the Syrian rebels how to use the weapons.

The next morning I left with Pete and a handful of Sameer's men in two low-profile Nissan sedans and two Toyota SUVs. We set out west on a smooth paved road through rocky, sandy land with patches of green to the town of Gogjali, then continued another five miles to the city of Mosul, which was still in Iraqi Kurdistan and an al-Nusra stronghold. (As I write this, Mosul is controlled by ISIS. Many of the al-Nusra units and commanders I dealt with in 2012 later switched allegiances to ISIS.)

Outside Mosul, we caught the 715 Highway, which took us southwest to Tal Afar, where we stopped to relieve ourselves and stretch our legs. Then we pushed another fifty-five miles to the Syria border. The crossing at the highway was heavily guarded on both sides, so we drove five miles northeast to the crossing at Khwaibyra Road. Here, the border guards were General Sameer's men, so we had no problem getting through.

Once in Syria, we headed west until the road was no longer paved. On either side we saw expanses of dust and dirt—inhospitable territory, to put it mildly, made more forbidding by the danger of being discovered by the odd Syrian air force patrol. The only vehicles we passed were occasional bongo trucks.

After fifty miles of desolate landscape, we reached the town of al-Hasakah and proceeded to the football stadium, which al-Nusra was using as a staging area. The town itself had taken a beating during recent fighting, but most roads were solid and still intact.

General Sabir had set up his headquarters in a collection of five compounds slightly south of the football stadium. That's where the arms were being stored. Waiting to greet me with a smile and embrace was Dana.

"Mr. Chase, welcome," he said. "General Sabir and I cannot thank you enough for everything you have done."

"Thank you, Dana. It's good to see you again. Our work has just begun."

We decamped there and set up a mini-training area where we could teach dry drills, line firing, and small contact drills.

Active fighting was going on all around us; rebel units would turn up at any time, resupply, and go back out into the field to fight. Pete and I would literally put a weapon in their hands, quickly show them how to take it apart, clean it, and use it, then send them out the door.

Throughout April and May of 2012, things were going surprisingly well on the ground in both Libya and Syria. The arms consignments were getting into the hands of the Syrian rebels. Now that they were better trained and armed, General Sabir became immensely hopeful.

While the guys in Libya and Erbil worked on three-weeks-on, one-week-at-home rotation schedules, I continued to bounce back and forth from Benghazi to Erbil to DC to California. Wherever I was, I'd get daily sitreps via Skype from Wyatt, Andy, and Asso in Erbil; Robbo, Reilly, and Pete in Benghazi; and Dana in al-Hasakah.

The only minor hiccup came from DC, where Ted and Michael S. sometimes had trouble getting the money approved in a timely manner. Red-tape hurdles, they explained. To my mind, another example of the men on the ground being more efficient than the more educated suits in DC. Suits and boots.

In early June I was at my home office in Malibu when Robbo called from Zero Alpha to report that the last meeting he'd had with Gassan and Ayid Ghali had been somewhat tense for reasons that weren't readily apparent. We were both aware that homemade bombs had been hurled at the walls of the US compound and the motorcade of UN special envoy Ian Martin in early April. In May a rocket-propelled grenade had struck the Benghazi offices of the International Red Cross. A previously unknown group called Omar Abdul Rahman had taken responsibility, but rumors circulated that both incidents were carried out by Ansar al-Sharia on the orders of AQIM.

Still, we didn't understand what those incidents had to do with our program and how they might have impacted Ayid Ghali. Robbo suggested that I come to Benghazi to meet with him, so I flew to Tripoli and caught an Egypt Air flight to Benina Airport. After a brief with the guys at Alpha One, I set out with Pete, Fatty Ahmed, and Robbo to the compound in al-Marj.

In the conference room at the back of the villa, Ayid Ghali greeted us with the same polite, businesslike reserve. I handed him a laundry list of weapons and told him that the operation was running efficiently. He seemed pleased. I didn't sense any hostility or distrust from him.

But Robbo and some of the guys waiting outside with the vehicles felt that tension was mounting in the compound. They also noted an increase in the number of militiamen present.

I left wondering if Ghali had been growing his forces in the area, and whether or not he had done so for offensive or defensive purposes.

With no more information to work with and no answers, I told the guys back at Zero Alpha to crack on as usual and returned to DC where I met with Michael and Ted. They, too, were concerned about the recent attacks on Western targets and asked about my impression of Ghali.

"He seemed the same," I answered. "My guys are telling me that they feel more tension coming from his militiamen, but Ghali seemed fine."

No sooner did I return to my home office in Malibu, when Robbo called with urgent news from Benghazi. Someone had attacked British ambassador Sir Dominic Asquith's convoy with RPGs and small arms as it drove through the city. The ambassador escaped unscathed, but two of his Brit mil guards were injured. The rumor in town was that Ansar al-Sharia and the Libyan Islamic Fighting Group were responsible.

Alarmed by this event, I returned to Benghazi.

Again, Fatty Ahmed set up a meeting at the al-Marj compound, and I rode out with Pete, Robbo, and Cowboy, feeling quite twitchy and worried I had missed something on my earlier visit. Again, Ayid Ghali sat waiting in the conference room. And once again, when we entered, he rose and greeted us with a smile.

Hoping to extend the positive feeling in the room, I told him that everything was going well and that the weapons were helping the rebels in Syria.

Ghali nodded and said, "I'm sure you are aware of the attacks on your ambassador and the Red Cross."

I looked him steadily in the eye, waiting for what was to come next, and wondered for an instant if we would make it out of the room alive.

Ghali leaned forward and said, "Simon, we have to trust each other one hundred percent if we're going to continue to do business."

"I agree," I said, and pushed a new shopping list across the table.

I didn't probe him further, and he said nothing more. When we got back into our SUVs, Robbo asked, "What the fuck was that all about?"

"I think he was saying that he knew about the attacks and that we can expect them to continue."

"Do you think his guys are behind them?"

"I have no way of knowing."

The boys back at Zero Alpha all agreed that the situation in and around the city was growing increasingly jittery, with truckloads of armed militiamen patrolling the streets. Pete had heard from other contractors that the guys from Janusian had picked up some of Libyan Islamic Fighting Group leader Abu Sufian bin Qumu's men and were questioning them about the recent attacks. Abu Sufian bin Qumu had worked for bin Laden in Afghanistan, was captured by the US and held at the Guantánamo Bay detention camp for six years, and released in 2007. Qumu's men did seem to be likely suspects, but no one was telling us what the other contracting teams in Benghazi were doing, so it was difficult to know what was really going on.

I flew to the US a couple days later in search of answers. Michael S. was in Erbil doing other work with General Sameer that I wasn't privy to. So I met with Ted and asked if he had any intel indicating that Ghali had played a role in the recent attacks, or if any of his relatives or close associates had been taken.

Ted answered, "No, I haven't heard anything about Ghali being involved. All I can tell you is that renditions are going on in Libya and Pakistan, and there have been recent drone strikes in Yemen. Maybe some of this activity has raised a red flag with Ghali."

"It's possible," I said. "All these jihadist groups are connected."

I returned to LA feeling troubled. So troubled, in fact, that I called Michael in Turkey.

He said, "Yes, I understand your concern. We need to talk about that. But not on the phone."

We made arrangements to meet in Istanbul. An hour after I hung up with him and was starting to pack, my laptop pinged. It was Pete calling from Benghazi via Skype. He didn't look happy.

"What's the matter, mate?" I asked.

"Reilly and I just got back from seeing Ghali, and things went very wrong. The atmospherics were off from our arrival."

"What do you mean?"

"There was some pushing and shoving from Ghali's men when we got out of the trucks. Then Gassan showed up to escort us into the villa with a very unfriendly look on his face. When Reilly and I arrived in the conference room, Ghali seemed angry. He said, 'Do you think I'm stupid? Do you think I'm an idiot? You think you can come here and do things in your Western way, and get away with it?'"

"What was he talking about?" I asked.

"We had no idea, at first," Pete answered. "Then he produced a knife and held it to my throat. He started screaming in my face, 'Where is my cousin? You have my cousin! Where is he?'"

"Holy fuck!"

"I was begging for my life, mate. I thought he was about to slice my throat. I kept shouting back, 'I have no idea! I have no idea!' Finally, Ghali backed off, but I've had the shakes ever since."

It sounded horrendous.

"Ghali also told us that the price of everything has now doubled. And he wants to meet with a top US official."

"Hunker down and hold fast. Don't do any more transfers. I'm leaving for Istanbul now to talk to Michael. I'll be in touch."

Reilly asked around town and found out that Ghali's cousin Umar had been taken a day earlier by another contracting group which was questioning him about the recent attacks. I suspected that meant he was being waterboarded.

Filled with anxiety, I flew from LAX to London, and London to Istanbul. I found Michael sipping coffee on the terrace of the elegant Istanbul Bosporus Hotel and quickly filled him in on events in Benghazi over the last couple weeks and the recent meeting with Ghali, Reilly, and Pete.

Michael looked back at me, nonplussed.

I said, "The whole operation is now in jeopardy, Michael. Is there any way you can get Umar released?"

He shook his head. "No. That had nothing to do with me. It's outside my remit."

More bullshit red tape, I thought. Then I told him about Ghali doubling the price of the arms.

Now Michael got annoyed. "What does he need more money for?"

Then he hit me with more ominous news. "Abu Yahya al-Libi, the number two operational leader of al-Qaeda and one of the founders of the Libyan Islamic Fighting Group, was recently killed in a US drone attack in the Mir Ali tribal region of Pakistan."

I had heard that Ghali and Abu Yahya al-Libi were distant relatives. Trying to understand the implications, I asked, "Michael, what the hell's going on? First, contractors working for the US grab and question the same people that we're trying to do business with. Then you take out a Libyan AQ leader who is a relative of Ghali. How is this supposed to work?"

Michael looked deep in thought. We both were.

After a few minutes, he said, "Let me think about this. Get back to Benghazi and keep the projects moving. Keep ordering weapons and keep an eye on Ghali."

I had every intention of going to Benghazi. But there was no way to do surveillance on Ghali without him finding out. So that was off the table. Nor were we likely to continue doing business with him after what had happened with his cousin. I was apprehensive, to say the least, and hoping that somehow the whole project didn't turn to shit.

CHAPTER SEVENTEEN

ATTACK ON THE US SPECIAL MISSION COMPOUND

THE MEETING with Michael S. left my head spinning like a bag of loose bolts. I'd learned there were more private contracting teams in Benghazi than I realized, all performing separate missions. More important, no one had been coordinating the teams' activities. This had resulted in a screwup of epic proportions that put the arms-transfer program in jeopardy, as well as the lives of my men.

Over the course of the last two months we had become friendly with operators on a few of the other contracting teams. Some of us had worked together in the past. We occasionally got together for a beer, and in the deteriorating security situation in Benghazi, we had agreed to back one another up if attacked. But since we all operated on a need-to-know basis, we never asked what the others were doing.

All of us boots on the ground assumed that the suits back in the US who had hired us were making sure that we didn't step on one another's toes. But what made absolute operational sense to us in the field had somehow never dawned on the decision makers in the US, which is why the guys working for another company had grabbed Ghali's cousin and were interrogating him at a time when we were carrying on important arms purchases with Ghali that required a high level of trust.

Filled with anxiety, I started to make my way back to Benghazi. What I didn't realize, and would learn soon after I landed, was that while I was in Istanbul talking to Michael, Ambassador Chris Stevens had flown to Benghazi.

Given Ghali's anger and the fact that his cousin had not been released, the ambassador's trip to Benghazi was obviously ill timed. But, again, no one asked me for my opinion.

Minutes after I arrived back at Zero Alpha on the afternoon of September 11, I brought the guys up to speed. My words were met with a wall of stunned silence. The guys seemed as gobsmacked as I had been.

After several minutes, old-school Reilly turned to me and asked, "How could this happen? I mean, you would think whoever approved the renditions would have said to leave Ghali's guys and relatives alone."

"The point is that they didn't," I answered.

"Well," Reilly continued, "Ambassador Stevens is at the US mission compound now, and the word I'm hearing is that Ghali is not going to meet him."

"How do you know that?" I asked.

"Fatty Ahmed heard it through the rumor mill."

The intel Fatty Ahmed got through his sources tended to be spot-on.

"Guys, does any of this make fucking sense?" I asked.

"It does if the ambassador is being set up," Reilly concluded.

We all looked at one another with alarm. Though we rode Reilly from time to time, we trusted his instincts. He understood tactics and strategy better than anyone I knew.

Robbo had a suggestion. "We need to have a face-to-face with Ghali immediately to sort this shit out."

I looked at my watch. It was almost 1815 local time. The sun was starting to set through the window to my right. The city outside sounded peaceful and quiet. Beyond the roof of a nearby house I saw the stripes of orange and gold reflected off the Mediterranean Sea.

I said, "Pack up, guys. Let's go see Ghali."

Meanwhile, approximately eight miles south and west in the leafy Western Fwayhat neighborhood, Ambassador Stevens was meeting with Turkish consul general Ali Sait Akin, discussing the movement of the AQIM arms through Turkey. They sat in a modern villa (referred to in congressional testimony as "Building C") in the US Special Mission Compound, which was approximately three hundred meters long and one hundred meters wide. It contained a beautiful Mediterranean-style house with a pool, where the ambassador stayed and worked, and three other structures—a smaller residence with bedrooms, a kitchen, and a dining room (Building A); a TOC (Building B) that housed the comms, a bedroom, and security cameras; and a barracks by the front gate that housed the Libyan security guards. Beyond the buildings, an orchard and a vineyard filled out the large, elegant expanse.

Occupying the compound were at least six Americans besides the ambassador: State Department information management officer (IMO) Sean Smith and five Diplomatic Security (DS) agents. Two of them, Scott Wickland and Dave Ubben, had traveled with the ambassador from Tripoli. Bolstering perimeter security were three local militiamen from the February 17 Martyrs Brigade. Five local unarmed guards hired and trained by the Blue Mountain Group manned the front gate and vehicle security barriers. By all accounts, they had no idea what was coming.

Pete, Fatty Ahmed, Reilly, Robbo, Cowboy, and Cory met me in the driveway of our compound, geared up and armed at around 1830. Ex-marine Cory was the youngest and stood six-two.

"Robbo," I said. "I want you, Cowboy, and Cory to stay here and monitor the comms."

Reilly, Pete, Moxie, Fatty Ahmed, and I packed into an SUV and sped out the gate. This wasn't going to be a regular meet, since we weren't dropping off money or picking up weapons. Nor did I have any idea what kind of reception we would get when we reached al-Marj. The best we could hope for was that Ghali and his militiamen would view our showing up as a gesture of good faith.

I planned to tell Ghali the truth—the ops teams in Benghazi were terribly disorganized. One hand didn't know what the other was doing. I would do everything I could to get to the bottom of the situation with his cousin and sort it out.

We set out north past the old prison, walls spray-painted with jihadist graffiti, piles of garbage, and the odd hookah shop. Ahead stood a crossroads that linked the local road to the northern highway. It had always been unobstructed in the past. But tonight as we approached we saw a pile of burning tires blocking the street and armed men standing near two HiLuxes with heavy-duty 762s mounted in back.

"What the fuck is this nonsense?" Pete asked out loud, readying his M4. Even in Benghazi the sight of armed militiamen after dark was cause for alarm.

Fatty Ahmed braked the SUV to a stop and got out. He sauntered back several minutes later to tell us that the guys up ahead were

Ghali's men from Ansar al-Sharia, and they weren't going to let us through.

"Tell them we've been working with Ghali," I said.

"They know that already."

"Then find out what they want."

He went back, smoked a cigarette with the dozen or more jihadists, and returned twenty minutes later. This time Ghali's men backed up one of the HiLuxes so we had room to pass. Once we had put a couple of miles between us, I instructed Fatty Ahmed to pull over and called Zero Alpha to give them a sitrep.

"Anything going on in town?" I asked.

"Nope," Cory answered. "All quiet. Robbo and Cowboy are up on the roof checking the city through binos. They report everything is quiet, too."

At around 1930, Ambassador Stevens ended his meeting with the Turkish consul general and escorted him to the front gate of the US Special Mission Compound in the company of DS agent Scott Wickland. The gravel street outside was empty.

Five more miles north of the prison we ran into another roadblock, which appeared less intimidating than the earlier one—a HiLux parked on the shoulder and five armed militiamen standing in the middle of the road. Again, Fatty Ahmed got out to speak to the men, and they let us pass.

Strange, but we were getting through. Since we'd never seen anything like this before, our anxiety grew. A few minutes later we saw headlights approaching at high speed. Then four flatbed trucks loaded with armed militiamen blew by.

Pete expressed what all of us were feeling: "What the fuck was that?"

I called Zero Alpha and spoke to Cowboy about the trucks loaded with militiamen speeding into town. "Ask Robbo to go on the roof and try to pick them up through the binos and see where they're going."

"Will do, bud."

"Also alert the other teams on Skype."

Skype was our preferred means of communication with the other teams, since it was encrypted and we could leave it open so guys on the teams scattered throughout town could jump on if they had something to report.

We talked our way through a third roadblock in the town of Tocra, then passed two technicals—HiLuxes with .50 cals mounted in back—speeding toward Benghazi, which added to our unease. When we finally entered al-Marj and turned onto the dirt track to Ghali's compound, we ran smack into trouble—a dozen technicals and a large group of militiamen were blocking the gate.

We hadn't seen this many armed men or technicals on any of our prior visits. Fatty Ahmed got out to talk to the militiamen, but they wouldn't let us in. As we sat there waiting and wondering what to do next, I called Zero Alpha to give the men a sitrep.

Cowboy, who had been in contact with the other teams, reported that the city remained quiet, but militiamen had been spotted setting checkpoints in town, particularly in the vicinity of the US Special Mission Compound.

As soon as I hung up, Fatty returned to the SUV and said, "Ghali's men say he isn't here."

"Then where is he?" I asked.

"He's in Benghazi."

A sick feeling hit my stomach, and I imagined an angry Ghali riding in one of the HiLuxes that had blown past. Clearly, he and his men were up to something, and I suspected it wasn't good. I said to Fatty, "Turn around and let's speed back into town."

At approximately the same time, 2140, Ambassador Stevens had retired to his bedroom and was writing in his diary when an explosion blew in the front gate of the US Special Mission Compound. A DS agent sat in the living room of the main house watching a video on TV. IMO Sean Smith was in his bedroom playing the online computer game EVE. Scott Wickland, the ambassador's personal security escort, lounged with two other DS agents outside by the swimming pool. DS agent Alec Henderson was in the TOC doing paperwork. On one of the security cameras above his desk, he saw several dozen men armed with AK-47s and carrying banners swarming through the pedestrian entrance at the main gate.

Some were bearded, some carried walkie-talkies, a few hid their faces behind scarves. Alec Henderson activated the alarm system, which blared a warning siren through the compound, then used his iPhone to alert the nearby CIA annex, approximately a mile away, and the US embassy in Tripoli.

Hearing shots, explosions, and men chanting in Arabic from the front of the compound, the three DS agents sitting by the pool slammed into action. Scott Wickland ran into Villa C to secure the ambassador and IMO Sean Smith while the others hurried to the TOC and cantina to retrieve their gear—which included body armor, helmets, radios, MP4 assault rifles, and extra mags.

As Ansar al-Sharia militants swarmed into the compound firing into the air and chanting *"Allahu akbar,"* the three armed February 17 militiamen and five unarmed Blue Mountain security guards who had been hired to secure the perimeter fled. Meeting with no resistance, the sixty or so attackers surged onto the compound's manicured grounds. Using diesel fuel in five-gallon cans that they found next to the February 17 barracks, they set the barracks and two nearby vehicles on fire.

Inside Villa C, DS agent Scott Wickland instructed Ambassador Stevens and IMO Smith to put on their body armor, then escorted them to the designated safe haven toward the back of the building, where he locked them behind metal gates. Rifle and shotgun at the ready, Wickland took up a defensive position within the safe area with a line of sight to the gate and possible intruders. Then he gave his cell phone to Ambassador Stevens, who began making frantic calls to the US embassy in Tripoli for help.

As we sped southwest toward the city, Robbo's anxious voice came over the comms. "We hear sporadic gunfire in the city. Some of the other teams are reporting smoke coming from the US compound."

"Fuck, no! Have you spoken to the guys at the CIA annex?"

"Wait, I'm getting something from them now. Skype has been going wild. Hold on…" A half minute later he came back. "The GRS [Global Response Staff] team at the annex has confirmed that the US compound is under attack. A mob has gathered outside, and the walls have been breached."

Everything we'd seen and heard earlier—the al-Sharia roadblocks, the technicals loaded with armed men speeding into town—now made horrible sense.

"Should I deploy to the US compound?" Robbo asked.

"No, Robbo. Wait until we get back."

I tried to get hold of Michael S. and Ted on my cell phone, but neither of them answered.

We were blasting south. As we approached the crossroads before the prison, we saw that the roadblock there was more heavily armed than before—with five technicals and more than twenty armed men. Hoping to slip around it, we turned east onto the Fifth Ring Road. No sooner had we swerved onto it than we saw another checkpoint twenty meters ahead. Fatty slammed on the brakes.

A discharge of weapons flashed in front of us. Fifty cals on the back of technicals swung in our direction.

"Contact front!" I shouted as Fatty slammed the SUV into reverse and bullets pounded into the hood and the walls on either side of us.

Fatty executed a J-turn onto a dirt side road, then slid into what seemed like a maze of little streets.

"Wait, Fatty!" I shouted. "Stop!"

Not wanting to get trapped or lost in the rabbit warren, I took a minute to get our bearings, then got Robbo on comms.

He told us that other teams had tried to get through to the US compound, but were stopped at checkpoints by al-Sharia.

Meanwhile, mayhem reigned inside the US compound. As many as sixty militiamen occupied the driveway between Villa C, the cantina, and TOC, firing in the air and shouting jihadist and anti-American slogans as dozens more militiamen and looters swarmed in the gate past the burning February 17 Martyrs Brigade barracks.

At least three very frightened Americans—Ambassador Stevens, DS agent Scott Wickland, and Sean Smith—hid in Villa C. The other four DS agents had barricaded themselves in the cantina and TOC with a number of other DOS employees.

Next, Ansar al-Sharia militiamen used rockets and grenades to blow through the reinforced wooden doors to Villa C. Scott Wickland watched from behind the protective bars inside the safe haven as men with AK-47s plundered the living room. He aimed his MP4 at several of them who approached the metal gate. Instead of trying to blow it open, the attackers doused the Persian rugs, overstuffed chairs, sofas, and pillows in the living room with diesel fuel and set the room on fire.

We blew across the Fifth and Fourth Ring Roads, skirting our way around two more checkpoints, and sped down Lebanon Street to our compound. Cory, Robbo, and Cowboy were crowded in the ops room monitoring developments in the city on laptops. The SERAC compound and CIA annex were closest to the US Special Mission Compound. Jace from SERAC was on Skype bringing us up to speed when we received the first SOS from the TOC in the US Special Mission Compound, which came via the annex, since we didn't have direct comms with the US compound. Why? Because our mission was off the books.

The GRS guys at the annex told us they were organizing a QRF and were determined to push through the roadblocks. I stood grasping my M4 Viper and weighing options in my head. There was no gunfire in our area. If we went to the US compound, we would be making our presence known, which would jeopardize our mission. On the other hand, we couldn't just sit in our compound and do nothing while US lives were in jeopardy. Besides, I had a sickening feeling that Ayid Ghali was behind the attack.

I said, "Fellows, our job is fucking burned! Now that this has gone down, our mission is over. So we're going to lift and shift. Moxie, Cowboy, Underpants…I need you guys to sanitize this place."

That meant burning all sensitive documents and smashing and burning all hard drives. We already had barrels with gasoline set up for that purpose. All the guys had to do was dump everything inside and toss in a thermal grenade.

I turned to my remaining mates and said, "I'm going to try to push through to the US mission. If you want to join me, fine. No one is getting paid for it, so it's completely up to you."

All of them—Robbo, Pete, Reilly, Cory, and Scots John—immediately reached for their weapons and plate carriers. We piled into two SUVs with all our gear, including wallets and passports. It was 2200.

At the US Special Mission Compound, minutes after al-Sharia militiamen had set Villa C on fire, the designated safe area where Scott Wickland, Sean Smith, and Ambassador Chris Stevens were hiding filled with thick black smoke, making it almost impossible to see or breathe. Figuring they would soon be overwhelmed, Wickland instructed the two other Americans to drop to their hands and knees and follow him to a bathroom, which had a barred exterior window. He stuffed wet towels into the gap between the door and the tile floor in an effort to deter the smoke, then opened the window to let in fresh air. But instead of fresh air, smoke from outside poured into the room, impairing visibility and hindering breathing further.

Visibility got so difficult that Wickland lost sight of the two men in the small four-by-six-foot space. Fearing that they would soon be overcome by smoke, he shouted at Ambassador Stevens and Smith to follow him into an adjoining bedroom, which also had bars over the window and an inside latch that would allow them to open the bars and escape. Unable to see them and hearing no reply to his shouts, Wickland banged on the floor to signal his route as gunfire and explosions continued outside.

At roughly the same time, a six-man GRS QRF—including Kris Paronto, Jack Silva, and Ty Woods, all former US mil Tier 1 operators who had been hired to guard the CIA annex—left their compound about a mile away from the US Special Mission.

The situation of the Americans there was growing increasingly more desperate. All the buildings were ablaze. At the cantina, two Tripoli-based DS agents and a Blue Mountain guard had barricaded themselves in a back room and were fighting off attackers who were trying to get in. At the TOC, DS agents Henderson and Ubben frantically shredded sensitive documents and destroyed hard drives as al-Sharia militiamen tried to slam their way through the secure metal door.

In the secure area of Villa C, Scott Wickland, his throat, eyes, and lungs burning from thick smoke, was desperately searching for a way out. Crawling on his belly, he managed to reach the window at the far end of the bedroom and unlatch the security grille. Feeling his strength waning, he climbed out, collapsed on the patio surface, and gasped for breath. He waited for Ambassador Stevens and Sean Smith to follow. When they didn't come, he turned back to the smoke-filled bedroom and called for them. They didn't respond.

We were on the Fourth Ring Road pushing south. I had the guys from SERAC on the radio guiding us and warning us that it would be hard to get through. As we blew past the al-Magrif Street intersection, we ran into our first roadblock.

I saw flashes from the barrels of AKs ahead and shouted, "Incoming!"

Cory, at the wheel, slammed on the brakes and swerved right onto a side road that took us to the Fifth Ring Road, which like the other ring roads looped around the city. The problem was that the US compound was off the Fourth Ring Road, not the Fifth, and the Fifth didn't travel far enough south. So when we reached one of the main thoroughfares into town, Abdun Nasir Street, we hung a right and then a left onto the Fourth Ring Road, where we encountered another roadblock and were hit by more incoming.

Cory veered south onto dirt roads and alleys, steering frantically around piles of rubble and garbage and hoping to avoid another roadblock or al-Sharia patrol. When I called Cowboy to help get our bearings, he told me that we were south of the US compound and needed to turn back.

Cory spun the SUV around and pushed north, cutting across a dirt field onto Tarik Arbu Highway, then onto the Fourth Ring Road. We could hear gunshots and chanting coming from the US Special Mission Compound, and we smelled the heavy stench of smoke.

We managed to cross Shari al-Andalus Street without resistance and then crept across an alley to the back of the US compound. Parked there were two Mercedes G-wagens and two Toyota pickups. Sitting in the Toyotas were Mike and Dave from SERAC.

Holding my M4 Viper, I ran over to the driver of one of the G-wagens who told me the vehicles belonged to the GRS team from the CIA annex and that Ty Woods and several other GRS contractors had already entered the compound.

"What's the sitrep in there?" I asked.

"Ty and the others are sweeping it for friendlies," the older American replied.

"Any casualties?" I asked.

"Three local nationals and one expat."

"The ambassador?"

He shrugged. "Don't know."

I ducked as a huge exchange of gunfire rang out from inside the compound and shrapnel rained over the roofs and hoods of the SUVs.

"Tell Ty more friendlies are coming in," I said to the driver.

"Roger that."

By this time Robbo, Reilly, and Scots John had also arrived. We quickly teamed in twos. Robbo and I would head for the main building while Reilly and Pete would clear the TOC and cantina. Cory and Scots John would stay with our SUVs and keep the engines running.

Reilly, Pete, Robbo, and I jumped on the hoods of the SUVs and climbed over the wall. We landed on the other side and immediately took up positions, eyes to scopes, scanning the compound in arcs. Ahead, on the other side of the orchard, we saw a scene of total mayhem. Vehicles and buildings were in flames. Armed militants were running from door to door, spreading the blaze with cans of fuel and torches, firing AKs and RPGs, all the while chanting slogans. Dead bodies littered the ground, the dark blood from them reflecting the glow of fire.

We weren't halfway through the orchard when we saw former Navy SEAL Ty Woods and a group of GRS guys leading a group of twenty or more haggard-looking expats out, their faces black with soot.

"Any more inside?" I asked.

"No idea," Ty shouted back.

"Ambassador Stevens?"

Ty shook his head. "Haven't found him. Not yet."

He turned back and waved to his men. Two of them then carried out the limp, lifeless body of a man who looked to be in his thirties. I later learned that his name was Sean Smith.

Ty shouted over the chanting and gunfire, "This guy didn't make it. The rest of them are ambulatory. We need to get them the fuck out of here. Fast."

I said, "We'll do another sweep. See if we can find the ambassador."

"Good luck."

I watched Ty hurry off with the injured men, then alerted Cory and Scots John via the headset radio.

"Ty's headed your way with some expats, no ambassador."

One of them double clicked to indicate that he'd received the message.

As Robbo and I approached the center of the compound, we took the odd blast of incoming, crouched behind whatever cover we could find, and returned fire. Strange shadows and images danced in front of us in the flickering light—a looter dragging a planter at eleven o'clock, a militiaman wearing a combat vest running past with a sub-machine gun at two.

The entire front of Villa C was engulfed in flames, so Robbo and I crossed quickly to the back door. Thick black smoke seeped out of the crack at the bottom. I removed the shemagh from around my neck, doused it with water from a bottle, and tied it around my mouth.

Robbo followed my example, then squeezed my shoulder. It was his way of saying *Time to move*.

I kicked open the door, ducked in low, and peeled right, looking through the sight of my M4 Viper. Robbo followed and peeled left. We scanned our sectors, sweeping the room as best we could through the billowing smoke.

"Clear," I said into my head mike.

"Clear. Move," Robbo echoed.

We pressed forward to the next door as the flames and smoke penetrated our makeshift masks and the heat started to sear our skin. We were entering a literal inferno. Looters were running in and out like locusts. I saw one sprinting out with a broken chair. Another carried a printer.

On the other side of the central driveway Pete and Reilly fought their way into the TOC, dropping militants along the way. They killed a number of them but found no Americans inside. The fire at the nearby cantina was so hot that Pete and Reilly couldn't even enter.

As we stumbled past a burning chair in Villa C, I heard Pete's voice over the radio.

"Simon. Pete."

"Send."

"The TOC has been cleared already, and the cantina is too fucking hot to get in. We're going to make our way back to the vehicles."

"Roger that."

Directly in front of me, a dark silhouette emerged from the smoke holding a towel over its face.

Robbo lased it and shouted, "Contact front!"

The man removed the towel from his mouth and held his arms up. He looked like a teenager and was unarmed, so we let him go.

We pushed forward into what looked to be a living room. The curtains, chairs, and rugs were all on fire. As I started to turn back to the rear of the house, a group of militants emerged from the smoke in front of us and opened fire. Robbo and I dove behind a corner and started hitting them with controlled bursts.

It was fucking chaos. Six or more of them against two of us. Hot shells spilled across the floor, and rounds ripped into the wall in front of us, spitting up pieces of concrete and dust. Cordite stung my nostrils. Dust and thick smoke clogged my throat.

What had started as a search and rescue was turning into a shitstorm with AK rounds coming from two directions. I signaled to Robbo, and we retreated through the back rooms, keeping low to the ground so as not to be overcome by smoke.

Lungs, skin, and eyes burning, we quickly scanned left and right, room to room, searching behind doors, inside closets, under desks. As we moved, it struck me that if the ambassador was still in the building, he must be dead by now. Either that, or he'd been grabbed by the militiamen and carted off.

We emerged from the back door coughing and filled our lungs with air. Friendly February 17 militiamen had arrived and were starting to clear looters from the compound. To the accompaniment of more small-arms fire, we retreated to the back wall, where Reilly, Pete, Scots John, and Cory stood waiting.

I coughed up some of the soot in my lungs, caught my breath, and got a sitrep from Cowboy back at Zero Alpha. "The militiamen are still running the streets. They seem to be regrouping, maybe in preparation for attacks on other compounds."

"Okay, copy."

"You want us to meet you there?" Cowboy asked.

"No. Sounds like the battle isn't over. We're coming to you."

CHAPTER EIGHTEEN
THE CIA ANNEX

WE HAD just left the US Special Mission Compound and were ripping south on the Fourth Ring Road with the smell of burning fuel still clinging to us when I spotted two SUVs stopped by the side of the road. Standing beside one of them was a chap I knew who worked for SERAC named Tony Parker—"Fez" to his mates.

I told Cory at the wheel to pull over and stop. Huddled with Tony was another contractor from SERAC named Tom and two guys from Global Security, Chris Cole and Tiny Lawler—a huge black man. I had worked with all four guys at various times in Afghanistan and Iraq.

All of us were armed for combat and covered with soot. I soon learned that Tiny, Tony, Tom, and Chris had been part of the initial QRF that arrived at the US Special Mission with Ty and the guys with GRS. We were all wondering if we should go to the CIA annex or return to our respective compounds—whose security was weakened by our absence.

Another question on all of our minds: were the militiamen from Ansar al-Sharia done for the night, or were they planning more attacks on other US and Western targets?

The SERAC compound had a direct line to the annex, so Tony established comms with his teammates who told him that Ty and the GRS boys had made it safely back to the annex with the twenty or so expats from the US Special Mission. They had seen militiamen milling about the area and were bracing themselves for a follow-up attack.

I called Cowboy and told him we were headed to the annex to see if they needed help and asked him to open a direct line of comms to the operators there. Cory and Robbo executed U-turns and turned onto a side road that ran parallel to Andaluc and took us to the front of the annex. Tony, in the lead SUV, radioed ahead to let them know we were coming.

We dashed through the open metal gates and parked, and local guards quickly closed the gates behind us. The time was roughly 2345. My men and I joined Tony in the driveway where Ty and a big sandy-haired GRS operator named Oz gave us a brief.

The annex compound consisted of four large one-story houses with ladders up their sides. Building D was lower than the others and didn't offer as good a vantage of the surrounding area, so we would concentrate our defense on A, B, and C, and put a smaller team on D. "What we want to do at the moment," said Ty, "is establish a security cordon so we can't be overrun."

As he spoke the occasional shot rang from beyond the annex walls. The compound itself was square, roughly two acres in area with lush lawns and foliage, and surrounded by ten-foot-high walls topped with barbed wire and surveillance cameras. Not exactly inconspicuous for a CIA compound.

Cory, Reilly, Robbo, Pete, Scots John, and I took the top of Building C, which housed the annex command post, including the secure Sensitive Compartmented Information Facility (SCIF), which was now being used as a medical center to treat the injured from the US Special Mission Compound. Tiny, Tony, Tom, Chris, and the GRS operators climbed to the roofs of A and B farther south, with A closest to the front gate. Building D stood behind us.

According to the practice in Benghazi, the roofs of all four structures were flat and made of concrete covered with tar and gravel. GRS operators had laid out boxes of 5.56, 7.72, and belt-fed ammo and crates of smoke and fragmentation grenades—as we had done on the top of our villa. In the event of an attack, you didn't want to have to carry boxes of ammo up to the roof.

As soon as we took up our positions, the firing directed at the compound picked up. Yellow, green, and blue tracers flew over our heads and smashed into the brick-and-concrete walls. It was generally coming from the northeast and south. Beyond the ten-foot annex wall to the northeast there was a stockyard with a dozen long tin-roofed sheds. Out to the east was a field of trees and shrubs. South and on the opposite side of what was known as Annex Road stood a four-story building under construction. All of these areas were sources of excellent cover.

Two explosions shook the compound, and the small-arms fire quickly grew in intensity and built into a constant fury. It came so hard and fast that we couldn't lift ours heads above the three-foot lip around the roof without the risk of getting them shot off. Automatically our training kicked in, and we bobbed up at intervals, lining up targets in our sights and taking them down with controlled bursts. If we didn't see a target, we didn't shoot, to conserve ammo.

Still, the battle was so intense that we were going through it quickly. There was no time to think or even scratch an itch. It was reload, pop up, pick out a target, and fire, all in a matter of seconds. Rounds slammed and ricocheted around us, and tracers, laser markers, and rockets formed elegant arcs in the night sky.

I estimated fifty to sixty attackers in what seemed like a coordinated attack. I saw them running across the street carrying RPGs and AKs, crouching behind garbage bins, and ducking in doorways as they fought their way closer. Clearly, their objective was to overwhelm the annex's defenses and gain access to the compound as they had at the US Special Mission. Occasional rocket rounds slammed into the lip of the roof in front of us and sprayed plaster and dust into our faces.

They outnumbered us, but we had the advantage in terms of cover and height, and we fought back furiously. All the time, we were in communication with the guys defending A, B, and D. All of them were trained operators and were holding fast. When guys ran out of ammo, we had to send someone down to lug more up.

I was covered in soot and sweating from head to toe, my ears ringing, my eyes sore and tired. Still, there's nothing like a firefight to focus one's attention. After what felt like sixty minutes—an eternity for a firefight—the shooting from outside let up. Fifteen more minutes of sporadic fire, and then it stopped completely. I took a deep breath and relaxed. Beyond the walls, we heard the sound of feet running away and vehicles speeding off.

I gulped down orange Gatorade and did a quick head count. No one on Building C had been hit. Ty called through the radio requesting my presence on the driveway for another sitrep.

Ty was upbeat as he informed us that we had taken no casualties and Tripoli was sending reinforcements. He made it sound like it would be a large team made up of Delta operators and SEALs. The implication was that his men had the situation under control.

Tony interjected the one ominous note, asking if anyone had heard anything about Ambassador Stevens.

"No," Ty answered. "Not yet."

On the roof of Building C, the guys were back to taking the piss out of one another, refreshing themselves with water, Gatorade, and energy bars and rebombing mags. I established comms with Zero Alpha and spoke to Moxie and Pants.

"Everything's quiet here," Moxie reported.

I didn't know whether we should stay at the annex or return to our compound.

Another forty-five minutes passed without incident. I climbed down again to hold another confab with Tony and Cole in the yard. Both of them had decided to leave with their guys and return to their compounds. The attack seemed to be over.

I checked with Ty one last time, who still had no word about the whereabouts of Ambassador Stevens. It was around 0200 the morning of the twelfth when the six of us exited the annex, turned left on Tarik Aruba Street heading into town, and right on the Third Ring Road as Cowboy at Zero Alpha monitored our progress on FalconView.

The city appeared to have returned to normal. We encountered no militia patrols or roadblocks, just an odd horse or two nosing through garbage by the side of the road.

Upon reaching our compound, we sat together in the living room (or team room, as we called it) and drank a cup of tea to calm our nerves. The six of us who had ventured out were exhausted and coughing up soot. Our faces and exposed skin had turned black.

Cowboy informed me that Zero Alpha had been completely sanitized. "What do we do now?" he asked.

"I don't know. Obviously all the State and agency guys are leaving. The other contracting teams will probably be leaving in droves."

Cowboy said, "Fatty heard a rumor that the annex was pounded because the CIA is holding two al-Sharia militiamen there and interrogating them."

"I didn't see any evidence of that," I responded. "But I didn't inspect all the buildings, either. So who knows."

I went to take a shower and wash off the soot. Then, exhaustion setting in, I tried to get Michael on the sat phone. As I was dialing, Cowboy ran in to inform me in his Tennessee accent that the Delta reinforcements had finally arrived at the annex after being held up at Benina Airport for hours waiting for a February 17 militia escort. It wasn't the large force Ty had expected and consisted of only two active-duty Delta Force members; four more GRS operators, including former SEAL Glen Doherty; and a translator.

Finally, after many tries, I contacted Michael and brought him up to speed. To my surprise, he knew nothing about the attacks on the US Special Mission and CIA annex.

Michael said, "Hang tight while I get more information."

"At the moment everything is calm where we are, but that could change in a second."

"Got it."

"Michael, the other teams are packing and leaving. Should we do the same?" I asked.

"Absolutely not."

Anxious and uncertain, we kept a steady rotation of guys monitoring comms in the ops room while others on the roof checked the surrounding streets through binos. At 0500, we got word via Skype that Ambassador Stevens had been located at the Benghazi Medical Center and was dead.

The news hit us hard. I sat wondering if killing Ambassador Stevens had been Ghali's intention all along. Was that his way of exacting revenge on the United States for kidnapping his cousin and killing Abu Yahya al-Libi in Pakistan? Would he attack us next?

A half hour later, we heard that the CIA annex had been hit again, and Ty and Glen Doherty had been killed by mortar fire on the roof of Building C, where we had been fighting just hours earlier. Other operators were wounded. According to reports from the annex, this second attack was more powerful and organized. Militiamen carried heavier arms this time, including mortars, rockets, and heavy machine guns.

Our instinct was rush to the annex and support them. Cowboy, Cory, Robbo, and Pete appeared in front of me kitted out with their plate carriers and holding their weapons and asked, "What should we do? Should we go?"

I knew what they wanted me to say but decided to check with Michael first. When I got him on the sat phone, Michael said, "No, stay put. The situation at the annex is under control."

"You sure about that?"

"Yes," he answered. "The assault has been repulsed. A convoy of about sixty February Seventeenth militiamen with technicals is on its way there now to escort everyone to the airport. The jet the Delta team flew in on is on the tarmac waiting."

"What about Ambassador Stevens?"

"My understanding is that other friendly February Seventeenth militiamen are going to the hospital to retrieve his body."

"What do you want us to do?" I asked.

"Lay low for the next forty-eight hours until the smoke clears and we sort things out."

"I'm not sure that's a good idea, mate," I countered. "We have no idea what's going on. Ghali's not at his compound. His men are armed to the max. We could be his next target."

"I understand. But stay put. Don't move until you hear from me. Are we clear?"

"Crystal clear, Michael."

I hung up, leaned back in my chair, and said, "Fuck it."

It was a strange situation to be in. All DOS and agency personnel were heading out, as were many private contractors, leaving us more alone and exposed. The guys on my team all asked the same question: Does Michael really think there's a chance to revive the arms-exchange program after what has happened?

At 0745 we learned via Skype that the first flight had left Benina Airport with the wounded. A second airplane, a big Libyan Air Force C-130, arrived two hours later to transport the remaining expats to Tripoli. We also found out that the guys from Control Risks, Hart, and SERAC had stayed behind to manage their own evacuation.

None of us was sleeping well, and our nerves were shot. We spent the remainder of the twelfth and the thirteenth on high alert with guards posted on the roof 24/7 watching the streets around us. Guys tried to lose themselves in games on Xbox or movies downloaded to their laptops or workouts in the gym. But nothing seemed to calm our nerves. Everywhere we went in the house, even the bathroom, we carried our weapons and grab bags.

Midday on the thirteenth, we got a call from Michael telling us to sanitize the compound and prepare to leave. I handed Fatty the cash we had left and told him to pay the guards. He'd worked with Michael and the DOS before and knew the score, which was that we were leaving and not coming back.

Good guy that he was, he wanted to stick around and help get us through the airport. Early the next morning, I got a call from Craig, who was piloting the An-70. He said he would be landing at Benina in thirty minutes.

We quickly collected our cell phones, sat phones, laptops, and gear and pushed to the airport, making sure to circumvent the US Special Mission Compound. The little airport departure lounge was crowded with expats waiting for a flight out. I ran into Tony from SERAC and Tiny from Global Security.

Big Tiny asked, "Popping smoke, mate? We're fucking off on the next flight. I'll catch up with you in the next war zone."

"Good luck."

Fatty Ahmed talked us through Immigration, which was being run by friends of his in the Libya Shield. Then he escorted us to the waiting Antonov, and we said goodbye.

"You going to be okay?" I asked him. After all, Ghali and members of the militia knew he was a friend of the Brits and Americans and had recently been working with us on the arms-transfer project. And I'd seen what anti-Western militias had done to locals who had worked with us in theater in Afghanistan and Iraq.

Fatty squeezed my hand and smiled. "All will be well, my friend," he said. "Until the next time."

I was hoping to myself that there wouldn't be a next time. "God be with you, my friend."

We sat on the tarmac in uncomfortable silence for twenty minutes before Craig was given the okay to depart. As we banked over the city, I looked down at the charred remains of the US Special Mission Compound as a thousand thoughts passed through my head. Ayid Ghali was down there somewhere, waiting for the US response. The families of Ambassador Stevens, Sean Smith, Glen Doherty, and Ty Woods were dealing with the painful aftermath of their tragic deaths. All of them had died heroically and unnecessarily. I wondered if the truth of what went down in Benghazi would ever come out.

At Heathrow, I said goodbye to the guys, who went their separate ways by plane, cab, and train—Pete to East London, Reilly and Moxie to north England, Robbo to Newcastle, Scots John to Glasgow, and Cory and Cowboy to the States. Carrying our five operational laptops I hopped a cab to the Landmark Hotel on Marylebone Road a half mile from Regent's Park.

I slept soundly for two hours—the first good rest I'd had in days. Then I dressed to meet an ex-spook named Ray in the tearoom at 1800. He was a huge, heavy man with the demeanor of an undertaker and had no time for small talk. He collected the five laptops, per Michael's instructions, and left me sipping my tea and mulling over the events of the last several days.

The newspapers were filled with headlines about the tragedy in Benghazi. The Obama administration claimed that the riot at the US Special Mission had been an angry and spontaneous reaction to a trailer for an amateurish anti-Islamic movie called *Innocence of Muslims* that had been posted on YouTube, which was total bunk. I wondered why they even bothered to float crap like that. Did they really think the public was that stupid?

Returning to my room, I called Michael in DC and told him I'd passed the laptops off to Ray.

"Good," he said. "That's it then. Now you can go home."

Instead I decided to stay an extra day to regroup and meet my mum, my stepfather, Paul, and half sister Lucy for lunch. My mum regaled us with stories about her adventures at the local supermarket where she worked. It was a huge relief to see them and hear about people living normal lives, where slights were dismissed with a quip rather than looting and burning down your house. They knew what I did for a living but understood not to ask where I'd been.

The next day I caught a flight to California and waited for a call from Michael. He instructed me to fold up Sion Resources LLC and bring the guys out of Erbil, which I did. Asso went back to selling used BMWs and helping his dad. Amada Bash—the security company we established with General Sameer—continues to win legitimate contracts and remains in business. Dana and General Sabir are still in Syria. Their situation improved considerably in June 2013 when President Obama finally authorized $500 million in military and medical assistance to the Syrian rebels.

In early 2014 their fortunes sagged again because the United States and its European allies had withheld military assistance and support for so long that the fundamentalist ISIS was able to gain a fervent following and foothold in northern Iraq and Syria. In the summer of 2014, ISIS took over the city of Mosul in Kurdistan and was pushing General Sabir and his fighters out of their bases in al-Hasakah, Syria.

I keep in touch with both Asso and Dana via Skype. In late 2014, Dana wrote, "The war is not far from us now as you know. Our battalion is right on the border with ISIS now. But everyone is good, Mr. Chase. Thanks for asking."

I wrote back a month later, "Hi, Dana. I've been following the news here closely. My heart really goes out to you. How are you getting along?"

"Mr. Chase," he replied. "Things are okay, but can be better. Yesterday was very dangerous. ISIS is near Kabat District now. They are less than ten kilometers from our compound."

"If you and General Sabir need my help, let me know, and I will try to fly back and train your men."

I didn't hear from him for another six weeks. Then in mid-

September I received another message: "We are now in a bad situation. The town is empty. Only Peshmerga are inside defending. We are trying to find a way to leave and get to Istanbul. I'm glad you want to help us and will never forget you, sir."

I haven't heard from him since.

Lesson number 13: Time passes and events fade in your memory, but the remarkable people you meet in the field stay with you.

CHAPTER NINETEEN
CALIFORNIA

THREE MONTHS after I had returned from Benghazi, I sat on a cot in a safe house in Kabul, Afghanistan, staring at the barrel of a gun, feeling completely disillusioned and thinking about ending my life.

The reason why didn't relate directly to events in Benghazi, though the deaths of Ambassador Chris Stevens and the three other Americans there, which had blown up into a huge political issue in the States, still weighed heavily on my mind. It didn't help that Obama administration spokespeople kept telling incomplete and misleading stories about what had led to the violence. I wondered when journalists and congressional investigations would start putting the pieces together and seek me out. And I asked myself how I would react when they did.

I admit, the tragic end of that mission had left me a bit paranoid. I kept in touch with people in Libya trying to find out if Ayid Ghali was still looking for me. Would some agent of the US government, the Assad regime, or some other shadowy agency jump me in the middle of the night? Would I start my car one morning and go up in flames?

What made the aftermath of Benghazi even more difficult was the fact that I couldn't discuss events in Syria and Libya with Mia and my civilian friends in California. The only people I could really trust were my mates Robbo, Reilly, and Pete, who were as much at odds and ends about the whole operation as I was.

My unresolved feeling about Benghazi and Syria was one of the main reasons I had taken this job in Kabul. I wanted to be hard to find, and I was hoping the challenges of a new assignment would help clear my head.

The irony was that even though California was my home, I felt safer in a war zone surrounded by teammates. It made sense from my perspective. Trust was everything in our line of work. It was the glue that held us together, made us effective, and kept us alive. We had fought beside one another, taken bullets for one another, and we were the only ones who really understood what we had been through.

While I kept in touch with friends and family back in Romford, I generally had a real hard time letting new people in. That seemed to have changed a few years ago when I met and fell in love with Mia. She and Olivia became my family and "safe place." They gave meaning to my world. Thinking of them had gotten me through the most difficult times in Iraq, Afghanistan, and Libya.

I carried pictures of the two of them everywhere, and Mia and I texted and Skyped each other several times a day. I filled her in on my activities in Afghanistan, and she told me about her life in Malibu as a singer-songwriter and mother of precious Olivia.

Minutes ago, I had written, "Hey love. Quiet day here and cold as hell. How are things in paradise?"

A minute or so later, my cell phone pinged with Mia's response.

271

I read it eagerly, expecting news about her recording career or an amusing story about Olivia. Instead she wrote, "Simon, sorry. Can't do this anymore. I'm not happy."

My breathing constricted and my hands started to tremble. "What?" I typed back. "I don't understand. What are you talking about?"

"It's over."

I couldn't believe what I was seeing at first, so I read the words again. As I did my body started to shake, and the room wobbled around me. I was losing control. The emotional foundation of everything I lived for had suddenly been pulled out from under me.

"Are you serious?" I typed back.

"Yes. It's over."

Feeling I had nothing to live for, I picked the Glock up off the cot, chambered a round, and held it to my head. I imagined myself standing in front of a blank canvas with a paintbrush in my hand. I painted a four-bedroom house with palm trees, a wife, a beautiful little girl, and a couple of nice cars. But when I dipped my brush in the pot to paint myself in the picture, there was no paint left.

Shattered, I started to squeeze the trigger.

Suddenly a voice told me to pick up my cell phone and scroll through the pictures I had taken with Olivia one last time. Tears streaming down my cheeks, I looked at dozens of photos of us splashing in the pool, walking down the beach, and playing.

I realized that in lots of ways I was a child myself. I had been running around the world from one adventure to the other, assuming I knew what was going on with my loved ones back home but not really understanding what it took to maintain a relationship and build a family. The nature of what I did for a living had caused me to compartmentalize my life—missions and mayhem in one box, family and

272

home in another. Because I loved Mia with all my heart, I assumed she loved me back with equal devotion.

Obviously, I was wrong.

Minutes later my teammate Ginge walked in the room, saw the expression on my face, and the tears dripping down my cheeks, and said, "Fuck, Sy. What the hell happened?"

"Mia..." was all I could manage to say.

"She okay?"

I nodded.

"Sy, whatever she's said or done to make you feel this way, you need to leave as soon as possible and sort it out."

The following day I was on a flight back to Los Angeles. I didn't tell Mia I was coming, and I didn't know what I was going to do when I got there. As I crossed oceans and continents heading west, I received more e-mails from her. One said, "I'll move your things to the spare bedroom. You can pick them up when you get back." Cold and clinical; she was putting me out like an old pairs of boots.

I landed at LAX around 1700 and took a cab straight to the house we shared in Malibu.

I entered through the back gate and sat in the backyard thinking. What had I done wrong? What could I say to Mia to patch things up? What could I do to be a more loving, supportive partner? Should I go in now, or check into a hotel and ring her in the morning?

More than an hour passed with the waves pounding in the background before I left through the gate, walked around to the front door, and rang the bell. The twenty-something babysitter we had used when Mia and I had gone out on date nights answered the door.

"Hi, Louise," I said.

"Oh, Simon, it's you. Mia didn't tell me you were coming home."

The word "home" reverberated in my head like an exploding rocket. I started to tremble.

She stepped aside and let me in. Olivia heard my voice from the living room, ran toward me, and threw herself in my arms. "Simon!" I felt like crying, but held it together.

A part of me said: *You can make this work. You can save this relationship. It's too important to lose.*

I spent twenty minutes talking and playing with Olivia. When I saw Louise again, I asked her, "How come you're here tonight?"

"Mia is out with friends."

"Well, since I'm home, I'll pay you and you can go."

"Okay," she said. "Are you going to pay me for the other nights, too?"

"You babysat other nights recently?" I asked.

"All four nights so far this week."

I paid her, but thought that was strange because I'd spoken to Mia every day on Skype, and she never told me anything about going out.

Louise left, Olivia and I watched a Disney movie together, and Mia returned at 2200 alone but all dolled up. She gave me a nervous kiss on the cheek and said that she had to put Olivia to bed.

"No, Mom," Olivia said. "I want Simon to do it."

I happily read her a book, tucked her in, and kissed her good night.

Mia sat waiting in the kitchen. She asked, "What are you doing here?"

"Do you think I could stay away after reading those texts from you?"

She said, "I don't want to talk about this now," and went to bed. Exhausted, I slipped in beside her and fell asleep.

The next morning was very awkward with me trying to talk to her and Mia trying to avoid me. At one point she said, "You know why this can't work? Because you're never here and I feel lonely. I don't get invited out, because people know we're together and you're not around."

"I understand, but that's the nature of my job," I responded. "You've known that all along. What has changed?"

"You told me you were going to give it up, but I don't think you ever will. I've just grown tired of this."

As best I could, I tried to explain that what I did was more than a job, more like a way of life. My teammates were my brothers. We had gone through hell together. Now we all lived in different places and only saw one another on the job. I didn't think I was ready to give that up. But I would, if I had to.

Mia insisted that she wanted to separate.

"Have you fallen out of love with me?" I asked her.

"It's not about that. No."

"Are you seeing someone else?"

"No."

I asked her the same questions a couple of days later, and she gave me the same answers. At the end of the week, I met my friend Diana for coffee. She was like a big sister to me and knew Mia.

When I told Diana about what had happened with Mia, she rolled her eyes.

I asked, "Is there something you want to tell me?"

"No," she answered. "It's not my place to tell you. You need to sort it out yourself."

That night I confronted Mia again. I said, "If you're seeing some-one else, just tell me so we can deal with this as adults and work something out."

She denied it again. "Your mind is messed up from doing the things you've been doing," she countered. "You're acting crazy and paranoid because you've been working with the CIA."

I didn't want to see the truth. I wanted to believe that if I opened up more to Mia about the work I did and how it had affected me, our relationship could be saved.

I almost begged her for a second chance. "The heart and mind of a little girl are involved here," I explained. "I don't want to hurt her by ripping this relationship apart unless it's completely necessary."

I explained the situation to Michael S., who had become a close friend and mentor. He said, "Obviously she's not telling you the whole story. If you give me her cell-phone number, I can give you every text and call that come in and go out, and every e-mail she has sent and received in the last six months." He also offered to give me access to a satellite feed that would track Mia's phone, telling me her location at every minute. "That way you can either put your mind at rest or prove that she's been fucking with you."

Not wanting to believe that about her, I said, "I don't know. Let me think about that."

That evening Mia, my actor friend Neal, and his wife, Tracy, took me out for a birthday dinner at Taverna Tony off the Pacific Coast Highway (PCH). Neal and I spent time together at the gym and cutting around when I was in Malibu. He had a habit of blurting out whatever was on his mind.

After dinner and before coffee and dessert, Neal leaned into me and whispered, "There's something I've got to tell you. Mia is totally cheating on you."

Before I had a chance to ask for details, I looked up and saw Mia and Tracy returning from the bathroom. Of course nothing else was said on the subject for the rest of the dinner.

Later that night, feeling betrayed and heartbroken, I called Michael and told him that I wanted to initiate what we had half jokingly dubbed Operation Janus, after the two-faced god from Roman mythology.

Via the tracking device, I found out that Mia was spending a lot of time with a guy named Robert. Since she was a singer-songwriter recording songs, and he was a drummer, this made sense. But when I mentioned him to my friend Diana the next time we met for coffee, she rolled her eyes.

Again I asked her, "Do you have something to tell me?"

And again, she answered, "It's not my place."

Despite the torment I was going through, Neal managed to provide some moments of levity. One night we were in his SUV following Mia to a recording session at some guy named Jeff's house. As we entered a narrow road that led into a canyon, Neal at the wheel kept asking me, "Are we on a follow, Simon? Am I on the team?"

"Yes, you're on the team, mate."

"Cool, man. This is so exciting!"

Mia parked in front of a house and entered. I told Neal to stop, which he did, directly under the only streetlamp on the block.

I turned to him and asked, "Do you think it would be possible to park somewhere else so we're not lit up like a birthday cake?"

"Oh, sorry." He backed up the car several feet and turned off the engine. But the interior light over the dashboard stayed on, illuminating our faces. Neal started flipping switches in an attempt to turn it off.

I finally asked, "Can you please just remove the bulb?"

"Sure." He unscrewed the hot bulb with his bare hand and dropped it somewhere on the floor. Now he couldn't find it, so he opened the driver's side door, which turned on other lights in the interior and caused the car to make an obnoxious pinging sound.

It was like a scene out of a Will Ferrell movie. I started laughing, and said, "Neal, this is crazy. Let's just drive home."

The following night, Mia told me that she was meeting her friend Joanna for a girls' night out.

I said, "Fine. I'll stay home with Olivia, and the two of us will watch a movie."

While *Cinderella* played on the flat-screen, I used my laptop to access the website Michael had set up and monitor the movement of Mia's car. It wasn't anywhere near Joanna's house in Point Dune. In fact, it was headed in the opposite direction, toward Santa Monica.

I called Neal. His wife, Tracy, answered and told me that he was in an acting class and wouldn't be home until midnight. Because I sounded so upset, she offered to hire a babysitter and come over. We left the babysitter with Olivia and her daughter at my house and took off for Santa Monica.

The tracker indicated that Mia had parked outside the upscale Huntley Hotel near the beach in Santa Monica.

"What do you want to do?" Tracy asked when we arrived there.

Mia was either meeting some guy in one of the rooms or was in the Penthouse bar having a drink with Joanna. Tracy offered to go up to the rooftop bar and have a look.

She came back ten minutes later to report that both the bar and restaurant were empty. Mia was not there. As I headed home, I asked myself: *What am I doing? Weeks ago I was hunting insurgents in Afghanistan. Now I'm tracking my girlfriend and acting like an idiot.*

Ready to confess to Mia that I had been following her, I pulled onto the shoulder of the PCH and called her.

"Hi, love," I said. "How's your night going?"

"Oh, fine," she answered. "I'm in the car with Joanna now, on my way home."

Soon as I hung up, I turned to Tracy and announced, "Everything's fine. She's behind us and is going to drive past any minute."

Sure enough, three minutes later Mia drove by in her car. *Alone.* I was so shaken, I had to go to Neal and Tracy's to calm down. An hour later, when I arrived at our house, I found Mia calmly sitting at the kitchen table.

"How was your night with Joanna at the Huntley?" I asked.

"Nice."

"Was the restaurant busy?"

"Yes, very."

I had caught her in several lies already. I said, "Mia, you actually have to go inside the restaurant to find out if it's busy or not."

She didn't respond. Then I confronted her with the information Michael had put together on one of the guys she was seeing— Robert. I said, "You've been treating me like shit for the last several weeks, telling me that I keep imagining things, and that hunting terrorists and the work I do has turned me into some kind of nut job. But here's the truth. All the while, you've been sleeping with this guy Robert behind my back."

Finally, she admitted the truth.

I said, "Mia, you know what I do for a living. Didn't you think I'd eventually find out?"

She didn't answer.

I said, "I realize now that I have no clue who you are," and turned around and left. I was shattered. I spent the next four days at Neal's house, sobbing like a baby and trying to figure out what to do next.

On the fifth day I pulled myself together, went back to the house, and spoke to Mia. "This is what we're going to do." I said. "Christmas is two weeks away. We're going to act like adults and hold Christmas in this house like I promised Olivia. It will also be the first Christmas I've had at home in eighteen years. After that, I'm going to pack my bags and leave, and we're done."

*   *   *

Maybe I was still hoping we could sort things out. But we didn't, and after Christmas I moved into the spare bedroom at Neal and Tracy's and hit rock bottom. I couldn't sleep and hadn't slept soundly since I returned from Benghazi, so I went to see a psychiatrist named Dr. Wilson.

He told me I hadn't developed any of the psychological tools to deal with a betrayal like this and was also suffering from PTSD. The trauma I experienced had eroded my faith that there was any safety, predictability, or meaning in the world. It had caused me to cling to the belief that Mia—a woman I didn't know very well—could provide the only safe harbor.

She clearly wasn't equipped to do that, and what I had expected of her was unrealistic. The first thing I needed to do was calm my nervous system and rest. Dr. Wilson explained that another symptom of PTSD was hyperarousal. If most people's minds operated at between thirty-three and forty-five rpm, mine normally ran at seventy-five. The stress I was under had upped that to ninety-five.

He prescribed powerful sleeping pills—one vial of blues, one vial of whites.

"Take one of each," he instructed. "They'll knock you out for eight hours and give your body a chance to reset."

That night after dinner, I took one of each and sat in the screening room at Neal and Tracy's watching *The Hobbit: An Unexpected Journey.* At the end of the three-hour movie, I popped my head up from the couch behind where they were sitting and asked, "What are we going to watch next?"

Neal turned around and gasped. "Holy fuck, Simon! How come you're not asleep?"

He called Dr. Wilson to solicit his advice. Dr. Wilson said, "Give him another two blues and one white. That's enough to knock out a horse."

Thirty minutes after taking the additional tablets, I passed out. Neal carried me to the spare princess bed in his daughter's room, which was equipped with a video camera.

He and Tracy retired to their bedroom and were watching TV. Forty minutes into the *Tonight Show,* he glanced at the monitor and gasped again.

Turning to Tracy, he said, "You're not going to believe this, but Simon's awake."

It took more pills from Dr. Wilson and many weeks before I was able to calm down and return to my quiet, low-profile life in the small community of Malibu. In the past, most people there had steered a wide berth around me because they had heard rumors that I was a spy, a British arms dealer, or some trigger-happy government assassin making piles of money. One thing the breakup with Mia did was humanize me to my neighbors. Now people I barely knew would come up to me in the gym or on the street and tell me they had heard about the breakup and were sorry about what had happened. They remarked that they had seen me playing with Olivia at various times and noted that behind the tough façade I seemed to be a very gentle, loving man.

That moved me, and helped me heal.

Now I understand better how hard it is for people to appreciate the challenges that warriors like myself face adjusting to the civilian world and the burden we put on our girlfriends, wives, friends, and children, who feel abandoned for long periods of time.

Lesson number 14: PMCs might look strong and hard, but our psyches are fragile.

*　　　*　　　*

One afternoon several months after the breakup I sat typing an e-mail to a friend when I noticed a message on Facebook Chat from my mate Rab. It read: "Are you there, Sy?"

"Yeah. What's up?"

"I've got bad news. Have you heard? Robbo's died."

I had seen Robbo seven days earlier in Afghanistan looking fit as a fiddle and happy-go-lucky. Rab's message didn't click.

I typed back, "Robbo who?"

"Our Robbo. Ian Robertson. He's killed himself."

"What the fuck are you talking about?"

I picked up the phone and called Rab in London. He told me that Robbo had been having problems with his missus and had hung himself two days earlier in his apartment in Manchester. Subsequent rumors claimed that he was also suffering from PTSD.

Either way, I had a hard time wrapping my head around it. Robbo had been one of my closest friends and the most vital, charming, seemingly secure guy I'd ever met; with a movie-star smile and a quick wit, he was always ready with a joke to lift everyone up. Chicks were all over him. His personality was magnetic.

I remembered running my two-miler fitness test just a couple weeks ago. When I reached the finish line, I looked back and saw Robbo grinning behind me.

How the fuck had this happened?

Losing a teammate in combat was hard enough, but this was almost unimaginable. None of his friends had seen it coming. None of us had any idea of the torment he had been secretly going through. But somewhere in the deepest recesses of my heart and mind, I knew how he felt.

CHAPTER TWENTY

BAGHDAD

OCTOBER 2013, I was back in Baghdad on the holy day of Eid—a joyous and important religious holiday that marks the end of Ramadan. The streets were packed with Iraqi men and women dressed in new clothes heading to their local mosque to perform special congregational prayers known as Salaat al-Eid. Their children, meanwhile, were in school singing songs and making cards and posters to mark the holiday. Later, families and friends would gather to exchange gifts and share a special meal of thanksgiving.

Six of my teammates and I had gone to the Shaab neighborhood of Sadr City—the large Shiite enclave that covers most of northeast Baghdad—to do an SRT (or pulse check) for a US-UK contracting company called Century International. The local leaders we sat down with reported increased attacks by the rising Sunni insurgent group ISIS, whose goal was to seize the central and western part of the country and turn it into a Sunni Islamic state.

The million Muslim Shiite residents of Sadr City—named after

Shia leader Mohammad Sadeq al-Sadr—stood in their way. After Mohammad Sadeq al-Sadr's assassination in 1999, his son Mustada al-Sadr had emerged as one of the most influential religious and political leaders in the country and a key representative of Iraq's Shiite majority. In 2004, he demanded the immediate withdrawal of all US-led coalition forces and raised his own militia known as the Mahdi Army to defend his people. Though he had remained a thorn in the side of the US coalition, most of his enmity and attention were focused on Sunni insurgents who were trying to terrorize his followers and drive them out of Iraq.

It was a hot, hazy Friday morning. Temperatures at this time of year often pushed into the nineties. As we slowly made our way through traffic in three white armored SUVs down Shafi al-Din al-Hilli Street, a main thoroughfare that would take us southeast and across the Tigris River to the International Zone, we received a radio report that a bomb had just gone off at Shami Middle School.

Sadr City had been the scene of many recent Sunni insurgent attacks. Our ops director Mike had advised us that if we happened to be passing through an area that had been hit and wanted to lend medical care, we could. But we would be doing so strictly on a volunteer basis.

The radio report stated that scores of children had been injured. Steve, Ginge, and I in the Alpha vehicle all exchanged looks. We were thinking the same thing: *Kids are kids. They're innocents in this conflict.*

Ginge was a brick shithouse six-four ex–Royal Marine with a face that said *Don't mess with me.* Steve was a former US Marine and Harley enthusiast from Dallas.

The school stood a half a mile behind us, in an area known as Sector 26 and in the vicinity of other schools. I radioed the guys in Bravo and Charlie—all of whom wanted to help—and our three vehicles looped north at the next turnaround. Immediately I saw five plumes of smoke rising into the blue sky ahead and to the right. We turned onto Gejara Street, which was jammed with traffic. Our white SUVs stood out in the melee of battered trucks, cars, motorbikes, and frantic people.

We had entered insurgent territory. Our muscles began to twitch. In the back of my mind, I worried about a secondary explosion, which was a common insurgent tactic. They'd set off a smaller IED, wait for the military, medical, and militia first responders to arrive, then detonate a more powerful one. It had gotten to the point where some militias, police, and medical teams no longer responded to attacks.

We veered off gridlocked Gejara Street and boxed east until we got within fifty meters of the school. Through the milling dust and smoke, I saw carnage everywhere. To our right stood the smoldering remains of the single-level school. Most of the front had been completely demolished.

"Fucking hell," Ginge muttered behind me.

In my head, I was preparing myself for the horror ahead. I knew we would be facing three main types of trauma—catastrophic bleeds, blunt-force internal damage, and loss of limbs. A catastrophic bleed could cause death in just three minutes. Time was precious.

I heard Ginge going through his med kit looking for tourniquets, fluid bags, and bandages. We got out and immediately went into our five-meter, ten-meter, twenty-meter cover maneuvers. Every time I dropped down and swept the area, I felt selfish for being concerned with my own safety while children were dying. But if we didn't do what we were doing, we could all be killed, and we'd be of zero utility.

People were scrambling about desperately—most of them appeared to be hysterical parents arriving to look for their kids. Their day of celebration had turned into an unbelievable nightmare.

The front gate of the school was missing. The only remnants: chunks of concrete and pieces of twisted metal. Cordite burning our nostrils, we climbed the four-foot wall on the right into the yard and entered.

Seconds later I was confronted by the sights and sounds of wounded and dead children scattered across a tile floor. One was missing half of his face. Another had had her arm blown off. A third had a huge wound in her chest. The pained, desperate screams of the children pierced my chest and reverberated.

Despite all my experience and training, nothing had prepared me for this. All of the kids were between the ages of eight and ten. The utter inhumanity of the attack chilled me to my bones.

I had designated one man to stay back to guard our vehicles. The six of us who entered went into triage mode, peeling off in different directions to attend to as many wounded children as we could in the shortest period of time. The first kid I reached was about ten. As he sat screaming for his mother, in a state of shock, I checked him for bleeds and broken bones. I felt along his chest, stomach, legs, arms, and back. He appeared intact.

I ran over and knelt beside another kid who was bleeding badly from a wound to his upper arm. As I wrapped a bandage around it, another man appeared dressed in khaki pants and an oxford shirt. He looked like a teacher. I directed him to hold the bandage while I turned the locking mechanism, which would keep it in place.

From him I bounded to a little girl of eight, named Hilema. She screamed in agony and stared at her arm, which was missing below the elbow. I gently pushed her head aside with one hand and wrapped a tourniquet around the shredded bone and flesh to stop the bleeding with the other. While I was doing this, a woman came over to me and started screaming in my face. I assumed it was the girl's mother, because she was telling me to stay with her daughter. I tried to explain the best I could that there was nothing else I could do for her now and had more kids to attend to.

I saw my buddy Ginge run to a girl lying on the ground, check her vitals, establish that she was dead, and hurry to another. We were all doing the same. It was fucking chaos. If you've never held a screaming child in your arms, his blood soaking your clothes as you try to wrap a tourniquet around his severed leg, you can't imagine.

After twenty minutes of blood, screams, and tourniquets, medical responders started to trickle in. Thankfully, there had been no secondary blast.

We kept working for another thirty minutes. By that time our flight suits were a mess, and our med bags were practically empty. I had gone through more than twenty pairs of latex gloves.

Numb from exhaustion, we started to carry the badly wounded children to waiting ambulances. There were two makeshift hospitals in the area—one called Juadr Hospital in Sector 32 to our east and a children's hospital called Ibn Balady. I didn't know if we should split up or not. Deciding to keep the team together, we headed toward Ibn Balady.

Since people were still rushing to the multiple bomb sites in the area, the streets were completely jammed. I kept shouting at Steve at the wheel, "Drive! Drive! Drive!" The poor guy was doing his best. Rich and Ginge behind me told me to relax.

When we got to Ibn Balady, we learned that it was a maternity hospital and not set up to handle trauma cases. So our convoy of SUVs and ambulances had to back up and push toward Juadr, which was on the other end of Sadr City. Precious time was running out.

On the way, I radioed the ops room to tell them where we were going. Juadr was one of the best hospitals in the area but terribly understaffed and underequipped. Sanitation fell way below Western standards. You wouldn't want to send your kid there for a routine checkup, let alone if one of his legs was missing and he had lost a lot of blood.

The hospital's director Zaid Kadin greeted us, and we immediately started applying sutures and fresh bandages, stabilizing kids' vital signs, and feeding them fluids. We worked there for twenty hours straight and managed to save nine children. Only nine. Twenty-seven other children died. Almost two hundred were wounded. The mere nine we saved seemed pathetic, but that was the best we could do.

Completely exhausted, angry, frustrated, and dehydrated, we headed back to the International Zone. The school had been hit on a Friday morning. Monday we were out doing another pulse check. As we crossed the Tigris River heading north, Steve said in his southern accent, "We should swing by the hospital later and see what's up."

"Good idea."

After we completed our mission, we stopped at shops and stands along the way to buy footballs, pens and paper, and any toys we could find, hoping to spread a little cheer and maybe buoy the kids' spirits.

At the front door of the hospital we were met by Zaid Kadin, who looked like he had gone several rounds in a boxing ring with Mike Tyson. Both of his eyes were blackened and practically swollen shut, his mouth was cut and bruised, his nose broken, and face, neck, and arms covered with bruises.

"What the hell happened to you?" I asked through my terp, Hadir.

"ISIS was here," he responded bluntly.

I ordered the men to pop the turrets on the gun trucks and put gunners up. Several stood guard at the entrance as I followed Zaid Kadin to his office. In a sad voice he told me that someone who had been working in the hospital on Friday had informed the insurgents that infidels had been here helping to save children. That night armed ISIS insurgents showed up at the hospital and demanded to see the kids who had been treated by the Westerners. Zaid Kadin had resisted at first but relented after they beat him within an inch of his life.

While he was being pummeled, other staff members managed to hide two of the children. The ISIS insurgents warned Kadin and his staff not to give any more medicines, fluids, food, or treatment to the remaining seven. If they did, the terrorists said, they would return and kill the staff and their families.

His voice choking with tears, Zaid Kadin reported that the seven children had received no further fluids or care, and had died.

The news was devastating. I thought I had seen the lowest forms of human depravity, but here was a new depth. My sense of failure, guilt, and despair was immense and felt inescapable. By trying to help those kids, we had condemned them.

What did their parents think of us now? If they hated us, how could I blame them?

The horror of that event struck deep and embedded itself in my soul. Those Iraqi children's faces have haunted me every day since— Hilema, Hamid, Bilial, and the others.

People like myself are trained to protect and defend the innocent. When we can't do that, we ask ourselves: *What purpose do we serve?*

Inevitably, we're called upon to perform another mission. And we go, hoping that next time we *will* make a difference by training brave boys and men who are trying to protect their village from rampaging terrorists, or rescuing injured children from the rubble of a bombed-out school.

Final lesson: The toll this work takes both physically and psychologically is enormous. Even when we're home with our loved ones, our minds are often far away, on a slain colleague or a rebel general whom you left with tears in his eyes as he pleaded for you to return with much-needed arms and support.

As in any other line of work, the PMC world has had its share of bad apples—like the Blackwater contractors who panicked and gunned down seventeen unarmed Iraqi civilians in Nisour Square. But the operators I've worked with have always conducted themselves with professionalism.

We didn't start the wars, or make the political decisions that resulted in the contracts overseas. We didn't approve the mission to Tora Bora in 2004, or send Ambassador Stevens to Benghazi under very dangerous circumstances, or authorize buying arms from Ansar al-Sharia. We're simply highly trained ex-military operators who have found a way to make a living doing what we were trained to do and hoping to contribute to the greater good.

When we served in uniform we were considered heroes. Now that we perform the same work in flight suits and desert boots, we're derided as mercenaries and war profiteers. Whatever you want to call us, we're still the same individuals with the same core beliefs, motivated by the same desire to protect and serve. And as long as companies and governments operate in dangerous corners of the world, and terrorist groups like ISIS and al-Qaeda oppose individual freedom and denigrate human life, we will answer the call. That's what we do.

We know not to expect parades and medals. But in my opinion, all wounded and fallen PMCs—including my mates Karl and Shaun who died in Iraq, and Danny, Stumpy, and Sam who perished in Tora Bora, and Ty Woods and Glen Doherty who lost their lives in Benghazi, and Robbo—are unsung heroes in the war on terrorism.

I dedicate this book to them and their loved ones.

INDEX

ABOUT THE AUTHORS

SIMON CHASE is the pseudonym of a former member of the elite Royal Marine Commandos. From there he was recruited into the British special forces, serving in the Special Boat Squadron, the naval partner of the infamous Special Air Service. While in the SBS he carried out top-secret missions around the world, working alongside other special-forces units, as well as the CIA and the Drug Enforcement Agency. Since leaving the British military, he has worked with a close-knit team of special-forces operatives from the UK and the United States to provide discreet high-level protection and intervention services for individuals, corporations, and governments all over the globe. He spends his downtime as a tactical adviser for feature films and TV shows and writing articles on counterterrorism.

RALPH PEZZULLO is a *New York Times* bestselling author and an award-winning playwright and screenwriter. His books have been published in over twenty languages and include *Jawbreaker* (with CIA operative

Gary Berntsen), *Inside SEAL Team Six* (with Don Mann), *The Walk-In, At the Fall of Somoza, Plunging into Haiti* (winner of the 2006 Douglas Dillon Prize for American Diplomacy), *Eve Missing, Blood of My Blood, Most Evil* (with Steve Hodel), the SEAL Team Six thrillers *Hunt the Wolf, Hunt the Scorpion, Hunt the Falcon, Hunt the Fox,* and *The Navy SEAL Survival Handbook* (also with Don Mann).